ROBERT S. COLE is vice president and director of communications for the New York State Bankers Association. He has taught public relations at Hunter College, American Management Association, American Institute of Banking, and Baruch College.

THE PRACTICAL HANDBOOK OF
PUBLIC
RELATIONS

ROBERT S. COLE

A SPECTRUM BOOK

PRENTICE-HALL, INC.
Englewood Cliffs, N.J. 07632

Library of Congress Cataloging in Publication Data

COLE, ROBERT S
    The practical handbook of public relations.
    (A Spectrum Book)
    Bibliography: p.
    Includes index.
    1. Public relations. I. Title.
HM263.C576   659.2   80-22443
ISBN 0-13-691162-5
ISBN 0-13-691154-4 (pbk.)

Printed in the United States of America

Editorial/production supervision and interior design by Frank Moorman
Cover design by Ira Shapiro
Manufacturing buyer: Barbara A. Frick

PRENTICE-HALL INTERNATIONAL, INC., *London*
PRENTICE-HALL OF AUSTRALIA PTY. LIMITED, *Sydney*
PRENTICE-HALL OF CANADA, LTD., *Toronto*
PRENTICE-HALL OF INDIA PRIVATE LIMITED, *New Delhi*
PRENTICE-HALL OF JAPAN, INC., *Tokyo*
PRENTICE-HALL OF SOUTHEAST ASIA PTE. LTD., *Singapore*
WHITEHALL BOOKS LIMITED, *Wellington, New Zealand*

CONTENTS

v

Contents

PREFACE

I GUESS one can't spend sixteen years in a given field without thinking it's a good one. That's the way I feel about public relations. It's interesting, it's fun, it's broadening, and it is occasionally financially rewarding.

Best of all, it's never boring. Practitioners get involved in a variety of endeavors (take a look at the table of contents), they deal with people at all levels of an organization, and they interact with journalists, community leaders, government officials, consumers, and other public relations professionals. There are new challenges and new, interesting people to meet on almost a daily basis. Consequently, one can face most assignments with a sense of wonder and eager anticipation of the lessons to be learned.

Some things do remain the same, however.

Basic PR tools and skills are required to meet each challenge, and there are numerous old standbys which prove handy in a variety of situations.

This is why there are probably so many books on PR—and why more will be forthcoming. The tools have to be explained and rapidly changing socioeconomic conditions dictate that they be explained in contemporary lights.

This book is aimed at newcomers to PR and at those considering a career in the field. It attempts to unravel the need for PR assistance and to show how the many skills can be used to positive effect. Hopefully, it will convey a feeling for the excitement that is part of the PR process and simultaneously serve as a desk reference for beginners in communications activities.

The text represents a good chunk of what

I've seen, experienced, and read over the past sixteen years, so I am grateful to the men and women who have worked with me, above me, and for me because they added to my store of knowledge.

I'm especially indebted to the people who taught me and served as models for me during my early years in the field: people such as Bill McGuire at Haire Publishing Company, Gladys Wurtenburg at Queens College, and Joe Nolan, Bill Carlin, and Joe Wicherski at Chase Manhattan. Additionally, there were several non-PR officials along the way whose willingness to cooperate in and/or help shape PR programs represent the kind of desired management attitudes I describe in chapter seventeen. Standing out in this regard are Jim Murphy at the New York State Bankers Association, Dave Palmer at Bank of America, and Luis Collazo at Chase Manhattan.

A special vote of thanks goes to my brother Larry, who found the time between his New York Daily News reporting duties and care for an infant daughter to do a masterful job of copy-reading. I had originally asked him to look the text over for typos and general observations—which he did—but he came up with at least several dozen valuable suggestions as well.

Also on the list of individuals I'm indebted to are my parents and former students at Hunter College, American Institute of Banking, and American Management Association. The former provided encouraging words over the years, and the latter showed sufficient interest in and enthusiasm for PR to convince me there is a market for another book on the subject.

And then there are my wife and children. There is no way in the world a person can write a book while maintaining a full-time job if his or her family isn't willing to make some sacrifices. My wife and children suffered my evening and weekend stays at my desk, and they helped me as well—Sue with proofreading and suggestions, Pete with some typing, and Debbie by helping me number the pages.

I'm looking forward to spending more free time with them.

THE PRACTICAL HANDBOOK
OF PUBLIC RELATIONS

TO Sue, who inspires me and helps me, and Pete and Debbie, two good kids.

1

WHAT PUBLIC RELATIONS IS ALL ABOUT

THE Ambassador Arms Hotel Company (a fictitious name in a fictitious situation) had what appeared to be a problem, perhaps a serious one.

Or maybe, as some of the organization's more optimistic officials pointed out, it was merely a minor inconvenience that would blow away in a few days or so.

A report had come across the chairman's desk detailing an incident in which the manager of the Kansas City branch refused to let a group of handicapped veterans use the hotel's facilities for the ex-soldiers' annual dinner dance. The manager, who expressed great regret in rendering his decision, explained that the grand ballroom was located on the top floor of the twenty-six-story structure and having seven hundred people exit from it simultaneously in an emergency was a difficult task. That a majority of the veterans were crippled, deaf, or blind made a sudden exodus seem impossible to the hotel executive.

"We are very sorry," the manager wrote to the president of the veterans' organization, "but we feel, in the interest of your own safety, that you will have to find other accommodations."

"Nonsense," retorted the veterans. "Worse, it's discrimination."

In a letter to the hotel signed by each member of the organization's board of directors, the veterans pointed out that the manager made no reference to the paucity of exits when he initially agreed to let them rent the ballroom during a telephone conversation.

"You didn't bring up the subject of a fire or other disaster until you noticed some of us were handicapped," the board members wrote. "Indeed, based on the way you extolled the virtues of your banquet facilities over the phone, you seemed very eager to have our business. However, it was obvious from your ill-at-ease manner when you saw us in person that you are not comfortable in dealing with the physically impaired and that you would prefer not to deal with them in the future.

"Moreover, in twelve years of holding dinner dances in and around Kansas City, your hotel is the first to refuse us access to its ballroom."

The ex-servicemen vigorously protested the manager's action and added that they would refrain from using Ambassador Arms facilities in the future and would urge members of out-of-state chapters to boycott the chain throughout the country. The letter closed with the hope that the organization's retaliatory measures would trigger a series of events leading to economic havoc for the company.

The chairman called his key lieutenants in, summarized the report, and asked, "What do we do about this?"

Two or three seconds of contemplative—and nervous—silence greeted the question before one of the officers rose, cleared his throat to gain another second for further thought, then suggested several activities.

"First, let's get all the facts," he said. "We've heard the veterans' side, now let's hear what our people in Kansas City have to say about the incident. It's possible they'll have a different story for us.

"Then let's determine how serious the problem is, which of our publics are or will be involved, if we can afford to ride it out, or, if not, what we can do to alleviate the situation and eventually turn it around.

"Assuming we have to respond to it," he added, "we should also make sure we establish mechanisms to measure the effectiveness of whatever we do."

An informal investigation revealed that the veterans' version of their discussions with the manager was completely accurate. And within a week the following statements were also on target in describing the situation:

• Room and meeting reservations at the Kansas City branch were below last year's figures.

• Other hotels in the chain were getting cancellation notices and letters of protest from groups representing veterans and/or the handicapped.

• Articles on the hotel's refusal to book the veterans' dinner dance had been featured prominently in the local press and were starting to appear elsewhere in the country.

• Questions about the incident—some of them decidedly hostile—were being directed to the company's head office.

• Three church groups and two colleges sold their shares in the company as a protest.

• Some state and federal legislators were initiating committee hearings on possible legislation concerning the right of hotels to bar groups from using their facilities.

2

"We have a problem, and I don't see it disappearing in the immediate future," stated the officer who had spoken up at the chairman's meeting. "Nor do I think our difficulties are confined to our relationships with veterans and the handicapped."

He then listed the following as publics with which the company would have to communicate on the issue, in addition to ex-servicemen and the physically impaired:

• The press
• Shareholders
• Employees
• Travel agents
• City, state, and federal legislators
• The general public

The official who initiated the investigation dug further and found that the Kansas City incident was a distinct exception to the policy of nondiscrimination generally maintained by the Ambassador Arms. However, many hotels in the chain had ballrooms from which an immediate group departure was difficult. And very few employees had experience or training in dealing with the physically impaired.

With the handicapped becoming increasingly aggressive in their demands for equal treatment—and dozens of social, educational, and political clubs representing veterans and the lame, deaf, or blind angrily focusing attention on the decision in Kansas City—the situation warranted not only a response, but one that would be widespread, rapid, and convincing.

The officer and his subordinates explored possible courses of action, evaluated them, selected the best, and then began budgeting and planning for their implementation.

Included among the weapons employed by the company in contending with the problem were the following:

• A letter to the handicapped-veterans' organization that said the Ambassador Arms management regretted the incident, recognized that the organization could properly assess its ability to react to emergencies, and in an effort to make amends for the inconvenience resulting from the Kansas City manager's decision, would host the following year's dinner dance free of charge.

• The introduction of a program to (a) evaluate all hotels in the chain in regard to ease of entry and departure for the handicapped; (b) evaluate means of communicating emergency instructions to the deaf and blind; and (c) make improvements where they are needed.

• Seminars for hotel employees on how to assist handicapped guests.

• The addition to the Ambassador Arms board of directors of a former government official (with twenty-five years experience supervising programs for the handicapped) who would represent the interests of the physically disadvantaged.

News of these developments and related activities were communicated to interested audiences via press releases, letters to government officials, employee publications, shareholder publications, speeches to community organizations, and open houses to display new facilities. And throughout the duration of the program, the officer and his staff monitored press coverage, studied incoming letters on the issue, followed legislative and regulatory developments, and kept close tabs on the chain's bookings, as well as those at rival hotels through publicly available information.

The group also watched its own activities closely to assure that they were being conducted as planned. And it constantly refined game plans in the event that new strategies and tactics would be needed.

In short, the officer and his lieutenants were practicing public relations, which consists of *activities aimed at generating awareness and appreciation of a concern's policies and performance. These activities are designed to maintain a two-way flow of information so that management can learn of its publics' wants and needs and the publics, in turn, can be informed of management's responses.*

Other definitions of the public relations that have struck my fancy over the years include the following:

• Public relations is a serious business. In fact, it is more than a business. It is an art and science that deals with difficult problems of how an individual or institution can get along satisfactorily with other people and other institutions.[1]

• Public relations is not the doing of deeds—it is

the mechanism for conveying impressions of deeds already done.[2]

• Public relations is more than a narrow set of rules—it is a broad concept. It is the entire body of relationships that go to make up our impression of an individual, an organization or an idea.[3]

• Public relations is organized conceit.[4] (This misses a lot about the practice, but it does have a point. If you're going to talk about yourself, it's better to do so in an organized rather than an unorganized manner.)

• To know ourselves and those around us, to understand our relationships with our fellow human beings and to guide our conduct so that those relationships will be more enjoyable and beneficial to ourselves as well as to others—those are the ideals of the art and science of public relations.[5]

• To gain and hold the favorable opinions of the publics of an institution or industry.[6]

For each of the previous definitions there are dozens that just as adequately describe public relations. So it is not fruitful, in terms of time and because of the difficulty involved in getting thousands of practitioners to agree on "the definitive" term, to dwell overly long on the meaning of the practice. It is, however, important to recognize that any explanation of public relations should take into account the following observations:

• It is not "public relations," but "publics relations." Practitioners are constantly dealing with many different groups, quite a few of which overlap and quite a few of which have interests in conflict with one another.

• Public relations must maintain a two-way flow of information. Qualified practitioners bring information to a concern's publics, and they alert management to its publics' wants and perceptions.

• Good public relations must be related to a concern's performance. If publicly disseminated information also describes an organization's success in meeting its goals, that is fine. But the key word is *performance*. If public relations material does not focus on what a concern is doing

when performance and goals are moving in different directions, then the material is misleading and not representative of ethical public relations practices.

• Public relations employs many tools, several of which do not require a typewriter, typesetter, or camera.

Now let's expand on these four points.

PUBLICS RELATIONS

Depending on how specifically one wants to break it down, it is not unreasonable to think that an individual can compile a list of fifty to a hundred different publics. For the purpose of both brevity and comprehensiveness, here is a list of one dozen groups with which a business interacts. (Nonprofit organizations would generally not deal with the second and sixth groups.)

Four of the publics have been broken down into subcategories to demonstrate the diversity of each group. It will be a useful exercise for readers to try to identify five subcategories in each of the remaining eight publics.

1. Employees
   Officials
   Clerical staff
   Retired employees
   New employees
   Potential employees
   Outstanding employees
   Families of employees
2. Shareholders
   New shareholders
   Large shareholders
   Institutional investors
   Vocal shareholders
   Employee shareholders
   Shareholders who have held the stock for more than five years
3. The media
   General press
   Business press
   Trade press
   Wire services
   Electronic media

4

Friendly journalists
Hostile journalists
Inaccurate journalists
Outstanding journalists
Local weeklies
Community publications
Foreign press

4. Customers
Large buyers (or users of services)
Satisfied customers
Dissatisfied customers
New customers
Old customers
Customers in different parts of the country
Former customers
Potential customers

5. The general public

6. Analysts and other financial intermediaries

7. Students

8. Educators

9. Government

10. Community leaders

11. Minorities

12. Members of the industry (or field) in which the concern operates

In order to understand the potential for conflict among an organization's publics, take a look at the differing points of view that employees and some shareholders may have on salaries. The employees, obviously, would like to see remuneration increased as much as possible. Shareholders, on the other hand, may prefer to have costs reduced so that earnings per share and dividends can rise.

Employees themselves can differ heatedly on the subject of pay. Older staff members, with families and medical expenses to worry about, tend to be more interested in employee benefits than their younger, unmarried colleagues. The latter individuals would prefer to see bursts of company generosity manifested in larger salaries as opposed to additional health or retirement benefits.

On the subject of disclosure, potential investors and government regulators constantly seek more information about publicly held cor-

porations. Customers, on the other hand, are often fearful that increased openness will reveal facts about their relationships with the company they would prefer to keep out of the limelight. At the same time, shareholders and employees may become concerned that corporate loquaciousness will provide competitors with too much information. As a result, debates on further disclosure pull some very key publics in different directions.

While lower prices, which reduce and occasionally eliminate the spread between expenses and income, are sources of delight to customers, the reduced earnings that occasionally accompany such pricing policies are of little cheer to stockholders and the staff.

It is, of course, possible to have reduced prices generate greater profits. But in attempting to find that one price from which customers and the company derive maximum pleasure, there are frequent trial runs, which dismay the buyer or the seller.

Compounding the lack of unanimity among publics is the emergence of one-issue special-interest groups: bodies of men and women who unite spiritedly behind causes such as reducing government expenditures, getting dog litter off the street, barring smoking in public places, or any other idea that catches their fancy. In severing boundary lines that normally separate publics, these one-issue groups are more difficult to reach than employees, for example. They're also harder to stay in contact with, because the resolution of an issue or birth of a more passionate one elsewhere dissolves them and sends their members hither and yon.

Public relations practitioners had better get used to dealing with them, however, because our constantly changing environment is creating new one-issue interest groups at a pace unprecedented in history. Responding to their concerns will become a way of life for many public relations departments.

But whether we deal with an easily identified public or a one-issue interest group, the most important thing to remember about the "publics" aspect of public relations is that each constituency is important to an organization. Any given public can, on a given issue at a given time or place, assume center stage and relegate all other interested parties to secondary roles.

PUBLIC RELATIONS MAINTAINS A TWO-WAY FLOW OF INFORMATION

Well-written press releases, persuasive speeches, beautiful photography, and creative community relations activities can often be a waste of valuable time and money if there aren't: (a) advance information on the attitudes of the targeted audience; and (b) follow-up research to measure feedback and uncover ideas for successful activities in the future.

The public relations department, which serves as the spokesmen and spokeswomen for the organization, must also function as its eyes and ears. It must know how the concern's publics are viewing major issues; it must determine how these attitudes affect the organization (and if these attitudes can be changed); and it must assess the publics' reactions to its activities.

If the department doesn't perform these tasks, some very important messages may be unheard by the people to whom they should be directed. And other themes may never get stated, because no one saw the need for their delivery.

The specific questions that should be asked in learning about the external environment will be discussed in chapter two. It will suffice at this point merely to state that bringing information into the organization encompasses careful examination of issues from the viewpoints of all publics. As the Ambassador Arms public relations office demonstrated in the Kansas City situation, management must be alerted to the seriousness, or lack of seriousness, of potential problems, the opinions of its publics, the potential for new problems, and the possible effects of alternate responses on publics and opinion leaders. Without such intelligence about the external environment, a public relations campaign starts off at a distinct disadvantage.

PUBLIC RELATIONS MUST BE RELATED TO PERFORMANCE

Discussing public relations in 1980, David Finn, chairman of Ruder & Finn, stated,

It is a presumption to say that public relations can secure public support for a cause or mold public opinion. A legitimate function of public relations is to make management's opinions public and to present the case for causes management believes in. Such efforts will win support if the opinions and causes prove to be consistent with public interests.[7]

Joseph T. Nolan, head of public affairs at Monsanto, made a similar point, focusing first on the importance of bringing information into the corporation. He used the *Harvard Business Review* as the vehicle for his message as he wrote:

The essence of improving the business image rests not in trying to conjure up a good story when performance fails, but in sharpening corporate perceptions of emerging social and political trends and in adjusting performance so there will, in fact, be a good story to tell.[8]

And Thomas W. Thompson, editor of *United States Banker,* writing in a three-part series on communicational planning, stated:

Words count. Deeds count more. And an organization's continuing conduct counts most of all.[9]

In somewhat less eloquent prose, I simply say that you shouldn't produce releases, speeches, and so forth, discussing your firm's innovativeness when it hasn't introduced a new product or service concept in twenty years and its executives still come to work in high-button shoes.

Nor should you expect the public relations department to lead a firm into the next decade by producing literature hailing its creativity. To be sure, the department can—and should—recommend activities that would encourage performance more in keeping with the times. But it can't introduce new products and services by itself. Its function, instead, is to gain support and understanding for what management is doing. Hopefully, the information and advice it gives senior officials will be helpful in shaping the policies that lead to profitable and forward-thinking performance.

PUBLIC RELATIONS USES MANY TOOLS

To many laymen, public relations primarily consists of working with the media, preparing speeches, and producing publications. To others, who may have seen the wrong movie or read the wrong book, its practitioners concentrate on selecting the proper wine for luncheons and dinners, obtaining tickets to successful Broadway shows, and getting seven inches of copy in *The New York Times* on the nuptials of the chairman's daughter.

The first trio of functions are, of course, exceedingly important parts of the public relations officer's job (the latter three are of little consequence, and deservedly so), but they only scratch the surface. There are numerous other tools to be used in the course of a public relations campaign, and any one of them can be crucial to the overall success of the effort.

The tools of public relations consist of the following:

- Research
- Planning
- Evaluation
- Counseling
- Press relations
- News and feature-article writing
- Letter writing
- Photography
- Investor relations
- Annual reports
- Other shareholder publications
- Community relations
- Government relations
- Philanthropy
- Internal communications
- Speeches
- Films, tapes, slides, closed-circuit television

They will be discussed in subsequent chapters.

SUMMARY

Regardless of the manner in which public relations is described, students should know that (a) the practice involves printed and verbal communication with many different publics; (b) this communication both goes out of and comes into the organization; (c) the outward communication focuses on performance; and (d) practitioners employ many tools in alerting publics to management's policies and actions.

Public relations is clearly a management function, although there are still some organizations that do not share this view. Fortunately, the trend is moving toward greater recognition of the public relations role in the shaping of organizational strategy and goal formation. Private- and public-sector firms are under siege from consumerists, the civil rights movement, disgruntled shareholders, women's groups, employees, the handicapped, and a host of one-issue constituencies who want immediate redress of the problems.

Public relations difficulties no longer merely raise fears of minor sales losses or damaged goodwill. In today's volatile world, they often threaten the very ability of an organization to survive.

The challenges of the 1980s and beyond are forcing stategists to look outside their company's headquarters more than ever before. The "public be damned" attitude of turn-of-the-century industrialists has definitely become a relic of the past. The public does count, and public relations departments, as the focal point for interaction between concerns and their external environments, are, by necessity, growing in importance.

FOR FURTHER EXPLORATION

1. Come up with your own definition of public relations.

2. Your company is the target of a take-over

attempt. List five publics you would concentrate on in shaping a public relations course of action.

3. How would shareholders and students on a

liberal college campus react to new company investments in a Latin American country accused of human rights violations?

4. Name some one-issue interest groups in the news today that would be of interest to a Fortune-500 company.

5. You are head of public relations for a tire-manufacturing company. Your boss wants to know why you spend so much time reading about community organizations, shareholders, and the public at large instead of bombarding them with information. What do you tell her?

2

THE NON-WRITING, NON-EDITING, NON-PICTURE-TAKING—BUT NEVERTHELESS VERY IMPORTANT—PUBLIC RELATIONS TOOLS

RESEARCH, planning, evaluation, and counseling are frequently omitted from lists of public relations activities and rarely thought of by outsiders as make-or-break factors in corporate- and nonprofit-sector communications programs. But they are, indeed, critical and are occasionally *the* critical factors in a campaign. They therefore deserve special attention.

RESEARCH

THE importance of research on issues and audiences has already been discussed in chapter one, so there is no need to belabor the point. A discussion of some fact-finding and fact-keeping methods is, however, worth including here. The methods include the following:

1. News monitoring—With approximately 1,700 daily newspapers, some 150 general-interest magazines, close to 8,000 weekly and monthly newspapers, and numerous periodicals zeroing in on almost every field of endeavor known to man—not to mention the hundreds of television and radio stations in this country—private- and public-sector organizations have a myriad of news-gathering organizations working, in effect, for them. If these organizations do nothing other than tap these sources on a daily basis, they've taken a critical first step in learning about their publics.

There are many ways to do this. Some public relations departments assign subject areas— disclosure, women's rights, South Africa, international business, privacy, human rights overseas, corporate ethics, and so on—to individual staff members and ask them to report on developments and potential impacts on the organization. Other corporations assign publications, television stations, and radio stations to different personnel with the admonition that they alert their superiors to developments that would be of interest to management.

Some firms may monitor the media on an informal basis, ask clipping services for transcripts and articles on given topics, or invite journalists to chat with management about major issues. Regardless of the method, the print and electronic media are indispensable sources of information that can't be overlooked in any research program.

2. Maintaining a library—A clipping or transcript once read is not nearly as valuable as a piece of information that's been perused and saved. Very few individuals can accurately recall everything they've seen. And one can't properly evaluate the importance of information unless it's measured against other writings and commentaries on the subject. A library of articles, reports, and speeches on topics of importance to an organization is therefore a must in keeping tabs on the external environment.

In addition to saving clippings, transcripts, speeches, and recent publications, a good library should also include standard reference books, the *Congressional Record,* recognized source books on the economy and the industry or field in which the organization operates, trade publications, histories of previous public relations programs, and public opinion surveys.

3. Analysis of mail—Letters, which often give a somewhat one-sided view, in that people are generally quicker to complain than to praise, provide valuable information on the attitudes of individuals and groups regarding company policy, performance, products, personnel, and prognosis. While they do represent a vocal minority, they are nevertheless tangible evidences of some people's reactions, and they often present clues to the thinking of the public at large. Equally important, when viewed in a historical context, they can show the formation of trends.

4. Analysis of sales records—This, too, provides meaningful evidence of how well or how badly a company is doing in the marketplace. And depending on how specific one wants to be, sales analyses can concentrate on a particular neighborhood, city, state, or country. They can also tell the future by identifying trends, which, if they are spotted at an early stage, can be reversed with promotional campaigns if so desired.

5. Analysis of speeches by opinion leaders—Recognizing that certain members of society have greater opportunity and ability to motivate people than others, public relations officials are wise to pay close attention to the utterances of legislators, heads of rival concerns, and leaders of organizations with which they interact. What better way to prepare responses to those who would regulate or otherwise influence your ability to meet annual goals than to hear or read their publicly announced intentions? Additionally, studying the speeches of opinion leaders over a period of years gives you insights into how they will react to external events in the present and future. It also fathers ideas on how to shape successful counteractions to their strategies.

6. Attendance at seminars, conferences, and workshops—Professional societies, think-tank organizations, academic institutions, and trade associations are continually sponsoring seminars, conferences, and workshops on issues of current interest. Although some merely rehash information previously reported in the media, many offer talks by noteworthy elected and appointed officials, business and community leaders, or journalists and academicians who have useful and previously unrevealed insights to share. These insights, in turn, spark discussions among the attendees that allow them to build on the knowledge acquired by listening to the speakers.

7. Culling information from personal contacts—All businesspeople tend to move in circles frequented by men and women with similar backgrounds, professional interests, and experiences. Discussions at luncheons, over cocktails, or during the course of a transaction provide information that can be of value on its own or when added to data accumulated elsewhere. It's not a bad idea to draft memorandums for your files—which can be useful immediately or at some time in the future—whenever new light is shed on a subject. These memos increase in value if copies are sent to all the parties in your

concern who might benefit from them. An added advantage of sharing the information is that thinking of the people to whom copies of a memo should go forces the author to look at the subject from the intended readers' viewpoints. This exercise can induce new interpretations.

8. Reading opinion polls and surveys—Public relations professionals would do well to subscribe to the reports on public opinion periodically disseminated by research firms. The studies cover a wide range of topics—what American housewives think of shopping by phone, how academicians react to open enrollment, what the man in the street thinks of tax reform, and so on—and direct readers' attention to shifts in national or local moods before they become the focus of media attention. It is not unusual that a minor change in consumer attitudes mentioned in a one-line comment on the bottom of page 6 will precede a powerful, nationwide movement for or against a particular product or company.

Research firms can also be commissioned to conduct detailed surveys of products, issues, services, organizations, politicans, and so forth. Depending on the amount of time and money the commissioning firm is willing to spend on the project, these endeavors can solicit the opinions of any number of individuals over any size geographic area.

These investigations can be performed at the direction of one enterprise or of a trade association representing all the members of a particular industry or field—or under the auspices of just several participants in a particular sector.

The advantages of joining with other concerns in designing a survey are the following:

- It's cheaper.
- With more people suggesting questions, it's likelier that all the important areas will be covered.
- It's a good way to stay in touch with counterparts at rival organizations.
- It's cheaper (given the pressures to keep operating costs down, many treasurers and financial vice-presidents count this argument twice).

The reasons for going it alone are the following:

- The sponsor has more control.
- The sponsor is less reluctant to ask embarrassing questions.
- The sponsor is not airing dirty laundry in front of competitors.
- The sponsor avoids the embarrassment of having competitors know that it ranks below them (if such is the case), as well as the pain of paying for information so pleasing to a rival.

9. *Company-conducted surveys*—Private concerns and public-sector organizations may not have the experience in polling that professional research firms possess, but this doesn't always stop them from conducting surveys of their own.

Nor should it. The advantage of such solo exercises, as opposed to the use of outside experts, is that they are generally cheaper, easier to change as circumstances warrant, less subject to misinterpretation between the orginators of the study and the pollsters, and are for the sponsoring concern's eyes only. The latter point takes on added importance when answers reveal marked hostility to an organization's performance or executives.

Typical self-service surveys are mail questionnaires for stockholders and employees. These investigations are not difficult to conduct, and they often elicit responses that are best kept within the family.

PLANNING

THE advantage of planning is comparable to the difference between knowing that you want to do, how you want to do it, with how much money, with which personnel, and with which publics *before* you launch a public relations campaign, and acting in a seat-of-the-pants, trial-and-error manner. It's possible that an organization may get lucky with a knee-jerk reaction to a public relations problem, but common sense, the odds, and the lessons of history all suggest that the longer, more thought-out approach is better.

If done well, planning results in the following:

- Better public relations performance
- Less-expensive public relations programs
- Messages being sent to the right publics
- Less surprises
- A greater ability to roll with the punches when surprises do occur, because there are activities held in reserve
- Less guessing
- More flexibility
- Less likelihood that the total budget will be expended midway through the campaign

- Greater knowledge by all the participants of what their colleagues are doing
- More support and involvement of senior executives, because they participate in the formulation of goals and strategies
- Better use of senior management's time
- Greater involvement and support from middle management, because it is known that senior management will be reviewing the results and looking askance at those who don't cooperate
- The ability to take an unhurried offensive role; that is, choosing the time, place, and means of contact with the public, as opposed to reacting to the initiatives of special-interest groups.

WHERE TO FOCUS PLANNERS' ATTENTION

In order to plan well, public relations people must look in the following directions:

- Outside the organization to determine moods and perceptions of publics. This includes careful monitoring of the competitive, legislative, regulatory, international, socioeconomic, and technological environments.

• Inside the organization in order to weigh the abilities of the concern and its people to answer the needs of its publics.

• From a macro-view, studying the entire organization and the total external environment.

• From a micro-view, carefully studying each unit in the organization and each of the external issues impacting on performance.

• Backward in order to determine how opinions were shaped, by whom, how issues evolved, and how they are dealt with.

• Forward in order to decide what the planners want to do, how the external environment will react to these plans, which resources will be used, and how activities will be monitored and evaluated.

HOW TO PLAN

Good planning includes the following activities:

• Gathering information
• Analyzing information
• Identifying problems
• Determining causes
• Identifying alternate courses of action
• Assessing strengths and weaknesses of public relations personnel
• Evaluating alternate plans
• Adapting plans
• Monitoring activities—and revising them when necessary
• Selecting methods of monitoring and measuring activities.

EVALUATION

WITHOUT feedback on the effectiveness or lack of effectiveness of a communications program, public relations people might do just as well tossing their speeches, press releases, community activities, and other measures at a brick wall instead of at specific publics, and hope for the best. Whether they target their activities or perform them indiscriminately, practitioners will have just as much knowledge of the success of their endeavors. And they will have learned nothing about what they should or shouldn't do when similar problems arise in the future.

Common sense tells us that informational and goodwill programs aimed at identifiable segments of society should do better than those directed at brick walls, no matter how forcefully they are tossed. But how do we know for sure? Perhaps well-planned messages and programs were so badly received that their creators would have been better off if they had colorfully decorated the aforementioned wall with them. Or perhaps the information and activities were gratefully accepted by a public that, for some

inexplicable reason, attributes them to a competing concern.

The best way to eliminate doubts on how the public relations programs are being perceived in the marketplace is to have a carefully orchestrated review operation that attempts to find out (a) if you accomplished your goals; and (b) how you can do better the next time around.

These two questions are rather broad, so the following questions are suggested as building blocks to getting the answers:

• Was our research adequate in terms of volume, timeliness, and freedom from bias and inaccuracies?
• Which were our best sources of information?
• Which were our worst sources of information?
• Did we stay within our budget?
• Did our planning touch all bases?
• Was our budget adequate?
• Did we follow our plan?

• Did we get the desired cooperation and participation from senior management?

• Did we get the desired cooperation and participation from all other non-PR personnel?

• Did we make appropriate use of our in-house experts, such as the organization's lawyers, accountants, purchasers, and so on?

• Did the public relations staff perform as expected?

• Which community leaders were most effective in opposing our activities?

• Which community leaders were least effective?

• How did we cope with the unexpected?

• Did we have to cope with the unexpected too frequently?

• Did we reach all of our intended audiences?

• Did our messages influence their attitudes?

• How good (or bad) was the media pickup of our material?

• How does this compare with the press coverage given our competitors?

• Which media were especially generous in their treatment of our side of the story?

• Which media disappointed us in their treatment of our material?

• Which of our activities and informational material could be used in future public relations campaigns?

• Are we getting feedback from all of the targeted publics?

• Are we satisfied that the feedback is representative of each public?

• Could we have achieved the same results with less expenditures of dollars, time, and personnel?

• Did we do a good job of keeping senior management and other involved personnel informed on all key developments?

• What does senior management think of our efforts? (Don't ignore the officers to whom the PR department reports. They're the ones who review public relations budgets and approve salary increases.)

SOME WORDS OF CAUTION

In many cases, public relations practitioners are dealing with intangibles that do not easily lend themselves to identification or measurement. How, for example, does one weigh goodwill, fear, anger, doubts, apathy, satisfaction, and so on?

One shouldn't expect program evaluations—no matter how thorough—always to provide clear-cut or lasting answers. In many cases, broad responses are all one can hope for. Nor should one assume that facts pointing to the successful realization of all program goals put a problem to rest for any extended period of time. Public opinion is very often a will-o'-the-wisp phenomenon (whatever happened to Fabian, Chubby Checker, hula hoops, mini-skirts, and maxi-skirts?) and is vulnerable to a multitude of happenings. As a result, evaluation has to be a continuous process.

It may be called research rather than evaluation if the monitoring takes place long after the termination of a public relations campaign. But regardless of its name, the study of external events has to be a 365-day-a-year process.

SOME CLUES ON WHAT TO LOOK AT

Despite the illusory aspects of communication between private- and public-sector organizations and their many publics, there are some solid facts and figures that can be used to help measure the effectiveness of public relations programs, especially those of corporations. These measures include the following.

1. Shareholder proxies—Getting a high percentage of votes supporting management positions prior to an annual meeting would indicate the existence of a contented shareholder body. If proxies were ignored or elicited a large number of antimanagement votes, one would have to ask some probing questions about the effectiveness of investor relations activities.

2. Share turnover—Frequent turnover indicates shareholder dissatisfaction or doubts about the company's ability to produce a satisfactory return on their investments. Stability, on the other hand, implies that shareholders are satisfied and bullish on the firm's outlook.

3. Press coverage—One method of measuring press coverage is to take all the favorable clippings and air time devoted to your organization and determine how much it would have cost to buy the space and minutes for advertisements. If the figure exceeds the cost of preparing the news releases and attendant press relations activities, you are somewhat ahead of the game.*

Another method is to determine the ratio of releases sent out to the number of articles and favorable mentions on television and radio. The ratio becomes more meaningful if you then compare it with those of your competitors.

Still another method is simply to ask yourself if you're satisfied with the quality and quantity of media attention. If you are capable of asking tough questions and giving honest answers, this subjective review may be the best way to determine if you're pleased or displeased with press coverage. But you must make sure you've identified the media that are most important to you, and also that you're including your competitors' press pickup in your analysis.

4. Number of press queries and requests for interviews—It's one thing to have editors transform releases into inches of type or seconds of air time; it's quite another to have them aggressively seek the opinion of your organization's officers when giving coverage to their areas of expertise. If reporters frequently call your PR department for assistance in gathering informa-

tion, it's because they consider it a reliable help and your concern's spokespeople knowledgeable and cooperative sources of information. If they only call the competition, you have a problem.

5. Media attendance at press conferences—Nothing gives a press relations operative more terrifying daydreams than the prospect of calling a press conference that no one attends. Poor turnouts can, on occasion, be the result of a major news happening elsewhere, a flu epidemic in the metropolitan area's city rooms, or bad luck, but if they occur repeatedly, they reflect a poor image. The press will stay away if they think the hosting organization has too many conferences at which nothing of significance is said, has executives who duck questions, or has spokespeople whose opinions don't interest journalists. Each of the preceding explanations represents a public relations problem.

6. Underwriting fees and loan charges—Financial intermediaries that assist a firm in bringing its obligations to market, or that finance its activities, are exceedingly astute observers of its performance, outlook, and image. Fees and interest rates above or below those normally charged the industry are important barometers of an organization's image.

7. The nature of legislation being introduced on the regulation of the industry or field in which the firm operates—It has been said that city, state, and federal lawmakers reflect rather than lead public opinion. This means that a spate of new bills

---

*There was the time I accompanied calling officers and an economist of a bank on a trip to Cincinnati. The lending personnel were there to oversee a seminar held for select customers in southwestern Ohio, the economist was on hand to present his forecasts, and I tagged along to arrange press interviews for our traveling experts.

At a last-minute coffee klatch to review seminar arrangements, the ranking bank officer on the trip looked around the table at the not insignificant number of colleagues present and wondered aloud if the cost of flying us all to Cincinnati, housing us, and feeding us made the effort worthwhile. It may have been my imagination, but I felt he was looking at me when he finished his question. And then again, it may not have been my imagination, since he seemed to be

a member of the vanishing breed of bankers who feel that if you're not making loans for your institution, you're among the great unwashed.

In any event, the interviews I arranged generated large and favorable articles that occupied space only a small fortune could have purchased. Petty and unforgiving for the imagined (or real) slight, I sent the officer the clips attached to a balance sheet showing the cost of the space on one side and my paltry travel expenses on the other.

Two months later he reviewed the new business resulting from the trip—which really wasn't bad considering loan demand at that time—and concluded that I had the best bottom line of all the officers who flew to Cincinnati. He even became a supporter of PR activities after that.

or hearings on ways to curtail alleged abuses are definite indications of disenchantment. Successful passage of these measures ceases to be an indication; it is a clear announcement that John Q. Public has an ax to grind.

8. The success of college recruiting programs, especially at the graduate level—Recent recipients of an M.B.A. are blessed with (a) the ability to dissect a company's financial statement and performance and make a good guess as to its future; and (b) a desire to go with a winner. Looking at a firm's batting average in terms of making job offers and getting affirmative responses is one way to decide whether it is perceived as a winner or a loser in its sphere of operation. (The same point can be made about the number of people working in the organization who previously held positions of responsibility at rival concerns.)

9. Personnel turnover—Chapter thirteen will discuss the importance of public relations activities in educating employees and improving their morale. If an unacceptable turnover rate is transformed into an acceptable one following the implementation of new internal communications strategies, the public relations department can accept a deserved pat on its collective back. Conversely, if the program fails to arrest the resignation pace—or, worse, speeds it up— public relations personnel would be wise to go back to their drawing boards.

10. Government use of products and services—With consumer groups and government agencies serving as diligent watchdogs of city, county, state, and federal use of corporate products and services, those who run government purchasing departments must base their decisions on the performance and image of the would-be suppliers. It follows that those firms that do more than their share of business with the government have successfully told their stories to highly critical audiences.

11. References to the organization in the speeches of community leaders and politicians—As we will point out in chapter fifteen, considerable and careful research is the cornerstone of a successful speech. Favorable references would imply that there have been positive comments in the media or marketplace about the organization, whereas negative statements reflect harsh judgments. No

comments could mean that a firm has failed to impress shapers of public opinion, which may be the harshest cut of all.

12. The direction in which the price of a firm's shares is moving—For the purposes of simplicity, up is good and down is bad, especially when the movement goes against the rest of the market.

13. The actions of institutional investors vis-a-vis a company's stock—Because institutional investors (a) buy in very large blocks, and (b) use other people's money, they must exercise extreme care in making buy-and-sell decisions. The tenor of their transactions is, as a result, of much greater interest to an organization's management than are the movements of individuals who are debating the ownership of ten shares.

14. Requests for annual reports—No company publication performs as many functions or has as many audiences as the annual report. In addition to being mailed to shareholders, analysts, pension fund managers, and other financial constituencies, the publication is made available to the media, customers, college placement offices, government officials, business school libraries, and a wide array of other interested parties. Many business enterprises print two or more copies for every shareholder. With some corporations having more than 100,000 investors, printing on a two-to-one ratio indicates strong confidence in the amount of interest the publication will be shown.

What a shame it would be—if not a public relations disaster of immense proportions—if only a handful of requests for the report arrived at company headquarters. While many executives would bemoan the cost of the extra, unwanted copies—a not insignificant figure— others would be wiser to concentrate on the causes for the lack of interest in the report, as well as methods to eliminate them.

15. Requests for contributions—An overload of requests for contributions to needy charities will, admittedly, create extra chores for some staff members who work on corporate philanthropy. But the attendant headaches are soothed by the awareness that people in the community recognize the company's generosity. Conversely, a minimal amount of requests from fund-raising entities mean the charities are unaware of the company's involvement in, and concern for, the affairs of the community.

16. Directorships offered company executives—There is a definite relationship between a corporation's or a nonprofit organization's image and the number of its officers who serve on boards of directors elsewhere. The officers would simply not be asked to serve as directors if their full-time affiliations wouldn't bring credit to the institutions seeking new board members.

17. Speech requests—These are similar to invitations to serve on boards of directors in that the principal speaker at any function worthy of distinction must be highly respected by the people in his or her field. Chief executive officers who are rarely invited to address major gatherings have image problems that must be tackled if they are to fulfill the roles they have been given.

18. Attendance at annual meetings—A sparse turnout is a sign of apathy and possibly disgust—unless the meeting is held at an isolated site.

19. The tone of questions at annual meetings—Having shareholders complain about performance or ask to have the chief executive dismissed on charges of incompetence—and it happens—would have to be interpreted as an absence of harmony. It is important, however, to study the vote counts on hostile stockholder proposals. It could be the advocates of aggressive amendments are out-of-sync minorities or spokespeople for a meaningful number of investors.

20. Interest by stock analysts—Every major brokerage house and financial intermediary employs analysts who prepare studies for internal and external use on the wisdom of buying and selling shares within given industries. If the analysts are not paying attention to your firm in their reports about your sector of the economy, the likely explanation is that they don't think the firm is important enough.

21. Nature of comments by analysts, stock brokers, pension fund managers, and so on—Attention or lack of attention by the intermediaries is important; favorable or unfavorable comments are crucial. Comments more critical of a firm than its financial performance would warrant are definitely symptoms of a public relations problem.

COUNSELING

BEFORE an organization embarks on an expansion program, introduction of a new product, involvement in a major community project, or effort to defeat a unionization attempt, it generally seeks the counsel and approval of its top management. The senior public relations official should be one of the executives participating in these planning and reviewing sessions.

This does not mean that a public relations director should have a veto power over such decisions—although the poignant cries of practitioners who wanted to know "why didn't they ask me" have frequently been heard in the wake of major disasters. (In fairness, there have even been one or two instances when the top communications official lamented, "Why did those fools listen to me?!")

It does, however, suggest that the personnel who serve as an organization's eyes and ears to the outside world should also perform as counselors in decision-making discussions impacting on various constituencies. Why not listen to what the people who have been monitoring publics' perceptions and needs have to say? Their advice is free and can be easily discarded.

For example, who besides the in-house spokesperson for the public can have the factual wherewithal to predict shareholder reaction to a new stock-purchase plan? Or the community's response to the relocation of a manufacturing plant? Or the government's counterproposal to a corporation's request to enter a field not mentioned in its charter?

If internal public relations departments or

outside counselors are not included in the higher councils of management, then the PR practitioners' first and most important priority is to convince their organization or client that they perform a management function.

Failure to do so often means that PR departments and counselors will, by necessity, spend too much time putting out fires instead of shaping long-range programs designed to eliminate difficulties before they become unmanageable.

SUMMARY

Good communications skills are helpful to any public relations campaign. Blend them with knowledge about publics and one's own capabilities and you have the prerequisites for a successful—if not very successful—effort.

In short, in order to get maximum mileage out of each communication, a considerable amount of time and energy is required both before and after the actual distribution of public relations messages gets underway. Practitioners must know how their publics feel about issues, how they can best be persuaded to share management's views, how messages can be carried to these publics, by whom, at what cost, and, last but not least, how to determine if the messages are being correctly interpreted by the targeted audiences.

One of the most serious dilemmas facing public relations personnel is that they are too often forced into defensive roles because problems weren't seen in advance. This causes them to spend much of their time writing, editing, and producing responses to the initiatives of others.

By fulfilling the management function of anticipating issues and shaping actions that can minimize negative impact and maximize gains, public relations executives make their jobs easier and much more satisfying. At the same time, they are doing their organizations a great service.

FOR FURTHER EXPLORATION

1. Your company's manufacturing plant in Flint, Michigan, has been accused of discharging harmful elements into the neighboring river. What would you look at to determine if you have a serious public relations problem or not?

2. Your company has been successful in defeating an attempt to unionize your operating departments at corporate headquarters. How long do you think you should wait before being on the alert to employee unrest or another unionization drive? What would you look at to determine if there is lingering discontent or the stirrings of another try at getting staff members to support a union vote?

3. One way of comparing the press coverage given your firm against that given your competitor is to count the number of clippings and minutes of air time devoted to each concern. There are, however, more subjective–and more meaningful–ways of assessing media treatment. Can you think of any?

4. Can you identify emerging issues facing American universities today that would require the attention and counsel of college public relations directors?

5. You are director of public relations for an organization that raises funds for cancer research. You've been told to set up a library for your department. What would you put in it?

3

PRESS RELATIONS

MAINTAINING good press relations, generally an enjoyable and rewarding endeavor, is ofttimes aggravating, difficult, time-consuming, and occasionally perilous.

This raises some interesting questions.

1. Why bother?

2. If performance is one of the most important ingredients in public relations, and we're satisfied that our actions are exemplary, why not let our deeds speak for themselves?

3. If we decide it is important to get information to our many publics, why use press releases—which are subject to editors' whims and fancies—when we can prepare advertisements, over which we have complete copy and art control?

I will now attempt to answer the questions in reverse numerical order.

ADVERTISING VERSUS PRESS RELATIONS

JUST about every PR practitioner who has had a press release ignored, reduced from twelve paragraphs to one, or totally botched by sloppy reporting at the media of his or her choice has longed at one time or another for that best of all possible worlds in which editors merely slap a headline on the prose and run it exactly as it was written. But such worlds do not exist. So communicators seek less aggravating fields of endeavor or else move across the hall to where the advertising department is domiciled.

If you don't like to see your copy played around with, there is much to be said for a career in advertising. The advantages include the following:

• Control of copy

• Control of size of ad or length of time it appears on radio or television

• Control of placement (that is, where the ad appears)

• Control of artwork (photography, models, color, and so on)

In short, the advertisement that leaves the company's headquarters en route to the media is the advertisement the public sees and/or hears. And it is seen or heard at the times and in the particular media chosen by the company. All the company has to do is pay for the privilege of having such control.

Sometimes through the nose.

This, then, induces some senior executives

to pause and wonder if perhaps there are some advantages to going the press-release route after all. I submit there are.

In comparison with advertising, there are two distinct benefits of publicity.

1. You don't have to pay for the time or space devoted to your release—Yes, there is no guarantee that the release will be used—or that it will be used to your satisfaction—but there is no charge when it does appear in print or on the air. So assuming the journalists don't badly misinterpret the release or end up ruining it by substituting your competitor's name for that of your company, chances are that the difference between your version and that of the media won't be worth the cost of purchasing a similar amount of space or air time.

2. The use of a release by the media gives it a third-party endorsement—Regardless of whether the press thinks the opening of a new business office or the appointment of a new member of a hospital's board of trustees is worthwhile, its mentions of these developments gives them an added legitimacy they wouldn't have without the media exposure. More important, the use of the release by a newspaper, magazine, or news program tells the general public that editors think it is deserving of mention, and that they are not running it because someone wanted to pay for an advertisement.

There is, nevertheless, no need to initiate an either-or-debate, because press relations and advertising work best when they work together. Publicity reinforces the information disseminated through paid advertisements, which, in turn, expand on the interest aroused by mentions in the news. Those who advocate the elimination of advertisements in favor of press relations activities are limiting the potential impact of news relations—and vice versa.

WHY NOT LET DEEDS SPEAK FOR THEMSELVES?

Let's pretend that the Jones Motor Company (a fictitious company) has decided that the reasons for the small number of minority automobile dealerships is that black and Hispanic would-be vendors of Jones vehicles lack the experience and capital to establish themselves in the business. Even though the percentage of minority dealers is no less at Jones than at other companies, the firm would like to rectify the situation. It initiates a program that provides minority men and women with three years of on-the-job training on automobile production, maintenance, and sales, then lends qualified graduates money (at rates below those charged by commercial banks) to open dealerships.

One hundred men and women are selected to participate in the first year, and the reports on their progress after the initial six months are most impressive. Furthermore, the participants are delighted with both the quality of the training and their outlook for the future.

But they are only one hundred out of the millions of blacks and Hispanics in the country. Many who are not in the program are less than thrilled with the minority representation among Jones auto dealers. And liberal whites, concerned about social injustice and economic disparities, are starting to vent their anger on the automobile industry. They picket showrooms of domestic manufacturers, they urge people to purchase foreign cars, and they bombard the media with press releases, letters to the editor, and op-ed-page features.

Now, Jones insensitivity or lack of meaningful actions in the past may have contributed to the misrepresentation of blacks and Hispanics in its showrooms, but there can be no denying that the company is making a sincere effort to correct the imbalances. Yet in the absence of an aggressive press relations program, who knows this?

Only the one hundred men and women in the program, their families, their friends, and very few others.

This does not constitute a sufficient body of spokespeople who can correct the inaccurate impressions held by thousands. Therefore, an obvious way to narrow the gap between Jones detractors and Jones supporters is to let the media know of the company's new program.

This leads to the first of several possible retorts to the initial question in the chapter.

WHY BOTHER?

1. Publicity gets useful information to key publics and allows influential audiences to learn more about you.

2. Sending press releases out allows the media to perform an invaluable middleman function—Standing on any New York City street corner and verbally extolling the virtues of the Jones Motor Company will only get the messages to a handful of passersby, no matter how well reasoned the arguments or how eloquent the speaker. Giving the same message to the media means it could reach millions of people in less than a day.

3. Communicating to the public through the media and openly answering questions enhances the credibility of the speakers and the institutions they represent.

4. Because of the diversity of the press—that is, daily newspapers, general-interest magazines, business publications, trade journals, local weeklies, news programs, talk shows, and so on—disseminators of information have a veritable smorgasbord of options to choose from in trying to reach select special-interest groups.

5. Publicity can counter false rumors.

6. Good press relations provide you with opportunities to air your side of the story—The difference between a news item presenting opposing points of view and one that tells only one person's side of the story is exceedingly sharp.

This point can be illustrated with references to two separate incidents that took place in the mid-1970s.

My brother, a reporter for the *New York Daily News,* received a call one day from a local politician he knew since grade-school. It seems the politician, who represented people in one of New York City's five boroughs, was vexed because his constituents had to pay more for phone calls to other boroughs than did residents of those areas. In a relatively angry tirade, the politician labeled this situation unfair and vowed to correct it. It appeared he had some sound arguments, but there are two sides to any issue, so my brother called the phone company to hear what its PR people had to say.

They had a lot to say. "The charge of bias against residents of the borough in question is unwarranted. Those people pay more for calls to other boroughs because they live farther from these areas than the residents of the other parts of the city. At the same time, they pay less for calls to their own borough than do nonresidents, because charges are based solely on distance. Mr._____ is merely engaging in a phony grandstand play," said the telephone company representatives.

Another New York paper, which has supported this politician throughout his career, wrote an article without bothering to contact anyone from the telephone company. The impressions left with readers of this publication were decidedly different from those of readers who were told both sides of the story.

In another incident, an automobile firm was accused by a discharged employee of favoritism and nepotism in the manner in which it supplied its dealerships. The employee made several derogatory statements to a major newspaper about the company and a like amount of favorable references to his years of service in the organization. The company replied that it couldn't comment on the charges because the matter was under litigation so the press focused only on the statements of the discharged employee and his friends.

Can you guess who the average reader, watcher, and listener thought was the injured party?

7. Sending useful information to the media prevents the competition from getting a disproportionate share of press coverage—There are numerous publications and news programs that are seriously understaffed. Without a sufficient number of reporters available to gather news, they are often dependent on the offerings of public relations people to fill their pages and air time. Those media relations officers who meet the editors' needs win the desired space and air time; those who don't distribute press releases don't get press coverage.

8. Good media relations tend to have snowballing effects—I remember joining a press relations office in New York for Bank of America at a time when it was receiving only two calls from journalists a month, primarily due to the fact that it was a California-based bank and there are scores of major financial institutions headquartered in New York. I started exposing the bank's executives to the media via press briefings, luncheons, and interviews. As reporters were helped on one story, it was only natural that they began assuming I could introduce them to other people in the organization who could assist them on still other articles. Within half a year we were getting up to fifty press calls per month.

9. Working with the press is fun—At the risk of appearing to apple-polish journalists (who probably wouldn't bother to read a book on public relations anyway, because they believe they are sufficiently versed in the subject), I find that an exceedingly high percentage of reporters and editors are fun to be with. They are conversant in a variety of topics, they are friendly, and they have a good sense of humor, acquired perhaps from coping with PR practitioners and hard-to-interview individuals. Some have become close friends of mine, and many others are people I'd like to know better. But regardless of our after-work-hours comings and goings, I have never met a journalist with whom it was difficult to establish a professional working relationship. Yes, we have occasionally differed on the treatment of a particular story or the amount of information that should be forthcoming from my office, but I've always felt that every relationship was marked by a feeling that each person could help the other and that neither was desirous of deceiving the other. While we should all be careful in what we say to journalists, PR people who are excessively distrustful of the media should find another line of work.

THE PRESS RELEASE

This is the bread and butter of any news relations office, because it is an easy way to disseminate information and it is *the* accepted manner of getting facts and figures to the press. It is not at all unusual for some news bureaus to distribute as many as fifty releases per week and for others to have 75 percent of their working days devoted to gathering, preparing, and distributing news.

Whether a release is being written for a major corporation, nonprofit organization, politician, or movie star, there are certain rules that should be followed by the person responsible for producing it.

1. Identify the organization sending the release— The chances are fairly good your release is one of many placed in editors' in-boxes. If deskmen are poring over several dozen at a time, they will want to know the source of each release very quickly. Having the name of the disseminating organization on the top of the first page is a good way to identify the source. Another is to use distinctive type or colored paper. All Bank of America press releases, for example, are printed on green paper.

*2. Identify the news contact—*It is very likely that editors will want additional information or have some questions about the text. If the name and phone number of the person who can serve as press contact is on the front of the release, obtaining additional data is not an overwhelmingly difficult task. If there is no name on the release, however, journalists may have to make two or three calls before reaching the appropriate person. That could be one or two more calls than the story is worth.

*3. Date the release—*Newspaper friends tell me they often file marginal releases in a separate drawer for possible use when there are holes to be filled. But if they go to that drawer and find an interesting but undated piece, they won't use it, out of fear they are holding something of ancient vintage.

*4. List a release date or time—*Editors want to know if the material is for immediate use or for release at a later date. State clearly at the top "for immediate release," "for release after 10 a.m., Tuesday, August 6," or whatever. Most releases are for immediate use, but if you find yourself listing specific times fairly frequently, try to be evenhanded in your treatment of morning and afternoon newspapers and news programs.

An example of when news bureaus may opt for a special release time is in the handling of speeches. The texts of major addresses are generally sent to the media with a press release before the speech is given so that reporters have time to go over them. The release, however, will state that the material is not to be used until after the speech has been delivered.

*5. Indicate the end of the release—*Releases of more than one page may be taken apart as they go along their merry route from editor's desk to reporter to copy desk and beyond. It is important to end the release with "30," "#," "The End," or any other sign you choose, so that journalists needn't worry that there is a fantastic ending floating somewhere around the office. Pages that are followed by more copy should have "more" written on the bottom.

*6. Type it double-space and leave plenty of room for editors' notations—*It is rare that major publications and stations will use press releases exactly as they are written. But weeklies, trade publications, and smaller stations may not be blessed with large news-writing staffs. They often are likely to slap a headline on a release, scribble in some instructions to the announcer or printer, maybe make a minor word change or two; then use it as it is written.

The double-spacing allows for minor editorial changes, and the space above the story and in the margins allows for instructions and headline creation. Single-spaced releases label the sender an amateur.

7. Put a headline on the release, one that summarizes the story without trying to be cute or attention getting—The purpose of the straightforward headline is to tell the editors, who have a mountain of mail in front of them, what the release is all about.

There are, however, PR departments that shun headlines on the theory that this forces editors to read more of the story and possibly see news angles not mentioned in the head. I would rather tell journalists what they are getting. Slowing news executives in their handling of the daily mail is not the fastest way to win friends in the newsroom.

WHEN TO RELEASE

The key rule about when to release is that yesterday's news is no news. Another pertinent thought is that the first three letters in *news* implies that something fresh and previously unseen or unheard is in the press release.

This means that the messages have to get to the media rapidly. The fastest methods are the press conference (which will be discussed later) and phone calls. After that, there is the use of outfits such as PR Newswire and Business Wire, which send stories to subscribing media in the same manner as wire services. Then comes the use of messengers. Then there is the mail. Anything slower than that is as useful as the Pony Express.

When handling major press releases at Chase Manhattan or Bank of America, news bureau personnel would call key media representatives after the release was distributed by messenger and placed on Business Wire or PR Newswire. The purpose of the call was to alert the media as to what the release was about and that it was on its way.

SUBJECT MATTER OF RELEASES

If you have no newsworthy items to share, don't send anything out. A release that wastes an editor's time is much more damaging to the relationship then not sending a release in the first place.

But an absence of releases doesn't do much for the relationship either, so press relations personnel should (a) look for news in their or-ganization; and (b) be able to recognize it when they see it.

The following are valid subjects for press releases at profit and nonprofit organizations:

- Physical expansions
- New personnel
- Personnel promotions and shifts
- Reorganizations
- Quarterly or yearly earnings (or, in the case of nonprofit institutions, expenditures on program goals)
- Significant participation in community, national, or international events
- Events that are open to the public
- Introduction of new products or services
- Major gifts to the community
- Formation of new subsidiaries
- Speeches or publications

It is equally important to know what not to release. Subjects that should be regarded as taboo include those that would do the following:

- Violate the confidentiality of customer relationships
- Reveal competitive information
- Violate good taste
- Invade the privacy of employees or clients
- Involve a matter in litigation

Perhaps the best method of determining what one should or should not send to the press is to become an avid student of the print and electronic media. Noting what editors consider news (and by their absence, what is not rated newsworthy) provides helpful clues to what should be in future press releases.

THE PRESS CONFERENCE

The advantage of a press conference is that the hosting organization gets to speak to several media at once, generally at a time and place of its choosing. Assuming that the host has a reputation for calling such get-togethers only when there is important news to announce, one can also list the assurance of good crowds as another benefit.

Two generally accepted rules in attracting good-sized and good-quality crowds (it's necessary to have good publications represented in addition to having many seats filled) are the following:

• Use the press conference tool rarely.
• Make sure the person who is fielding the questions is newsworthy.

The rationale for the first point is obvious. Unless you work for a major sports, political, or entertainment figure, it isn't likely you'll have many reasons to call press conferences. To have more than three or four annually means you are straining a bit too hard and are having sessions of dubious value. Trying to attract a decent number of journalists when your last press conference was a dud can be an imposing task.

The second point is based on the premise that certain people are more important than others. This doesn't mean, however, that only the very senior officers should be seated in front of the microphones at press conferences. It could be that a junior-level bookkeeper has discovered a new and time-saving method of maintaining the books. Or perhaps a gardener has uncovered a trace of prehistoric man on the grounds of the company's headquarters. Or maybe a member of middle management has been found after being kidnaped by terrorists two months ago. Trot these individuals—not your senior managers—out for the press.

But don't bring the people from the lower levels of the organizational hierarchy into the center ring if you're announcing the opening of an office in China or the creation of an ambitious ten-year growth plan. Those are subjects for executives at the top of the ladder.

Some acceptable justifications for a press conference, in addition to those just mentioned, include the following:

• A shake-up in senior management
• A major new product or service
• The hiring of a well-known person—a former senator, for example
• The need to present the organization's side in a dispute being covered on the front pages of the major newspapers
• The creation of a significant community relations program
• The visit by a chief executive officer to a foreign country or key city in the United States

It was at an out-of-town press conference, by the way, that I had my scariest moment as a public relations officer. The year was 1972, a time when I was younger and not as careful as I am today.

The locale was Sao Paulo, Brazil, and I was there to arrange a press conference for David Rockefeller, chairman of Chase Manhattan. It was one of three I was arranging during a seventeen-day swing through South America.

As luck would have it, A. W. Clausen, president and chief executive officer of Bank of America, was in Brazil at the same time. Luck further dictated that he would choose to hold a Sao Paulo press conference one day before Rockefeller's.

Now, part of any PR officer's job in setting up press conferences is to give the speaker an idea of what kinds of questions to expect. I had done a pretty good job of forecasting the topics that were brought up at a session in Buenos Aires one week earlier and was anxious to maintain my "winning streak."

Upon first hearing that Clausen would meet the press before Rockefeller, my reaction was "Oh, nuts," or words to that effect. Then I thought, "Hey, wait a minute; if I can figure out a way to sit in on Clausen's conference, it will help Rockefeller, because I'll be able to do a fantastic job of preparing him for the journalists." Moreover, I reasoned, I would have a realistic shot at the PR profession's equivalent of a hole-in-one—predicting all the questions at a press conference.

There were two problems, though. First, sneaking in struck me as not entirely ethical. Second, I had spent three days calling on journalists in and around Sao Paulo to tell them about Rockefeller's visit, so there was a chance I'd be recognized. Actually, it was a pretty good chance, because the president of one newspaper chain had a picture taken of us chatting about Rockefeller, and my likeness appeared on front pages throughout the country.

The reason for looking the other way on the first problem is that I found out about the Clausen conference thirty minutes before its start and didn't have time to think the dilemma through. And I downplayed the second problem by rationalizing that I could sit in the back of the room and not be seen.

I didn't know how much of the meeting would be conducted in Portuguese, so I decided to have the young translator our local advertising agency assigned to me sit in on the Clausen session as well.

"Grab a seat in the front row so that people will only see the back of your head, and don't call any attention to yourself. If anyone asks who you are, say you're a reporter for one of the suburban dailies," I cautioned him.

"Great idea," he responded, whereupon he went to the front of the room and sat, prepared to take accurate notes.

I waited in the lobby until the conference began, then steathily took a seat in the last row.

This was a mistake.

Two seats away sat the head of the bureau of a major U.S. wire service with whom I had chatted for two hours earlier in the week.

There were only two things to do. First, I stifled the groan a man with slower reflexes might have emitted. Then I moved my chair six inches to the rear of the room and kept my eyes riveted on the man between us. I leaned forward when he did and backward when he did, so that his head was continually between mine and that of the American journalist. And I fervently hoped the man next to me wouldn't have to go to the men's room.

My strategy worked beautifully, and I began to think I might pull the whole thing off. But twenty minutes into the conference my translator raised his hand to ask a question. Fortunately, his query was insignificant and went unnoticed. Another twenty minutes went by, and when I noticed Clausen glancing at his watch, my relief knew no bounds.

Then my translator rose to ask another question. Not wishing to attract attention by hurling a shoe at his head, there was naught but to watch silently and painfully. "Mr. Clausen," he said aggressively, shattering the mood of good fellowship that had prevailed until then, "is it true that Bank of America is financing the war in Vietnam?"

Heads spun—including Clausen's—pens began scribbling, and all eyes except mine focused on the bank executive. My eyes were riveted on the translator's back, and I was wishing looks could kill.

I thought Clausen handled the question well by responding that the bank wasn't financing the war or the manufacture of arms, but it did have relationships with some of the companies manufacturing weaponry.

This didn't satisfy my colleague. "But what about all the deaths, all the displaced persons, all the damage to Vietnam?" the lad shouted. It took Clausen about five minutes to extricate himself, although I don't remember how, being somewhat agitated at the time.

The meeting ended shortly thereafter, and surprisingly no one thought to learn the identity of the hostile "journalist" in the front row. Rockefeller benefited from the briefing I gave him, but I vowed then—and now in writing—to refrain from ever doing anything like that again.

I learned another lesson at a different out-of-town Rockefeller press conference. This one was in 1969, and the setting was Montreal. I had spent two days alerting local scribes about the conference and was happily awaiting the crowd when Rockefeller and my boss, Bill Carlin, arrived at the hotel just before the session was to begin.

"How many people do you expect?," Carlin asked.

"I have twenty-seven definites and four-teens maybes," I answered proudly, because none of Rockefeller's previous Montreal press conferences had attracted more than twenty-two reporters.

Carlin shot me down fast. "Then why do you have forty-five chairs in the room? Get at least fifteen of them out of here. You can bring them back in if we get an SRO crowd. In the meantime, everyone will be impressed by Rockefeller's importance and his ability to attract journalists," he said.

He was right.

Now, let's get back to press conferences in our headquarters city. A frequently asked question is, Do we hold them in our building or at a hotel that is more conveniently located for the media? The advantages of each alternative are listed below.

Hotel

Generally closer to the press

More meeting rooms to choose from

Easier to serve food

Nicer facilities

More experience at hosting such events

Generally better equipped in terms of lighting and electrical outlets

Headquarters

More control over the people doing the work*

Cheaper

Gets reporters used to visiting us

Less drain on executive's time

Can rehearse in the actual location if we think it is necessary

Can bring in other officers and materials at the last minute if necessary

The second set of arguments, it seems, carry more weight, so on-site sessions are generally favored by PR people.

In inviting reporters to a press conference, I favor a three-step approach:

1. Call to extend the invitation.
2. Follow this up with a memo to the invitees.
3. Call again on the day of the event.

In terms of providing material for the journalists, I suggest the following:

• Pads, pencils, and phones
• A biography and photograph of each speaker

---

*I once was arranging a press breakfast in a Winston-Salem hotel and showed up thirty minutes early to find the wrong room being set up. I also noticed that the announcement on the lobby bulletin board listed the wrong time. That's why I feel more comfortable having people from my organization handling such details.

• Background material on the hosting organization (annual report, marketing literature, a history, and so on)
• A press release

In addition, make sure there are electrical outlets for reporters in need of them and spare tapes and batteries for people using tape recorders.

THE BACKGROUND MEMO

The background memo is helpful when you're trying to sell the media on a feature-story idea. Suppose, for example, the news relations department of Jones Motor Company, the progressive automobile manufacturer mentioned at the beginning of this chapter, wanted to get maximum exposure out of its minority-training program.

They might call a press conference to announce the inception of the program, they should definitely distribute a press release on it, and they should issue a background memo after the program is well underway.

The memo, which should be sent to all potentially interested media, should present a complete overview of the program, covering topics such as the following:

• Rationale for the program
• How it was put together
• How the participants are selected
• How the participants are reacting to the program
• How their families are reacting to it
• Typical classroom sessions
• Who conducts the training
• Anticipated results
• Anything else that would be of interest

The memo would be sent to journalists with a covering letter along the following lines:

Memo to Editors:

The attached is a background memorandum on a Jones Motor Company program designed to help members of ethnic minorities acquire the necessary skills and capital to establish their own automobile dealerships.

Introduced in [month of inception], the program is offering one hundred black and Hispanic individuals three years of on-the-job training in automobile production, maintenance, and sales at Jones' headquarters in Huntington Park, Michigan. Graduates of the program will be given ten-year loans at below commercial bank rates in order to establish their dealerships.

The enclosed memorandum explains the rationale for the program and describes the participants' progress thus far.

I hope you will find it of interest and that you will feel free to call me at [list phone number] if you would like additional information.

In attempting to spark media interest, the author of the memo should present word pictures to give editors an understanding of the story's photographic and television appeal. He or she should also write about several interesting people in the program in order to point editors in the direction of individual profiles.

Including photographs is another good idea. Just make sure the individuals in the pictures are mentioned in the memo.

PHOTOGRAPHY

Good photographs can embellish just about any press release—and some are capable of standing on their own and going to newsrooms without a release.

Seven rules on press relations photography follow:

1. Unless you are specifically asked to produce a color photograph, shoot in black and white.

2. If you are sending out a group shot, try not to have more than four people in it. There are two reasons for this. First, more than four people could make for a very long caption, especially if you have to add the title and organiza-

tion after each name. Second, including many people in a picture could reduce the size of their faces to that of a button.

3. Group shots tend to be fairly similar—three or four people around a table or standing side by side—so try to have the photographer take them from different angles. The photographer can shoot them looking down, up, or from off to one side. There is no law that says everyone must be seen full-face; profiles are allowed.

4. If possible, try to send publications both a vertical and a horizontal of the same shot. This gives them more flexibility when doing makeup.

5. Most editors prefer shots that look as if they weren't posed. Theoretically, the photographer should be trying to capture the event as it happens. Tell your subjects to please—aw c'mon, pretty please—not look at the camera.

6. Make sure captions are firmly affixed to the back of the photograph. Many people will handle the shot at each publication, and the caption could be separated from the picture if it was put on loosely in the first place.

7. When possible, take more posed shots than you need. It is possible someone will blink, have a silly expression, or simply look horrible. Give yourself a choice by taking many pictures.

OP-ED PIECES AND OTHER GHOSTED ARTICLES

Op-ed pieces are important if for no other reason than that they are read by people concerned enough about what's happening in the world to find out what opinion leaders have to say. That they tend to be written for senior executives also enhances their significance.

Basically, the way the system works is that the PR department selects an issue to which it would like to have the organization address itself. It then contacts an op-ed page or publication editor and asks if he or she would like to have an article on the topic under the by-line of a senior official. If the response is affirmative, an article is produced and submitted.

INTERVIEWS

PR practitioners can be either on the offense or on the defense in regard to interviews. When they are on the offense, they suggest interviews to reporters. They assume a defensive stance when a reporter calls asking to interview someone in the organization.

When receiving such a call, the PR person must decide if it is appropriate for the organization to respond. Then, and only then, is thought given to who the respondee will be. More will be said about this in chapter four.

In going on the offense, news bureau operatives will look for topics worth discussing, then call reporters and suggest that they have an informed source who would be happy to answer questions. For example, suppose much has been written over a two-day period on a political development in Italy. A PR officer could call local editors, say that there is a person at his organization who is an expert on Italy, and who would be happy to answer questions. Or he or she may simply call a reporter and suggest an interview. Or he or she may simply call a reporter and suggest an interview appropos of nothing. It has been done.

BACKGROUND BRIEFINGS

Background briefings are somewhat similar to press conferences and suggesting interviews. News relations specialists may invite journalists to a luncheon or coffee session at which a knowledgeable individual is to provide an update on a topic of current interest. The ensuing discussions can be either "on the record" or "off the record."

These sessions are similar to press conferences in that they are held for more than one journalist at a time—and they resemble "offensive" interviews in that they are initiated by the PR team.

PRESS KITS

Press kits can be handed out at a news conference or major event to which journalists are invited—for example, a tour of a new plant, the inauguration of a college president, or the opening of a concert hall. They are somewhat related to background memos in that they give the media just about everything of potential interest in the hope that some of the material may be used—and not just immediately, but in the future as well.

In order to demonstrate this "shotgun" aspect of the press kit, I will list the material that might be used at (a) a press conference announcing the introduction of a new product, and (b) the opening night of a road-company version of Neil Simon's *Chapter Two* in Dayton, Ohio.

The New-Product Press Conference
• A press release
• A feature article on the research over the years that led to the new product
• Biographies of members of the research team
• A chronological listing of other company innovations
• An annual report
• A fact sheet on the product
• Pictures of the product, the researchers, and the person making the announcement
• A discussion of marketing plans for the product

Opening Night for "Chapter Two"
• A press release
• A biography of Neil Simon
• Biographies of the cast, director, and producer
• Copies of reviews from the New York and national press following its Broadway opening
• A synopsis of the play
• A feature on how and why Simon wrote the play
• A Q-and-A piece with Simon
• Features on Dayton-area people involved in the production
• A feature on the theater
• Pictures of the author, director, producer, lead players, and Dayton-area people
• Pictures of the cast in rehearsal

1. What are the respective merits of getting information to the public via a press release and an advertisement?

2. You are the new director of information at your local college. Design press-release paper for the school, making sure you include all the information journalists will need.

3. You are the director of information at a municipal hospital. List ten types of stories you may have to put into press-release form.

4. You are publicity director for the Boston Symphony Orchestra. List three developments that would justify calling a press conference.

5. You are preparing a background memo on your company's oil exploration project in Canada. List seven topics you would include in the memo.

4

WORKING WITH THE PRESS

WITH very few exceptions, reporters and editors I have known over the years are easy to meet and receptive to initiatives by PR people. They're savvy enough to realize that media relations personnel are potential sources of help and that good professional working relationships reap nicer rewards if they are founded on admiration, respect, and compatibility.

Remember, a good percentage of the calls reporters make to PR offices can just as easily be directed to a competitive concern. All other things being equal, the reporter is most likely to choose the PR office with the best track record as a source of useful, accurate, and fast information. If the reporter happens to like the people in the PR office as well, so much the better, because that's another good reason to call.

So how do we get reporters and editors to think of us as reliable and likable?

Let's start from the beginning by pretending that you have been named director of news relations for a corporation or a nonprofit organization based in a city in which you have never lived. You don't know any of the journalists in town, and they have never heard of you.

The first thing to do is produce an up-to-date roster of the working press in the area. There may be an old one floating around the office—or you may have to start from scratch—but regardless of the age of any written or word-of-mouth information, your arrival on the scene is a good reason for compiling a new list.

Some people are hesitant to phone publications and radio and television stations for the names of journalists, out of fear that the respondee will retort, "Shouldn't you already know that?" There is no need to be embarrassed. After all, you're not going to get exercised because the journalists didn't know you're in town.

Besides, there's an easy way to avoid having to make the calls yourself. Just let your secretary do it. After all, who at the media will get upset if a secretary calls, announces that the firm is updating its press lists, and asks if the person at the other end of the line would be kind enough to give him or her the names of various editors? If the secretary already has some of the information that's been floating around the office, he or she can ask if the information is accurate.

Once you have the names, the next step is to send out a letter in which you introduce yourself and remind the journalists that they should feel free to call you for information, either at the office or after hours at your home phone number, which you list.

But that doesn't mean that you sit around waiting for their calls. Instead, you'll call them one at a time, over a period of a month or two, suggesting that you get together for lunch so that you (the news relations director) can explain how your operation works and find out if there are any story ideas they'd like to pursue.

One of my female students at a Hunter College PR course raised her hand in protest when I made this point in a lecture several years ago. "That's easy for you to say; you're a man. It's difficult for a woman to call a man up and invite him to lunch," she complained.

To which I replied then—and reply now as well—that it probably was difficult years ago, but it is an accepted practice today. Women may still have additional battles to win, but their right to pick up a check attracts few, if any, arguments in this era of growing male enlightenment and rising restaurant costs.

There are, of course, other ways to meet journalists. One is to find out where their favorite watering spots are and meet them for an after-hours cocktail. Or simply pop in for a drink alone and initiate conversations at the bar.*

---

*There was a time when PR people were required to hold impressive quantities of liquor without telltale traces in their behavior, because journalists were reputedly heavy drinkers who disliked imbibing alone. This isn't so today, as most members of the fourth estate rarely have more than one pre-luncheon drink—and some opt for a club soda or ginger ale. If, however, you're at a cocktail party where most people are walking around with a drink in their hand, and you find it hard not to intake liquid refreshment, I have a tip for you. Order a drink you despise. It will probably take you an hour to get one of them down, as opposed to the four or five glasses you might have drained if you enjoyed your drink.

Another is the "just happened to be passing by your office, so I thought I'd deliver this release in person and say hello" gambit. If you don't do this too frequently—and never at deadline time—this is not a bad idea, because editors and reporters like to connect a face to the voice at the other end of the phone line. Occasional in-person visits make them feel more comfortable chatting with you.

Still another technique is to invite a reporter and spouse (or friend) out for an evening at the theater or an athletic event. Chase Manhattan's PR department has, for many years, owned four good season tickets to all New York Ranger home hockey games. They are used by media relations people who would like to spend a relaxing evening with a journalist totally devoid of business discussions.

Regardless of how the initial contact is made, it *should* be made, because there are numerous things to be discussed with newspeople. In addition to explaining your operations and that of the company, you may wish to suggest possible story ideas and ascertain what subjects are of special interest to them.

Furthermore, you should learn what their deadlines are and find out if they put out separate supplements on certain days. Some papers, for example, will put out a food section on Wednesday, a science section on another day, and a health care section on still another. News bureau executives must know when they come out and what is the last day for submitting copy for them.

RESPONDING TO PRESS QUERIES

Responding to press queries can be an art, because it is not as easy as it sounds. Rather than simply answering questions with all the facts at your disposal, certain questions should be asked by you first.

1. Who is the person at the other end of the line?—Is he really who he says he is, or is he someone else? Whenever I get a call from a journalist I don't know and something about the conversation doesn't ring true, I say I'm on my way to a meeting and will call back. When I make the return call, I phone the switchboard number of the organization the journalist claims to represent and ask to be switched to him. If the

reporter says that he's working at home, I'll call a friend at the publication or station and check him out.

2. Do we want to respond?—Perhaps the reporter represents a publication that specializes in yellow journalism and delights in attacking concerns such as yours. If he or she is going to distort what you say, you might decide that getting blasted for refusing to cooperate is the lesser evil.

Another reason for not responding occurs when the reporter is seeking information you don't want to divulge. For example, he or she may want data that would reveal competitive secrets or violate the confidentiality of a customer relationship.

3. Is it appropriate for you to respond?—Suppose the reporter is calling the Kansas City field office of a multinational organization to find out what the company's European plans are. The head of the field office would be foolish to respond; the answers have to come from the main office or from European headquarters.

Satisfying a journalist's desire for information is, obviously, not the only reason for responding to questions.

4. Do you have a ready answer?—If you don't, then the best thing to do is to promise to get back at a later time or date. Just because the reporter is on deadline is no reason to give a response that hasn't been thoroughly thought out or approved.

5. Do you have all the information you need from the reporter?—If the only person asking questions during a journalist's call to a PR office is the newsperson, the response probably won't be as helpful as it could be—especially if the PR officer has to find someone to field the queries. Indeed, there are several things the press representative has to find out before asking a company official to speak with the reporter.

• Will the interview be on or off the record?

• Is the reporter on deadline, and when is the latest you can respond?

• Where does the reporter want to conduct the interview—in the subject's office, over the phone, or elsewhere?

• Will your person be the only one interviewed for the story, or are other people from other organizations also to be included?

• Will you get a chance to see the copy before the story is printed or aired? (This is a ticklish question, which should not be raised all the time—or even half the time. But I will ask it if the reporter seems unsure about the topic and is likely to make an honest mistake. I may, however, couch it in terms such as, "Look, this is an extremely complicated topic, and I'm not sure we'll be able to cover it completely in the time you've allotted to us. Would you have any objection to our seeing the copy in case we want to add something or clarify a point we didn't explain succinctly the first time around?" If the reporter refuses, I wouldn't ask the question again.

• How much time does the reporter think he or she will need with the interviewee?

In addition to the preceding questions, the person who is to be interviewed would probably want us to be able to tell him or her if the reporter is

• Accurate

• Unbiased

• Knowledgeable on the subject

• Working for a publication or station that is fair or unfair

Whether these questions are voiced or not, the PR person should be able to answer them.

HANDLING THE PRESS IN AN EMERGENCY

Several years ago I attended a Continental Oil Corporation presentation on coping with the press. It made some interesting points, not by lecturing, but, rather, by taking the audience through a role-playing case study that had us actually responding to queries.

The case study was along the following lines:

We had to pretend we were the plant manager of an overseas-based operation in a country in which our corporation had no

PR personnel. We are driving to work one morning when the music on the car radio is interrupted by an announcement of an explosion at the plant.

What should we do?

We finally arrive at the plant, rush to our office (which has escaped the damage) and are greeted by a call from a journalist wanting to know what's what.

What do we tell her?

We spend thirty minutes getting the pertinent facts, when the phone rings again. The speaker identifies himself as a local official calling at the request of the mayor. He wants to know if the local government can be of assistance and what is the extent of the damage.

What do we tell him?

Another twenty minutes go by, then the first reporter and several other journalists arrive. They want an update and the names of the injured persons.

What do we tell them?

It is now noon, and we have all the necessary facts.

What do we do?

The case study was designed primarily for people not given the press relations function, but the questions can and should be addressed to neophyte PR professionals as well. So let's look at the answers.

What do we do after hearing the radio announcement?

First, we get to the nearest phone, call the plant, and ask if there has, in fact, been an explosion. It's possible the announcement was in error.

If we're told the explosion did occur, we tell the person on the other end of the line when we expect to arrive and that all press calls should be held for us. We also ask that person to alert the head office.

If it is only four in the morning at corporate headquarters and the explosion was fairly significant, then we have someone called at his or her home.

What do we tell our reporter friend?

Not a heck of a lot, because we don't know a heck of a lot. All we can do at this point is confirm that there was an explosion and that we'll try to get back with additional facts. We add that we'll be extremely busy, so she may want to call us again in about thirty minutes if we haven't had a chance to call back ourselves.

Then we do our best to get all the facts we can.

What do we tell the man from the mayor's office?

We say we will call him back because we're in the process of gathering information. But that's not the real reason. We're putting him off because we don't know the man. For all we know, he's the guy who planted the bomb.

We'll call the mayor's switchboard number and ask to be connected to the man. If we get connected, we answer his questions. If not, we know he was a phony.

What do we tell the journalists asking for the update and the names of the explosion victims?

We give an update, emphasizing that further information will have to be forthcoming because all the facts are not yet in. We don't, however, give the names of the victims until they have been verified and their families have been notified.

What do we do when we have all the facts?

Issue a statement to the media.

There are several things this exercise should tell would-be PR professionals.

• There should be a written guide in each office on emergency procedures.

• Each field office should have one person designated as its spokesperson.

• Offices should have a list of local publications and stations—with the names of key reporters and journalists at each office.

• Each office should have the home phone numbers of key personnel, including those at the head office.

• Make sure you know who you're talking to at the other end of the telephone line.

• Don't refrain from answering questions until you have a final report. Periodic reports are permissible—and desired by reporters on deadline.

• Don't release the names of injured or deceased personnel until they have been verified and the families have been notified.

HOW TO DEVELOP THE ABILITY TO SPOT GOOD STORY IDEAS

YEARS ago, when I was manager of retail banking public relations at Chase Manhattan, I would periodically call branch managers and ask if there was anything going on in their offices worth publicizing. Invariably, the answer was no.

But I'm occasionally a persistent fellow, so I would sometimes suggest getting together for a cup of coffee the next time I was in their neighborhood. The appointed day would arrive, we'd chat for ten or fifteen minutes, and I would walk away with at least one feature- or news-story idea.

The point of this is not to brag about my creativity but to emphasize that people trained in digging up news will do a much better job

than individuals who are schooled in other disciplines—retail banking, for example.

How, then, does one become adroit at spotting potential news and feature articles?

• Be a student of the media and learn what interests them.

• Be curious about what you see and hear. Ask questions.

• Be willing to invest the time required to learn more about a situation. If there is no news on the surface, there may be a story one or two levels below.

• Look at a situation and ask what's unusual here.

• Know the subjects you cover so that you can recognize the unusual.

The next question that comes to mind is, How does one recognize the unusual?

Let's start with a concern's staff. Have any of them been with the organization for an unusually long period of time? Are there any staff members with three or more relatives also employed by the concern? Do any employees have weird but effective working habits? Do any have interesting off-hour activities? (One coffee break conversation at Chase Manhattan led me to a branch manager who headed a troop of physically handicapped Boy Scouts. We got a lot of press pickup from the ensuing release and photographs.) Are any of the employees physically handicapped?

You can also ask the same questions of customers or clients. For example, colleges get a tremendous amount of publicity mileage out of interesting students.

Now let's look around a bit. Do you work in an unusual building? Can you make interesting comparisons to previous activities? Any interesting forecasts for the future—or methods of forecasting developments? Do you have programs on training, recruiting, marketing, product development, sales, and so on that differ drastically from the norms in your field?

And so on and so on. Sight unseen, I'm confident there are untold feature stories at just about every organization. It is simply a question of digging long enough and hard enough until they are uncovered.

WORKING WITH IN-HOUSE PERSONNEL TO PROMOTE GOOD PRESS RELATIONS

OUTSTANDING organizational performance and professionalism in the PR department are the two major ingredients in creating and maintaining good press relations. But there's a third ingredient that also affects journalists' treatment of the organization: the attitudes and actions of the men and women who are called upon to interface with the press.

There are certain attitudes and actions that are required of them—and it is the PR department's responsibility to see that these requirements are met. The correct attitudes and actions include the following.

1. Know the policies and positions of the organization—It is one thing to spout off as a private citizen; it's another to do so as an officer of a particular organization. The next day's headlines could be, "John Doe Blasts Senators as Incompetent" in the former case and "XYZ Corporation Official Calls Senators Incompetent" in the latter.

The second headline could be perceived as helpful if the corporation agrees with John Doe and wants his views aired. But if the corporation is not critical of the Senate, or is critical but

doesn't want this assessment made public, such a statement in the press will be highly detrimental to John Doe's career and the chairman's blood pressure.

When personnel are representing an organization, it is the organization's opinions that are stated, not those of the spokespeople.

2. Be willing to meet the press—It has been recognized that good publicity is helpful to an organization, but the good media relations that precede or accompany favorable mentions by the press can't be maintained if no one in the organization will respond to queries. The PR department simply can't do it alone, because journalists aren't interested in quoting them; they want statements from senior officers or the individuals directly involved in a given story.

3. Don't be hostile or distrustful when you do meet the press—Some people have approached interviews with the attitude that the journalist is biased, out to embarrass them and the organization, and responsible for the misquotes and distortions of every bad reporter they have ever encountered.

This confrontation mentality immediately

breeds suspicion on the part of the reporter—and sometimes a desire to retaliate in kind. It is hardly conducive to a productive exchange.

It's all right to be careful about what one says, but hostility and obfuscation clearly should not be present. If subjects aren't willing to be responsive, their time and that of the reporters is wasted. And the concern's image is likely to suffer, too, because its side of a story won't get aired.

4. *Let the PR department know when reporters are bullying, biased, and inaccurate*—Yes, there are some unethical journalists. A small minority perhaps, but they exist in sufficient quantity to keep PR departments and organization spokespeople on their toes.

Since many interviews are conducted over the phone without a news relations person present, it is important that individuals who are misquoted not keep this information to themselves.

The news relations personnel, in turn, may be able to complain effectively to the reporter or editor. At the very least, they can keep a scorecard on the "good guys" and "bad guys" so that potential spokespeople can be spared unpleasant encounters in the future.

The role of the PR department in assuring that the proper attitudes and actions on the part of all personnel become the behavioral norms can be summed up in two words: *education* and *training*.

When wearing the educational hat, PR practitioners alert their colleagues to the concern's positions and policies, sell them on the importance of good press relations, and prepare them for interviews by anticipating questions and briefing them on the individuals who will be doing the asking.

Additionally, there should be follow-up action to demonstrate the benefits of cooperating with the press and the price one pays for lack of cooperation. This means that clips of printed articles and transcripts of radio and television coverage should be sent to the spokesperson as soon as possible.

If, on the other hand, officers refuse to cooperate with the press, the PR department should show them the clips that people from rival concerns received because reporters had to

go elsewhere for information. And if officers reject advice from the PR department, they should be shown all the negative clippings and transcripts that ensue.

Training might consist of running mock interviews and critiquing officers' performances afterward. One recent trend at organizations wealthy enough to afford the equipment is to video-tape the staged occasions and then show the participants where and why they went wrong.

This is not unlike shock therapy. After years of watching polished politicians and corporate leaders field queries, the officers are shocked by their own relatively amateurish performances and become eager for counseling.

It should be pointed out that taping sessions are not for television interviews only. It's important for would-be subjects to see how they react to questions regardless of whether the interview is for television, radio, or a publication. The manner in which interviewees respond can be as informative to some journalists as the answers they give.

Equally important, the potential spokespeople need practice in thinking on their feet and participating in conversations in which most, if not all, of the control of subject selection belongs to the interviewer.

This can be particularly frustrating to the interviewee if there's a point that he or she wants to make but is unable to move the discussion in the proper direction. Practice, however, can teach subjects how to turn questions around so that the points they want to air can be made. Politicians are outstanding practitioners of this little trick. Watch them during interviews and note how often their answers are only remotely related to the questions.

Practice can also help subjects anticipate questions, make their answers quotable, and, most important, feel confident that their mental faculties are sharp enough to react in the desired manner.

I have seen people appear nervous and unsure before the interviewer and I have seen others respond eagerly and confidently. The quality of the answers by the former group may have been slightly superior to those of the latter group, but the enthusiastic respondees always made the better impression.

One of the all-time masters of the art of

enjoying himself during exchanges with the press is Walter Hoadley, executive vice-president and chief economist at Bank of America. He is also an exceedingly well-informed and prescient economist, but his exuberance and apparent joy in sharing ideas with the media are equally responsible for the favorable impact he makes on audiences. He obviously relishes reporters' questions, respects their professionalism, and occasionally asks a question himself to make the sessions a useful exchange of ideas.

It is no accident that I've had more thank-you calls after a press conference for Hoadley than for anyone else. I'm certain there's a direct relation between his good image with the press and his enjoyment—which comes from practice—in dealing with the media.

SOME WORDS ABOUT THE DIFFERENCES BETWEEN PRINT AND ELECTRONIC MEDIA INTERVIEWS —AND SOME TIPS FOR PREPARING FOR TELEVISION INTERVIEWS

THE major difference between an interview for a newspaper or magazine and an interview for television or radio is that the former tells what the interviewee said, whereas the latter presents him or her saying it.

This is a considerable difference for both the audience and the spokesperson. For example, if John Doe says "I, er, think that, er, the economy—I mean the U.S. economy—will enjoy, oh no, have a growth rate of, oh let me think, 6 percent in 1990," the printed version would likely state, " 'The U.S. economy will have a growth rate of 6 percent in 1990,' said John Doe."

The radio or television program will have the entire statement, because there is no middleman playing around with the words. Rather than reading a report of what was said, television and radio audiences get it directly.

Of course, some editing is done, so that not all of what was stated is included in the news program. But what *is* included is a more complete version than printed text, because the pauses and inflections are there for all to hear—and see, in the case of television. And if the interview is live, there is no such thing as a do-over. Or calling the reporter thirty minutes later to ask if something can be added.

This means that casual preparation for a television or radio interview by someone who hasn't been interviewed too often is unwise. The size of audiences, especially those of network television programs, the scarcity of opportunities to undo the damage from a bad interview quickly, and the fact that most answers can only be given once, dictate that considerable care be given by PR people to readying their colleagues for on-camera or radio interviews. The following hints are suggested:

• See or listen to the program beforehand to familiarize yourself with the format and the interviewer's style.

• Make sure that the subjects are up-to-date on their areas of expertise.

• Go to the studio thirty minutes before the interview to familiarize the subjects with the surroundings.

• Don't be afraid to ask in advance what topics will be covered during the interview.

• Encourage the subjects to correct the interviewer if an incorrect statement is made. There may not be a chance to do this later on.

• Don't let the subjects get into arguments with the interviewer. The journalist is more experienced in debating before a live microphone and is likely to cut your colleagues to ribbons if sufficiently aroused.

• Encourage the subjects to have an idea of the key points they want to make, so that they can, if necessary, turn questions around in order to sound out their arguments.

• Encourage them to practice the 30-second drill, which has prospective interviewees pretend they've been told they will have 30 seconds at the end of the interview to summarize their major points.

• Encourage the subjects to be relaxed (admittedly easier said than done) and informal. Although they may be speaking to millions of viewers at once, most of the audience is catching the remarks in the privacy of their homes. This requires that pulpit-type lecturing be avoided in favor of down-to-earth chatting.

• Make sure the subjects are aware that it is not their responsibility to fill pregnant silences. Some radio and television reporters like to coax additional remarks out of their subjects by keeping the microphone in their face after a question has been answered. More often than not, the person confronted with the mike feels obliged to embellish the original comment rather than remain silent, and then comes out with a foolish or unneccesary statement.*

DO'S AND DON'TS OF PRESS RELATIONS

IF the reader looks hard enough, he or she can find upward of several dozen do's and don'ts in the previous pages. The following suggestions are listed separately because (a) they haven't been covered and deserve special mention; or (b) they have fallen between the lines of the text.

• **Do** update your press lists at least once a year. Journalists move around a lot, and they don't enjoy getting mail addressed to their predecessors, especially if they feel they are established in their new slot.

• **Don't** count on getting special privileges from editors because you advertise. It may help a bit on small-town weeklies and financially troubled trade magazines, but it counts for nothing at major publications and network stations.

• **Don't** ignore the trade press. They are widely read by executives in the industries they cover, even if they don't sound as impressive as *The New York Times* or the *Wall Street Journal*.

• **Don't** ignore local weekly newspapers either.

There are close to 8,000 of them in the United States.

• **Don't** overwhelm journalists with half a dozen to a dozen people sitting next to an executive during an interview. Executives are big boys and girls who don't need a supporting cast to field questions. If they do need help, the reporter is liable to assume they're idiots.

• **Don't** hold back publicly available information just because you don't like a journalist.

• **Don't** blame reporters for a headline, caption, or editing that detracts from the story. And don't let people blame the PR department if a headline, caption, or editing by someone unfamiliar with the story louses it up.†

• **Do** reemphasize key points in an interview. Reporters may not have heard them the first time.

• **Do** keep a photo library of head shots of key officers, important buildings, products, and the like. You never know when a publication will request a picture.

• If you use freelance photographers, **do** consider calling photographers from the local

---

*My wife and I have always been irked by television reporters who force unsuspecting interviewees to make dumb statements via the mike-in-the-face trick. We were therefore delighted one evening to see a woman permanently reduce a reporter's use of this gambit. She was one of several supermarket shoppers being asked for "man in the street" comments on rising food prices. She answered the newsman's query about soaring grocery bills and seemed surprised when the microphone stayed in front of her. She waited a few seconds, smiled, waited two more seconds, and said, "What do *you* think about the prices?" My wife and I rose to our feet applauding as the reporter literally crumpled before our eyes, stammering, "Er, I, er, only ask questions, not answer them."

†One of my greatest moments at Bank of America was hearing that Associated Press had selected our New York foreign exchange head for a profile on a trader and that the ensuing interview resulted in lead business stories throughout the country. But my pleasure didn't last long. During the interview, the New York–based trader mentioned that his operation was relatively small because we only had a subsidiary bank in the city. An editor in San Francisco, wanting to call attention on page 1 to the lead business story, wrote a box that said, "Read about Bank of America's small foreign exchange operation on page 43."

media. It's a good way to win friends among journalists, and it might give you an in-house advocate for a picture's use at a particular publication.

• **Don't** go over an editor's head if you disagree with his or her news judgment.

• But **do** speak to the editor's boss if you feel that he or she has been guilty of distortion or unethical journalism.

• **Don't** ask to have pictures returned or that the editor sign a messenger's receipt verifying that your release has arrived.

• **Don't** have an interview in an executive's office interrupted by phone calls. The executive would have a secretary hold all calls if entertaining a customer; the same courtesy should be extended the media.

• **Don't** call editors to ask if they have received your release and if they are planning to use it.

• **Don't** be afraid to stand up to unethical investigative reporters who are out to embarrass your organization. You don't have to answer hostile questions, put up with rudeness, or refrain from verbally attacking them.

• If a reporter comes to your organization to interview one of your officers, **do** give her the officer's business card. This eliminates the risk of a misspelled name or erroneous title.

• **Don't** be afraid to say, "I don't know; I'll have to get back to you later with an answer." It's much better to be ignorant than to be deceitful, but **don't** be ignorant too often.

• **Do** get your spokespeople to relax. About 90 percent of press queries are routine and are best dealt with in a friendly atmosphere.

• But **do** have them be on guard at the same time. The other 10 percent of journalists' questions could lead to an adversary discussion.

• **Do** make sure the subjects know the media the reporter represents so that they'll also know to whom their remarks should really be addressed.

• **Don't** take a friendly journalist for granted. If the facts suggest a negative story, then that is what will appear. All you can hope for is the opportunity to tell your side of the story.

• **Don't** expect all stories about your organization to be 100 percent favorable. There are occasions when warts will appear or when the reporter will emphasize aspects of the story you would hope he or she would ignore. Articles and radio and television presentations that are favorable on balance should be regarded as plusses for the organization.

• **Don't** think your refusal to respond will kill a negative story. It won't. Your choice is simply whether the story appears with or without your side of it, not whether the story appears at all. That choice belongs to the editor.

• **Don't** lie. Omit, beg off, or carefully edit if you have to, but don't give out information you know to be untrue. Credibility is one of the best things PR people have going for them. It can't be replaced.

FOR FURTHER EXPLORATION

1. Pretend you are news director for a hotel chain. A reporter calls and asks if she can interview the chairman about the chain's operations in the Caribbean. The chairman is out of town, so you tell the reporter you'll get back to her when he returns next week. Write a memo to the chairman asking him if he wants to do the interview. Give him all the information he'll need to make a decision.

2. Prepare a one-page guide on dealing with the press in an emergency.

3. You are trying to get your branch manager in Dayton, Ohio, to appear on a local television interview program, but she is reluctant to do so. She says most journalists are left-wing radicals who only want to embarrass businesspeople. What do you tell her?

4. What tips would you give a colleague who is getting ready for a live television interview that would not be necessary for a magazine interview?

5. Add two more do's and don'ts to the list at the end of the chapter.

5

NEWS AND FEATURE WRITING

ASIDE from pleasing personality traits, the quality required of public relations more than all others is an ability to write. This is obvious if you consider speeches, press relations, and internal communications, but it applies to *all* external relations disciplines. There is no getting around the fact that sooner or later one has to sit down at a typewriter and put some thoughts on paper.

The resulting prose might be an interoffice memo, a letter, or an advertisement—in addition to articles or speeches—but regardless of its ultimate shape, it's going to appear on paper. The written word has always been a major form of corporate and public-sector communications, and it is unlikely that it will ever be replaced.

A second reason to study the art of communicating by the printed word is that most, though not all, beginner's jobs require incumbents to compose articles for internal publications or for use as press releases.

So not only should PR neophytes know how to write, they should know how to write news.

NEWS WRITING

AS walking is to running, so is news writing to feature article, editorial, investigative article, and column production. And just as walking is generally performed by placing one foot about a yard in front of the other and repeating the process continuously, there is little dissimilarity in the way straight news stories are written.

The news writing equivalent of walking is the inverted pyramid.

WHY THE INVERTED PYRAMID?

The inverted pyramid style of writing requires reporters to place the most important facts first and have each succeeding paragraph decline in importance. It is called inverted pyramid because the top is much fatter in facts than the bottom and there is a steady tapering from wide to narrow.*

Writers employ this technique by using leads that answer most if not all, of the five W's and an H—who, what, why, where, when, and how.

An example of a lead that employs the five W's and an H is the following:

The Queens County Democratic Club [*who*] elected [*what*] John Jefferson its president by a 51–40 vote [*how*] at a special election [*why*] in its Forest Hills headquarters [*where*] last night [*when*].

The remaining text would then expand on

---

*I once asked my students to write a news story in inverted pyramid style. One gentleman handed me a paper that read like this:

The Chase Manhattan Bank announced this morning that it would open its
fifth branch in Albany on Monday, January 24, at the corner of State
and Ryan Streets. The new, full-service office, which will have
a staff of twelve people, is to be managed by Lydia Jones.
Individuals who come into the branch during its two-
week opening celebration will be able to
participate in a special drawing for
a color television set. In
addition, gifts will be
given to men and
women who open
new savings
accounts.

That wasn't quite what I had in mind.

these facts, with the most important information at the top and the least important data bringing up the rear.

There are three very good reasons for using inverted pyramid news writing.

First, hurried readers need only glance at the beginning of a story to get the pertinent facts.

Second, if an editor has to make cuts in the article to create space for other material, he or she can make cuts anywhere and be reasonably certain that no facts were omitted that were more important than the salvaged text. It is for this reason that wire services (Associated Press, United Press International, Reuters, Dow Jones, and so on) use the inverted pyramid style when dispatching news stories. Students looking for examples of this form of prose would be well advised to search for the wire service articles in their local newspapers.

Third, news editors don't have time to read an entire release before deciding if it is to be rejected or used. They need to know rapidly what the story is all about, and it isn't likely that they'll wait until the eighth or ninth paragraph to get some meaningful clues. Writers who don't place the key information at the top aren't putting their best foot forward for the editors. If they don't want their handiwork to end up in the wastepaper baskets, they must learn to use the inverted pyramid form.

HOW TO WRITE AN INVERTED PYRAMID NEWS STORY

Let's look at a series of facts gathered by a reporter and see how they would be organized into a news story.

• John Williams was promoted at Johnson College in Aberdeen, South Dakota, yesterday.

• The promotion was announced by college president William Smathers.

• Williams has been on the faculty since 1974.

• His new assignment is chairman of the political science department.

• He was formerly lieutenant governor of South Dakota for one term.

• He has been a professor of political science at the college since 1976, after starting as an associate professor.

• He and his wife, Carolyn, live in Aberdeen.

• They have two sons.

• At thirty-eight, he is the youngest department head in the school's history.

• The political science department has a faculty of twenty.

• Williams plans to make the department known throughout the country as a leading center of thought on state and local government.

• He was a state assemblyman for two terms prior to his election as lieutenant governor in 1970. He also taught at the University of South Dakota before running for office.

• He has an M.A. in political science from Yale University.

• He was born in Twin Brooks, South Dakota.

• He is the author of *Passing through the State House: A Lieutenant Governor's Diary* and *The Care and Feeding of New Laws.*

• Johnson College has 650 political science majors.

• In making the announcement, Smathers said, "John's promotion is an indication of our interest in the study of state and local government. His experience in local politics and his books and articles on the subject make him the ideal person to head our expansion in this area."

• Smathers estimated that the school will have over two thousand political science majors and at least a tripling of the number of course offerings in the subject within ten years.

• Williams will head a massive recruiting drive for students and faculty over the next several years.

• Williams left active participation in politics in 1975 after he and ex-Governor Patrick Torming were defeated in their bid for reelection.

Now study these random facts. Put a check next to the very important pieces of information and an *X* next to those that aren't very important and could easily be placed at the bottom of the story. Then put a circle next to those facts that fall between the two extremes.

The ensuing news story in the next day's local newspaper would be along the following lines:

The appointment of John Williams, former lieutenant governor of South

43

Dakota, as head of Johnson College's department of political science, was announced yesterday by William Smathers, president of the Aberdeen-based school.

Williams, at 38 the youngest department head in the school's 51-year history, will spearhead a drive to make Johnson a leading center for the study of state and local government.

"John's experience in local politics and his books and articles on the subject make him the ideal person to head our expansion in this area," said Smathers.

He added that Williams plans to concentrate on recruiting new faculty and students over the next several years.

A professor of political science at the school since 1976, Williams was lieutenant governor of the state from 1971 to 1975.

He and running mate Governor Patrick Torming were narrowly defeated by Grover Kington and Alexander Narovansky in 1974, and he joined the Johnson faculty as an associate professor shortly after leaving office.

In his new assignment, Williams will head a faculty of 20 and oversee the political science course program for a student body of 6,000.

According to President Smathers, the department's expansion plans call for a tripling of the number of political science course offerings and an increase in the number of students majoring in the subject from 650 to more than 2,000 within the next 10 years.

A native of Twin Brooks, S.D., Williams is the author of *Passing through the State House: A Lieutenant Governor's Diary, The Care and Feeding of New Laws,* and numerous articles for academic journals.

He also served two terms as a state assemblyman and was an assistant professor of political science at the University of South Dakota before running for office.

He has an M.A. in political science from Yale University.

Williams and his wife, Carolyn, reside in Aberdeen. They have two sons.

The foregoing does not represent the only—nor the best—way to write the story, but it is an example of inverted pyramid writing. I think an editor could start at the end of the article and eliminate any number of paragraphs up to the initial four and not lose the essential elements of the story. Would-be reporters and press-release authors should examine their newspapers for other examples and should practice by rewriting them or doing stories of their own. And practice, and practice, and practice.

Beginners must ask themselves, which of the available facts and figures would be of the greatest interest to readers? Or how would one summarize the available information into one sentence?

The answers to these questions should present writers with the essential ingredients for the lead. Subsequent paragraphs should then contain the facts, which embellish, or flesh out, points made in the opening sentence.

For example, after announcing the John Williams appointment, the writer would want to say what Williams will do in the job, why he was selected for it, and how he'll go about achieving his goals.

Another cardinal rule is to avoid editorializing (presenting reporters' opinions as fact). If, for example, someone were to write, "John Williams, the ideal person to head an expansion program, will . . ." he or she would be editorializing. But if the reporter were to quote the college president calling Williams "the ideal person," he or she would merely be reporting a fact.

Another rule is to keep the prose tight. Every news article—whether it appears in a company publication, daily newspaper, or trade magazine—competes for the time and attention of potential readers. A good way to battle for that attention is to put as much information into as little space as possible.

The following are examples of how one word can easily replace two or more without losing any meaning:

wordy	*good, tight writing*
every now and then	occasionally
tendered his resignation	resigned
be that as it may	however
at that time	then
on one occasion	once

taken to jail	arrested
once in a great while	rarely
in the event that	if
breathed his last breath	died
departed from the premises	left
declared in loud tones	shouted
at the present time	now
is of the belief that	believes
conducted a study of	studied
united in wedded bliss	married
told her audience that	said

Despite the ease with which lengthy word groupings can be replaced by pithier phrasing, redundancy will occasionally appear in articles by the sharpest of writers. The best way to guard against such excesses is to practice tightening your prose.

One useful exercise is to shoot for a 5- to 10-percent reduction in the number of words from first to second draft without sacrificing factual content.

FEATURE WRITING

THE first question that comes up in discussing the art of feature writing is, how does it differ from news writing? Or, more to the point, what is the difference between a news article and a feature story?

One of the key distinguishing characteristics between the two is timeliness—or the lack of it.

If an explosion occurs at the gas station on Fillmore and Third Streets today, a story on the event in tomorrow's newspaper would be considered a news article. But it wouldn't be considered a terribly worthwhile news story next week or next month.

If, however, a journalist chose to write a piece on major gas explosions over the years, it might make an interesting feature. Such an article would probably attract more attention if it ran with the coverage of a new disaster, but it could, if sufficiently interesting, be used at just about any time.

Basically, if it is news, it has to be used almost immediately. If it is a feature, it can generally run whenever there is space for it.

THE USE OF PYRAMID WRITING IN FEATURE ARTICLES

The inverted pyramid can be used for feature articles, but variations of the style are more likely to be employed. They make for livelier reading and they're more fun to compose as well.

Some of the more common variations are the pyramid, the small pyramid on top of a large inverted pyramid, and the small inverted pyramid on top of a larger pyramid.

1. The pyramid—Writers using this form merely tell the story from beginning to end, with the real punch line coming in the last two or three paragraphs. One could, for example, begin a feature article with a statement such as, "It all began with a remark made in jest." The next few paragraphs would describe the setting in which the remark was uttered, then the story would be told from start to finish.

2. Small pyramid on top of a large inverted pyramid—In this form, the writer also initiates the text with a statement that describes the genesis of the event. Again, something like, "It all started with a remark made in jest" can be used. Then there is an additional paragraph or two to describe the setting and let some of the developments unfold.

Then the writer skips to the end and sums up the event by writing something like, "And by the time the dust had cleared, four people were treated for bruises at Jefferson City hospital, an estranged couple were reconciled, and little Mary Ann Morris became a neighborhood heroine."

Such a statement is bound to arouse some curiosity, which the writer will then attempt to satisfy by telling the rest of the story in inverted pyramid style.

3. Small inverted pyramid on top of a larger pyramid—This is the opposite of the previous example. Here the writer wraps up the article in a tight one-, two-, or three-paragraph lead and then tells the story from the beginning.

For example . . .

When Jake Findlay asks his wife Sally what kind of day she had at the office, he's not making small talk; he—and his sons, cousin, and sister—really want to know.

For the past two years, the Findlay clan have all been working for First National Bank of Arizona, each as a branch manager in the Phoenix metropolitan area.

They attribute their mutual interest in banking to an evening course Jake took twelve years ago.

From here on, the reporter tells the story of how the evening course changed the Findlays' lives. She sprinkles the tale with some anecdotes, too, and she has a fairly marketable feature.

COMPONENTS OF THE FEATURE STORY

THE THEME

The theme of a feature is what editors refer to in explaining why their publication or television or radio station has decided to include the story in its daily, weekly, or monthly fare. It tells what the story is all about and why it is worth sharing.

Equally important, the theme holds the feature together. It isn't necessary that each paragraph of text explain why the story is deserving of the reader's, listener's, or viewer's attention, but all the paragraphs should have some relation to the theme. If not, the article would read or sound like a series of uncollected thoughts.

Unfortunately, finding a theme and using it to hold the story together are two of the more difficult challenges for rookie writers. They're not easy things to do, but these tasks can be mastered with practice, a study of how professional journalists handle features, and more practice.

The following are random facts I gave students for a feature-writing assignment, as well as some representative samples of their work.

• Ms. Margaret Moraker has worked at your insurance company for four years.

• She began her career as an administrative assistant and is now a claims manager in the main office.

• You are doing a house-organ article on her because she has been attending classes four nights a week at Baruch College since joining the company.

• She will get a bachelor's degree in business administration next January. She plans to continue her studies as a graduate student and is undecided at this time whether to major in marketing or accounting while seeking her master's degree.

• According to the dean of faculty at Baruch (Dr. Joseph Baker) only 5 percent of the school's evening students take courses four nights a week. "Well over 90 percent of the evening student body takes courses only one or two evenings a week."

• Ms. Moraker is taking the heavy schedule because she's anxious to get a bachelor's degree. She even studies during the summer, explaining, "I have to work during the summer, so why should I take a vacation from school?"

• She has been on the Dean's List since starting at the school. Her average is 3.7 out of a possible 4.0.

• She works in the auto insurance division and handles claims from heavily populated sections of Manhattan. Supervisor Tom Mangano says, "She turns in an effective performance in a delicate role."

• She attributes her good grades to the facts that she finds the subjects very interesting, that she spends two hours a day riding the subway to and from work and therefore has ten hours a week of "enforced study time," that she takes good notes, and that she has an excellent memory.

• When not working or studying, she devotes time to horseback riding, tennis, and dating. She often dates fellow students.

• What's a typical date? "We study together at the library for an hour or two and then grab a cup of coffee."

• Ms. Moraker's tuition is paid for under the company's tuition refund program.

• Margaret lives in Brooklyn, New York, with her parents and fifteen-year-old sister.

The following article was prepared by a professional writer, and the next two were written by students.

Margaret Moraker doesn't believe in doing things the easy way.

Rather than pursue an evening education at the leisurely pace adopted by most full-time workers, the claims manager at the head office has been attending classes at Baruch College four nights a week for the past four years—summers included. ("I have to work during the summer, so why take a vacation from school?" she asks.)

And rather than just barely meeting the minimum requirements for each course, Margaret has been on the Dean's List every semester she has been at the school.

"It hasn't been easy, but I find that I have a lot of time for studying on weekends. And since I almost always get a seat on the subway (she commutes from Brooklyn), I can read my textbooks to and from work. That adds up to 10 hours a week of enforced study time," she said.

Her fellow students will verify that her work load isn't easy, because few will attempt to imitate it. According to Dr. Joseph Baker, dean of faculty at the school, only 5% of the student body matriculates four evenings a week.

Margaret's schedule calls for her to receive a bachelor's degree in business administration next January. Then she'll decide whether or not to continue her studies under the company tuition refund plan as

a graduate student majoring in either marketing or accounting.

In the meantime, she works as a claims manager in the auto insurance division where she also receives "good grades."

"She turns in an effective performance in a delicate role," said supervisor Tom Mangano.

Margaret handles claims from several heavily populated sections of Manhattan and says she "very much enjoys the customer contact and the busy pace in the office."

When not working or studying, Margaret finds time to see friends, go horseback riding, or date—most often with fellow students.

And what's a typical date with a classmate?

"Well, sometimes we'll go to the library and study together," she said.

STUDENT SAMPLE NUMBER ONE

Margaret Moraker, a claims manager at the head office, will get a bachelor's degree in business administration from Baruch College this coming January after four years of hard work.

An excellent student at the college, she has a 3.7 average out of a possible 4.0.

She says her grades are good because she likes her subjects and spends 10 hours a week on the subway going to and from work, which, she adds, gives her enforced study time.

She lives in Brooklyn with her parents and 15-year-old sister.

Unlike most of the students at the college, who matriculate only one or two evenings a week, Margaret has been going to school four nights a week.

She even goes in the summer.

"I have to work during the summer, so why should I take a vacation from school?"

After getting her degree, she'll continue

her studies as a graduate student, but is undecided about whether to major in marketing or accounting.

She has been working for the company during the past four years and currently handles auto insurance claims for sections of Manhattan.

She performs as well on the job as she does in school.

When not studying or working, she occasionally dates, sometimes with men from school.

Margaret is such a dedicated student that a typical date on campus is to go to the library and study together and then go out for coffee.

STUDENT SAMPLE NUMBER TWO

Most commuters read during their subway commute, some snooze or stare off into space. Margaret Moraker, full-time claims manager, auto insurance division, fills her daily two hours' travel time to and from her parents' home in Brooklyn and XYZ Insurance Company's main office studying for the courses she takes four nights a week toward her bachelor's degree in business administration.

Juggling her busy schedule with determination and persistence seems to have paid off for Ms. Moraker.

"She turns in an effective performance in a delicate role," says supervisor Tom Mangano, of her work handling claims from heavily populated Manhattan sections.

At the same time, in the four years since she began with the company as an administrative assistant, she has been going to school four nights a week and has maintained a Dean's List average of 3.7.

She attributes her success at school to the fact that she finds the subjects interesting, takes good notes, has an excellent memory and spends as much time as possible studying.

"Even my dates with fellow students mean

studying together at the library for an hour or two, then grabbing a cup of coffee," she said.

Ms. Moraker's tuition is paid for under the company's tuition refund program, which will enable her also to begin graduate studies toward her master's degree after she receives her bachelor's degree next January.

Note that the professional's theme was "Margaret Moraker is a hardworking young lady who not only is taking on a difficult task, she is performing it in an unusually competent manner." Notice, too, that most of the paragraphs in the professional's copy touched on the theme, and that each one seemed to flow logically into the next.

Most of the students, all of whom were beginners, failed to find the right theme. And those who did didn't stay with it.

They also displayed a penchant for editorializing and an understandable inability to connect the paragraphs. Indeed, many of the assignments handed in read as if it wouldn't have made any difference at all if the paragraphs were rearranged at random.

HOW TO FIND THE THEME

In looking at a disconnected series of facts such as the data on Ms. Moraker, there are several questions writers should ask themselves.

• What is unusual about all this?

• Are there any interesting comparisons that can be made with the past?

• Do the facts tell me anything about the future?

• Are there any interesting conflicts suggested by the facts?

• Is there anything here that would be of special interest to the readers of the publication I write for?

• Are there any interesting anecdotes that could serve as the basis of a theme?

• Are any of the facts a large surprise? For example, do four-night-a-week students usually have a 3.7 average?

• Were any normal practices reversed or accentuated to get improved results?

It is important to zero in on a theme, because it should provide the reason for doing the story in the first place. It should also make composing a story easier, because the writer now has something with which he or she can tie everything together. And, perhaps most important of all, its existence tells the writer there is, in fact, a story to write. Without a strong central idea, the writer would be better off looking for another feature.

THE LEAD

The function of the lead, which is the beginning of the story, is to get readers' attention and motivate them to read on. The writer must accept the fact that there are other articles and scores of other activities competing for people's attention, so an audience isn't going to suffer through six or seven paragraphs before deciding whether the story is worth continuing or is a waste of time.

If the article doesn't get and hold readers' interest rapidly, the chances of it doing so at all are very slim.

In selecting a good opener, writers have several lead options open to them. It is important for beginners to become familiar with them all, because the same kind of lead, story after story, can start to get boring.

Let's take a look at some random facts from two separate feature stories and then show how different types of leads can be used for each of them.

Story A

Jose Rivera is a teller at the Main Street branch of First Valley Bank.

He has been a teller at the bank for the past three years.

He is not sure he wants to be a banker, however, as his first love is acting.

He majored in drama at the University of Pennsylvania and starred in close to a dozen shows.

He is a part-time professional actor and has appeared in twenty-five television shows and scores of commercials.

Most of his appearances have been bit parts or extra parts as a villain. He has spoken dialogue in only ten of his appearances and never more than two or three lines.

He takes acting classes one night a week and studies for his master of business administration one night a week, too.

He enjoys his double life but isn't sure he can continue in show business much longer without any juicy parts on the horizon.

He is married and has one son, age four.

He says customers come up to him about once a month to ask if he's the person they saw on television the other night.

He had to turn down a lucrative commercial last month because the advertising agency was looking for someone to act the part of a teller at a rival bank.

Story B

Al and Betty Sample have been working for Taylor Manufacturing Company for seven years; Al as a computer salesman, Betty as a personnel assistant.

They go away on vacation every year.

Rather than go to Caribbean resorts, Europe, or other vacation spots, they go on African safaris.

A typical vacation is a two- or three-week trip through a jungle.

Sometimes they go with other couples, sometimes with a guide, and sometimes alone.

They've had encounters with animals quite frequently but nothing that they can describe as dangerous.

One time, as they camped near a river, a crocodile came on shore and chewed on several pieces of their clothing. Fortunately, they weren't wearing the clothes at the time.

Another time, a pair of chimpanzees took a liking to the Samples and followed them wherever they went.

Then there was the vacation during which a giraffe developed a fondness for their Jeep and slept next to it two nights in a row.

They went to a luxurious resort seven years ago but found it boring. They also don't like people waiting on them hand and foot.

The Samples always take a lot of slides and movies for home showings over the winter. Some friends enjoy the shows, others don't.

1. The question lead—An old standby, this is an easy way to attract attention and set the stage for the next several paragraphs as the writer attempts to provide an answer. For some reason, this lead has been very popular with students.

For story A: Although friendly and amiable, Jose Rivera is not an unusually handsome man. So why is it that customers of First Valley Bank often stare at him upon visiting his branch office?

For story B: Riddle: What offers snakes, crocodiles, giraffes, al fresco bathroom facilities, and an occasional element of fear?

Answer: A typical Al and Betty Sample vacation.

2. The news summary lead—Using the five *W's* and an *H,* the writer brings the key facts of the story to his readers right at the outset.

For story A: Jose Rivera is a bank teller by day, an actor by night and he still finds time to raise a family.

For story B: Plush resorts, picturesque European cities, and luxurious cruises hold no vacation-time allure for Al and Betty Sample; they much prefer to rough it in African jungles.

3. The contrast lead—The advantage of this type of lead is that people enjoy reading about conflicts. It is interesting to sit on the sidelines and watch people or ideas slug it out.

For story A: The way Jose Rivera figures it, the banking profession is interesting and secure. Acting, on the other hand, is risky, but, oh, what a nice pot at the end of the rainbow.

With a steady job in the former field and ambitious hopes for the second, Rivera spends a lot of time trying to decide between the two.

For story B: Friends of Al and Betty Sample who entertain thoughts of vacationing with them face an interesting debate every year: Do they put up with snakes or do they refrain from putting up with the Samples?

4. The narrative lead—Most people like to read or hear a story. Get it in the lead, make it interesting enough, and people will read on.

For story A: First Valley Bank teller Jose Rivera calmly reached across his counter to accept a customer's deposit ticket, when she suddenly shrieked.

"You're the one, you're the one. I know it. You're the one. I saw you kill that woman last night."

Heads turned, conversations stopped, and one customer stealthily crossed the branch to alert the guard.

"Yes, I'm sure," the woman continued shouting. You're the one who was on that made-for-television movie last night. Right?"

Right.

For story B: Four thousand miles away from home and alone in an African jungle, Al and Betty Sample had an uneasy feeling they were being watched.

"I keep hearing noises behind us," Betty said.

"Maybe it's only our imagination," said Al. They walked some more and heard more noises. They stopped, and the noises stopped.

With one hand firmly clutching his penknife, Al threw a stone at a clump of bushes behind him. Out came two frightened chimpanzees.

5. The descriptive lead—Here, writers use words to draw a picture of people, locations, or incidents.

For story A: He stands at his teller's cage in a pin-striped suit, white shirt, rep tie, horn-rimmed glasses, and a pleasant smile. It's an interesting outfit for a guy who will be wearing a soiled sweatshirt and aged jeans six hours later as he mugs a drunken derelict.

For story B: It's the fourth day of Betty Sample's vacation, and she's washing clothes in a muddy river. Upstream about 30 yards, her husband Al, is trying to catch fish so that they'll have something to eat for dinner.

6. *The tabular lead*—If writers have many interesting facts at their disposal, they can simply list them to arouse curiosity.

For story A: White shirt. Wig. Pin-striped suit. Attaché case. Monster makeup.

These are the tools of Jose Rivera's trades.

For story B: Snakes, crocodiles, outdoor facilities if they can find them, friendly chimpanzees, and dining in the mud are just some of the features of a typical Al and Betty Sample vacation.

7. *The striking-statement lead*—There's nothing like a sudden punch to the stomach to attract attention. The striking-statement lead is the writer's equivalent of a fast punch.

For story A: The thing of it is Jose Rivera likes helping people by day and killing them at night.

For story B: Betty Sample would have worn her favorite green blouse on the second day of her vacation, but a crocodile ate it that morning.

8. *The dialogue lead*—This is similar to a narrative lead in that it attracts attention with storylike prose. The only difference is that it focuses on dialogue rather than on observation.

For story A: He: Here's your passbook, madam.

She: Thank you. Hey, didn't I see you kill a policeman last night?

For story B: Said Betty Sample to her husband, Al, on the third morning of their vacation: "Why don't you back our Jeep out of the ditch while I put out the campfire?"

"I can't," Al replied, "there's a giraffe sleeping right behind it."

9. *The direct-address lead*—This stops readers, because the writer is communicating directly to them.

For story A: So you think bankers are dull? There's a teller at First Valley Bank who puts on old clothes and kills someone a couple of nights per month.

For story B: You say you'd like something different in a vacation this year? How about a week in the jungle with two chimpanzees for companionship?

10. *The quotation lead*—When all else fails, you can always fall back on a well-known quote to focus on the theme of the story.

For story A: "Variety is the spice of life," it has been said.

"Ditto," says Jose Rivera, who's a bank teller by day and a villainous actor by night.

For story B: It is written in Genesis II that "It is not good that man should be alone."

It therefore only seemed fitting to a pair of friendly African chimpanzees that they follow Al and Betty Sample around on their recent vacation.

The common ingredients in these examples—ingredients all novice writers should strive for—are imagination and direct relationship to the facts at hand.

There are those who feel imagination is a natural gift one either has or doesn't have at birth. I am not one of them.

Imagination can most assuredly be developed with practice and by learning how to look at things from different angles.

To cite an example, one can look at a situation by focusing on one of its many parts, many of its parts, or all of them. Or one can look at a situation by focusing on what it tells us about the past or on what it says about the future. Or one can view the facts from the viewpoints of one or more of the people involved, or from the perspective of outsiders.

Writers can also get ideas by magnifying situations, showing how they relate to other settings, focusing on a particular aspect; and by reversing facts, rearranging them, or combining them.

Or—and here comes the final *or*—they can simply look at the facts at hand and force themselves to come up with twenty different leads before picking one they like best.

Proponents of the teaching of creativity have shown in tests at numerous academic institutions that practice and the use of techniques such as those just mentioned *can* facilitate and increase idea generation.

Novice writers who have difficulty with leads would be well advised to read a book on creative problem solving. One source of information on such literature is the Creative Education Foundation, located at 1300 Elmwood Avenue, Chase Hall, Buffalo, New York, 14222.

The second key ingredient of good leads—direct relation to the facts—is obvious. The most effective, attention-getting device in the world isn't going to work very well if it has nothing to do with the subject under discussion. If readers have to start guessing what the remaining paragraphs have to do with the lead, they will start getting annoyed. Ultimately, they will lose interest.

THE STORY AFTER THE LEAD

Most writers will find that after identifying the theme and finding a good lead, the actual writing of a feature article isn't very difficult. It may be somewhat time-consuming as writers wrestle with certain phrases and fine-tune the copy, but the major hurdles are generally behind them by the time they get to the fourth or fifth paragraph.

At this stage, writers should have a good idea of where they are going. All that remains is that the facts be used to tell the story in a logical sequence.

Regardless of where they start the sequence—at the beginning, middle, or end—writers must also strive to stay with the theme. The theme explains why the story is interesting in the first place, so unless most of the text stays close to the theme, the interesting aspects of the story will be missed.

THE CLOSE

Many features can simply wind to an end when the story has been told. There's no special trick to this; simply get up from your typewriter and leave the room when there is nothing more to write.

Occasionally, however, a writer will opt to end the piece with a punch line to leave the audience laughing, crying, rueful, angry or whatever.

There are several different types of closings. Let's go back to the features on Jose Rivera and the Samples to see how these different closings can be employed.

1. *The restatement close*—This merely wraps up the story (and subtly reminds the readers what it was all about).

For story A: Juggling two diverse careers may cost Rivera an hour or two of sleep each night, but he figures it's a fair price to pay for his enjoyment of both worlds.

For story B: The Samples admit their vacations are not the type travel agents market aggressively, but they have no intention of changing their plans in the future.

2. *The gag-line close*—This is effective in humorous stories because the last reader reaction—a laugh—reinforces the mood maintained in the earlier paragraphs.

For story A: An added benefit of his double life, Rivera points out, is that he's had so much experience playing criminals, he's certain he can spot a bank robber if one ever ventured into his branch.

For story B: The only objection the Samples had to their last trip was that they shelled out $1,400 while the chimpanzees travelled free.

3. *The question close*—A question at the beginning gets readers thinking about the topic and anxious for more information. The purpose of the query at the end of the article is that it *keeps* people thinking about it.

For story A: One wonders if it is possible to find two professions as dissimilar as banking and acting.

For story B: With seven African journeys behind them, Al and Betty are fearful they'll soon exhaust their options on the continent. Where can they go next?

4. *The additional-data close*—There is nothing wrong with taking some of the facts that haven't been mentioned and putting them into a final paragraph.

For story A: Rivera's next picture will be "Sing-Sing Breakout." It should reach neighborhood theaters in August.

For story B: Betty added that Jim Day, president of the Taylor Employee Club, said he'll include a showing of the Samples' slides from their most recent trip in the Monday, Aug. 15, meeting program.

5. *The quotation close*—Here, the reporter ends a story by quoting someone.

For story A: "One of the best parts of this double life is the looks of recognition that I get from customers," Jose said.

For story B: "We tried luxury and we tried roughing it. Roughing it is much more fun." Betty grinned.

COMMON BEGINNERS' ERRORS IN FEATURE WRITING

1. Poor leads—Poor leads are generally a symptom of insufficient practice, an unwillingness to experiment with "off the wall" leads, or of failure to study professionals by reading newspapers and magazines. Beginners must do a lot of writing at home, they must force themselves to develop creativity, and they have to watch how the pros do it. Even if reading the best-written publications doesn't give novices the skills to write well, it will at least enable them to recognize a good lead when they accidentally produce one.

2. Failure to find the theme—Many of the students who tried to write a feature on Margaret Moraker focused on the fact that she was graduating soon or that she studied on the subway. Neither of these accomplishments distinguish her from thousands of other college students. Stories with those secondary topics as themes can only elicit a "so what?" response.

3. Failure to stay with the theme—Some students may hit upon Ms. Moraker's academic accomplishments in the face of an exceedingly heavy schedule as the most interesting fact about her. But they soon lose their readers by quickly moving on to other things that aren't terribly interesting.

4. Editorializing—It is not necessary to write that Ms. Moraker is a hard worker unless you are quoting someone making that statement. The mere mention of her schedule and grades can get that fact across without having to hit readers over the head with it.

Let facts speak for themselves. Readers feel insulted when writers make obvious assumptions for them. Just give them the facts, and they'll arrive at the appropriate conclusions on their own.

And don't overstate or telegraph your punches. Watch Johnny Carson, or any other good comedian, deliver a monologue. The laughs tend to be loudest when the punch line comes as a surprise. The surprise is lost, however, if the comic shouts the punch line to let everyone know it has arrived.

5. Failure to connect paragraphs—This is probably the most difficult task for new writers. One way to get around the challenge is to tell the story from beginning to end, so that every paragraph logically follows the preceding one.

Another way is to make use of transitional phrases such as "this was followed by . . .," "as a result . . .," "Sampson responded to this by . . .," "he added that . . .," "three weeks later . . .," and so on.

THE INTERVIEW

IT is always nice to be handed facts such as those presented earlier in the chapter, but writers in the real world are more often forced to produce copy from information they uncover on their own.

Some of the necessary data are available in previously printed reports, but most come from interviews. Which means that a few words on the art of asking questions and getting answers (which don't always go hand in hand) are in order.

BEFORE THE INTERVIEW

1. Setting it up—Interviews can be conducted over the phone, by mail, or in person. In person is best. If you can do the interview at the subject's home or office (assuming that that is where the action of the story occurred), so much the better. The advantages are that the subject is relaxed and you can describe his or her reactions in the appropriate setting.

2. Establish a time limit–Make sure that you know, when the interview begins, exactly how much time you will have with the interviewee. Otherwise, just as you're getting to the good questions, he or she could rise to announce it is time for another appointment.

3. List your questions—Never go into an interview thinking you can ad-lib all of the questions. The usual by-product of such an exercise is the realization by the reporter upon returning to the office that there were two or three critical points that never got raised.

In listing the questions that you do want to ask, make sure the five W's and an H are covered, that you're hitting the points a curious person would want to read about, and that you are taking into account the interests of the audience. Once you have a list in front of you, it is perfectly all right to ad-lib queries if you are not satisfied with an answer or you want to follow up on a comment made by the subject. The only time ad-libbing is wrong is when it is the sole form of question formation.

DURING THE INTERVIEW

1. Start slowly—The average interviewee is understandably on guard at the outset, fearful he or she may say the wrong thing. Unless you've been told in advance you only have five minutes or so for the interview, a few minutes of friendly small talk and then some simple questions for starters can be effective in exorcising tenseness and laying the groundwork for some meaningful exchanges.

2. Don't lead the interviewee—Questions that begin with "isn't it true that . . ." aren't as conducive to a friendly atmosphere as "what hap-pened . . ."–type inquiries. It is always best to let the subject talk at a pace he or she finds comfortable. You still have the option of choosing which comments get included in your text, so what is it going to cost you to sit back and listen (assuming that the person across from you isn't stalling or obfuscating)? The chances are the more the subject talks, the more quotable comments you are going to get.

3. Watch as well as listen—How a person looks or acts when answering questions can be almost as telling as the responses themselves. Is the subject chain-smoking? Or very nervous? Or looking up facts and figures she should know off the top of her head? The answers to these and similar questions could be of interest to readers.

4. Don't argue—You are there to report what the subject has to say: Whether you agree or disagree with the comments is unimportant. If you are obvious in your displeasure with the interviewee's statements, it could lead to a sudden termination of the interview.

For example, if you feel a remark is inaccurate, it is decidedly unprofessional to declare, "That's a lot of baloney, chum." It is far more effective to state, "Mr. Smith's version is in direct conflict with yours. How do you explain the disparity?"

5. Don't rely on memory; take notes—It is very disconcerting to speak to a reporter who is listening but not taking notes. It makes subjects think that (a) the reporter feels that what they are saying is unimportant; or (b) the reporter is going to mess up the statements thoroughly and will have the subject looking like a jerk. If keeping up with interviewees is hard for you, study shorthand or speed writing—or ask permission to tape the interview. Failure to do this could result in a lot of shortened interviews.

6. End the meeting courteously—This can be accomplished by the voicing of two questions and a statement.

• Are there any points not covered by my questions that you would like to bring up? (This doesn't mean that the reporter is then obliged to include the additional comments in the story.)

• May I call you later on if I think of any additional questions?

• Please feel free to call me if you think of something you'd like to add.

AFTER THE INTERVIEW

1. Review your notes quickly—If you used a tape recorder, make sure you got it all on tape. If you relied on notes, make sure you understand your scribbling while the interview is still fresh in your mind.

2. Don't violate a trust—Any remarks prefaced with "off the record" must remain off the record.

3. Weigh remarks against acknowledged facts—A point is not necessarily a fact just because an important person said it. If you have doubts about some of the spokesperson's facts, go to another source or two. (This is especially important when writing for internal publications, because you don't want to embarrass someone in the organization.)

4. Write a thank-you note—Subjects usually have a choice as to whether or not they are going to be interviewed. It is therefore incumbent on the reporter to make the experience as pleasant as possible, especially if there might be a need for a follow-up interview. One way to leave the subject in a pleasant frame of mind is to send a thank-you note for his or her time and cooperation and a tear sheet of the article.

FOR FURTHER EXPLORATION

1. Take five news stories from your local paper and cut out the unnecessary verbiage. Don't stop until you've deleted at least fifteen words.

2. Frank Sinatra and Billy Martin got into a fistfight with each other at a Manhattan night club in the early morning hours today. Write a straight news lead and a feature lead.

3. Your twelve-year-old cousin was asked to write a news story for his school paper. He knows nothing about news writing but he was told by his mother that you are an expert in public relations, so he asks you for some tips. What do you tell him?

4. Take an inverted pyramid news story from your local paper. Rewrite it in pyramid style.

5. Pick three features from your Sunday newspaper. State what the theme is in one sentence for each. Then, just for the heck of it, write better leads.

ELECTRONIC COMMUNICATIONS

INCLUDING text about telecommunications (audio-visuals) and their implications for public relations is almost a waste of time. The field is growing so rapidly and new discoveries are taking place so frequently that it is impossible to be current. All an author should therefore attempt to do is to present an overview of the state of the art and a description of the various tools.

THE OVERVIEW

THERE is no doubt that the printed word has been giving way to the electronically communicated word. We've a long way to go before the former is replaced by the latter—actually the likelihood of that ever happening is extremely remote—but the two are learning to exist side by side, and the day of print's total dominance will not reappear.

There are good reasons for this. Aside from the fact that a message featuring moving images and sound has more impact than the unmoving word, electronics is an easier and more entertaining medium for most audiences.

The statistics back this contention. According to *Ad Age,* a publication covering the advertising industry, more than nine out of ten adults listen to radio. *Broadcasting Magazine* observes that after doctors and dentists, most Americans get health information from television.

Other observers of American mores have noted that anywhere from 50 to 85 percent of the people get most of their news from television.

Electronics has much to offer the public. In addition to providing sound and motion (or in the case of radio, sound alone), electronically communicated information:

• Reaches most audiences in the privacy of their homes, and, as a consequence, becomes a part of their everyday lives

• Often shows what has happened as opposed to merely reporting about the events

• Can be very immediate because it isn't difficult to show news live or to interrupt regular broadcasting shortly after the news occurs

• Can reach both large and small audiences all over the country

Given these selling points, it is no wonder audio-visuals are growing in importance as a private- and public-sector medium.

As their popularity increases, the uses for these wonders of modern science increase as well. Within organizations audio-visuals are becoming *the* medium for employee education. Slides, movies, and tapes make for entertaining and informative ways to enlighten audiences, and—on top of that—they are easily updated.

These features are the justifications for a new and rapidly spreading phenomenon in internal communications: the taped house organ. Shown on closed-circuit television or video recorders at employee gathering spots (that is, the staff lounge or cafeteria), these presentations are valuable supplements to company magazines and newsletters. In some cases they even serve as replacements for their printed counterparts.

At present there are more than three hundred major U.S. companies using newscasts for employees. These programs run from five to thirty minutes and are aired on a repetitive basis during lunch hours. More will be said about them later.

Still another internal use of audio-visual equipment is the training of senior executives for on-the-air interviews. Such priming is sorely needed. Most executives spent their formative years in their chosen professions when print was king. As a consequence, they are more comfortable facing journalists who come bearing pads and pencils than those who are equipped with microphones and television cameras. As stated in chapter four, "do-overs" are allowed, and flubs are generally omitted by print journalists attempting to recreate the highlights of a given interview. The subject need only worry about what is said. Once the television camera and/or recording devices are turned on, however, interviewees must also concern themselves with *how* the information is conveyed.

This generates a need for help. Countless firms are now bringing senior officials to their in-house studios, where they are tutored in the art of responding to questions in "live" discussions with make-believe journalists. This exercise almost always includes a torturous session or two in which the "students" are put through rough interviews, then given the dubious pleasure of watching instant replays.

As painful as these drills are, they're exceedingly useful in pruning budding bad habits. Equally important, they allow potential spokespeople to practice putting the tutoring to use and to develop new skills before—not after—they are placed in the limelight.

Outside the organization, the uses of audio-visuals are many, although they all fall under the broad heading of "communication." Subheadings such as "education" and "entertainment" also come into play as organizations take their stories to a multitude of publics in a variety of shapes and forms.

The basic tools of audio-visuals are slides, films, and videotape. All are making inroads on print and are "must-study" topics for newcomers to public relations—and not only upon entry into the field, but at periodic intervals throughout one's career—in order to appreciate the potential advantages of these vehicles and the advent of new discoveries.

SLIDES

AMONG the many advantages of slides, price and flexibility stand at the top of the list. Depending on what you want to put in them, you can have slides made for as little as 50¢ apiece. The more common range for the preparation of a slide, it should be noted, is $10 to $75, but good ones can still be had for less. Just go to your neighborhood processor with a roll of color film, pay about 50¢ for the developing of each slide, and examine the results.

The flexibility feature is most appreciated when the slides are being placed in a projector. A flick of the wrist here, some minor manipulations with two or three fingers there, and a slide can move in order from first to last—and anywhere in between. All other slides can be repositioned just as easily or replaced by better depictions of the same scene or data.

In addition, each slide can be shown for any length of time; it can be shown alone or with others at the same time; it can be embellished by a variety of audio accompaniments; and its size can be played around with. Not bad for 50¢ (or more) a pop.

And, if you are using an overhead projector and transparencies, as well, the material can be created and edited before the audience's eyes.

Readers should not, however, conclude that slide shows can be produced in a helter-skelter fashion. The best presentations are the results of detailed planning that takes into account a multitude of factors including:

• Budget

• Audience

• Objective of the presentation

• Production schedule

• Type of meeting at which the slides are to be exhibited

Once these elements have been studied and appropriate strategies have been formulated, planners must arrange to have the photographs taken or acquired, tie the visual aspect of the program into a script, and set up the sequential order of the slides.

The use of a script implies that a person will accompany the slide show to (a) introduce the presentation to the audience; (b) press the appropriate buttons so that the audio portion (usually on tape) is not forgotten; or (c) do the voice-over live.

The last is, obviously, the most demanding of the three tasks, but all require a strong familiarity with the slides and the purpose for which they are being displayed. The presentation also requires rehearsal to:

• Make sure the equipment works
• Know how long the show runs
• Guarantee that the audio portion and the visuals are properly synchronized
• Make sure the slides are easily seen from every seat

Presentation planners who feel that their slides are so outstanding that there is no need to worry about the role of the "live accompanist" are guilty of a gross error of judgment. They can also be accurately accused of throwing a lot of time and money down the drain.

FILMS

FILM is a very effective instrument for taking messages to large audiences. While it does, naturally, have many internal uses, its ability to blend movement and sound on large screens makes film an increasingly popular vehicle for external gatherings.

The rationales for using this medium with large and small groups throughout the world are the following:

• Once a film is made, it can be reproduced easily and cheaply, and thus is capable of being used in a variety of locations at the same time.
• It is very portable.
• Its sharpness is such that it can be blown up many times its original size and still be seen clearly by hundreds of people.
• It can be divided so that some portions of a film are shown to one audience, while other segments are presented elsewhere.
• There are many outlets for films. In addition to public theaters, there are clubs, schools, resorts, network television, cable television, and foreign television, to name just a few.

It is not hard to understand why businesses and nonprofit organizations spend millions of dollars each year on celluloid to tell the outside world of their activities. There is an awful lot that can be accomplished with film.

These corporate and public-sector filmmaking ventures may not come up for mention at the Academy Awards ceremony, but they are quite Hollywood-like in their sophisticated use of contemporary techniques and talents.

MAKING FILMS

Public relations personnel who are asked to produce a film for their organization should accept one basic premise at the outset: There's a lot more expertise outside their place of business than there is inside. Since even the companies with fairly sophisticated audio-visual operations don't make too many films each year, it is not at all unreasonable to assume that outside consultants with numerous productions under their belts should be called in.

The PR operatives will still maintain control, but the individuals who deal with lighting, staging, film supplies, sound, cinematography, editing, and the like on a near-daily basis should handle the nuts-and-bolts decisions.

Once the key players have been assembled, there will be a meeting or two to discuss broad goals, targeted audiences, and budget. (The last subject must be brought up, because a filet mignon appetite and hamburger supply of cash just don't go together.)

Then there's the film treatment, which is a detailed description of what will be in the movie—story, locations, characters—and how.

When that is approved, production begins. Actors are hired, a script is prepared, film is shot, footage is edited, and management is informed just about every step of the way. Failure to perform the last chore could result in a large accumulation of useless film.

As the production work nears an end, management will have a screening of unedited footage, followed by the interlock (working print) and the answer (near final) print.

With these hurdles cleared, a final print is made, copies are produced, and the film is ready for distribution.

SOME ADDITIONAL WORDS ON PRODUCTION

Students need not confine their studies to the ten-minute-plus documentary or feature movie when exploring films. There are uses that can be made for film clips ranging from thirty to one hundred twenty seconds in length.

For example, short clips can accompany a new-product press release or personal-promotion announcement that is sent to a television station. They can capture company spokespeople making short statements on topical issues, or they can contain timeless feature material for use on slow news days.

Another point worth noting is that the printed word can be helpful as an embellishment to films. Producers should not ignore the value of handouts that describe the making of the movie, rephrase the message, or feature some of the key people behind the production. Nor should they forget that posters can be effective in attracting interest and eventually audiences, while brochures can reinforce many of the films' messages.

DISTRIBUTION

That there are so many outlets for films made by both private- and public-sector entities is one of the beauties of this medium. But the impressive number of potential viewing places alone doesn't guarantee that each movie will be seen by scores of appreciative citizens. The proper placement of films requires care.

As with the film production itself, distribution can benefit from outside help. Here, assistance can be found in the form of film distributors who maintain contact with theater owners, television systems, service clubs, resorts, academia, and a host of other possible users. Many of these distributors will also give film producers feedback on audience reaction, reporting what viewers liked, what they disliked, what they remembered best, and what, if any, suggestions they had.

Some distributors even provide promotional material—posters, catalogues, mailers, and so on. And all give their clients periodic reports on where the film is being shown and to how many people.

These services are not offered gratis, but the money used to obtain them is well spent. It is folly to invest thousands of dollars (a good twenty-minute film can cost between $50,000 and $300,000) without permitting additional expenditures to strive for a full booking schedule.

In a 1977 poll conducted by Modern Talking Picture Services, theater owners were asked about their interest in company-sponsored films—which are, incidentally, loaned to them free of charge. The following is extrapolated from the findings:

• Short subjects are shown with every feature program by 33 percent of the theaters.

• Films of eleven to fifteen minutes were designated the desired length by 67 percent of the respondees.

• A lobby poster was thought to be helpful by 68 percent of the respondees.[1]

The firm, based in New Hyde Park, New York, also polled social studies teachers about sponsored films and found that:

• Films of twenty-one to thirty minutes are wanted by 75 percent.

• Well-known personalities are wanted in the films by 79 percent.

• Collateral materials are wanted by 92 percent.[2]

It is important to conduct studies of this nature from time to time, because the potential audiences in schools and theaters represent fairly high numbers.

For example, there are some sixteen thousand theaters in the United States today. Most are in the market for shorts because they like to offer two-hour programs and the majority of feature films run between 105 and 110 minutes. This leaves between seven and fifteen minutes for sponsored films.

It is not unusual for good shorts to get booked in five thousand theaters a year and reach audiences well in excess of one million. Those aren't bad numbers for vehicles that cost less than $300,000 to produce.

IT took a while to convince skeptical managers of video's potential value, but once the message got through, it spread quickly. By 1977, U.S. private- and public-sector organizations were producing more television programs for internal use than were carried by the three major networks and public service systems combined.

This is quite a change from the early days of company video, when the use of internal television activities was reserved for personnel and training-department services alone. But video is an excellent communications tool, there are more external than internal audiences for it, and people enjoy getting their information from television sets. It's not surprising that public relations units have taken over the video function or that expenditures for equipment fail to induce harsh questions from budget-conscious bureaucrats.

Most major profit and non-profit firms now have production studios, many of them with investments of more than $200,000 in equipment. Small organizations are joining the bandwagon too.

According to a 1977 book entitled *Private Television Communications: An Awakening Giant,* over half of the organizations using video equipment had less than ten thousand employees. Three years earlier, these smaller firms accounted for less than one-third of the user organizations.[3]

The book also showed that the typical video user produced more than twenty programs a year and distributed them to an average of eighteen locations. Annual budgets ranged from $50,000 to $100,000, and the average staff had two and a half people.[4]

The uses for video are many. In addition to the television version of a house organ, video can be used to

• Cover press conferences
• Cover annual meetings
• Service television news programs
• Beam important conferences via satellite to other sites
• Help executives who are to appear on television

The in-house television news/feature program is deserving of special mention because it is often a nesting place for beginners in telecommunications.

With names like *Televiews, Video Communication,* and [name of company] *Update,* these programs are changed daily, weekly, monthly, or quarterly and cover topics such as quarterly earnings reports, employee club news, workers with interesting hobbies, benefits, major product introductions, reorganizations; in short, just about anything that would appear in a company newspaper or magazine.

Their advantages, in addition to the blending of sight and sound, are that they make top officials seem more credible and personable than do publications, and they are shown to audiences composed in large part of people who grew up in homes with the television set on at least three hours per day.

Also, employees who serve as on-camera subjects tend to get a bigger thrill out of seeing themselves on television than they do from similar "appearances" in house organs—and their co-workers react the same way.

But the thrill will soon wear off if the appearance is not backed up by professional programming and planning. The following are some of the features of successful video packages for employees:

• Likable anchor people who stay with the show long enough to develop a following.

• An adequate distribution system so that the shows are seen by a majority of the people in a given organization.

• Efforts to ensure that there is some upward communication in addition to downward communication.

• Programs that don't try to be the sole source of news for staff members, because there are certain informational assignments that are better met by other media.

• Programs that focus on what's happening in and to the company, not on unrelated items.

• Sales pitches on company products that are kept to a minimum. On the other hand, staff members should know of major new company offerings. If a new product story is treated as news rather than advertising, it is all right to air it.

• Programs that are not too long. Employees are seeing them on their own time, so ten to fifteen minutes comes very close to the maximum amount of time they'll give to a company television offering.

Looking to the future, satellite distribution of video programs significantly increases the promise of telecommunications.

The advantages of satellites are that they lower costs, make it possible to reach great distances, and allow producers to pinpoint audiences. It is therefore not unusual to have annual meetings in New York beamed by satellite to boardrooms in Tokyo, Frankfurt, Buenos Aires, and other distant locales. And video phone calls can easily be arranged to allow individuals in one country to chat with people in another land.

Then there is the videocassette recorder-player, a highly individualized message delivery system that offers considerable potential for home use.

One executive can take company data home, press some buttons, and see the information on her television set. Another can tape himself giving a lecture in his living room, then have it replayed later in the day back at the office. Other staff members can slip news programs in an envelope for home viewing over the weekend.

Some problems of standardization and compatibility among the VCRs still loom on the horizon; however, they seem minor compared to the difficulties of inventing and designing the equipment in the first place. Mass use of video playback equipment is definitely one of the waves of the near future.

As for the distant future, it appears there are no limits to what telecommunications engineers can come up with. It will be interesting to compare this text with a description of audio-visual capabilities in 1990.

ORGANIZING FOR AUDIO-VISUALS

FIRST, a general rule. Audio-visual units (or individuals) may have started out as arms of the training department, but now that they perform so many communications functions, they should be part of the public relations department. Fortunately, in most cases they are.

Once under the PR umbrella, three options suggest themselves: (a) the unit can be a separate operation reporting directly to the top public relations executive; (b) it can be part of internal communications; or (c) it can be part of the news bureau.

There are no hard and fast rules on this, because the field is still evolving, and it will be a while before the dust settles. But logic suggests that since the potential uses and skills are so many, a separate unit should eventually become standard.

In the meantime the proper course in the present is the one that meshes best with the organization's use of telecommunications. If audio-visuals are primarily used as a press rela-tions tool, the unit belongs in the news bureau; if it focuses on internal needs, it belongs with internal communications; and if it's fulfilling a variety of functions, it may be ready to stand on its own.

Those making a go of it on their own are generally subdivided into mini-units focusing on production services (films), photographic services, television services, print and artwork services, and administration.

There are even less hard and fast rules regarding equipment. And in view of the rapidly evolving nature of new machines and uses, it serves little purpose to present a shopping list complete with prices. It would be outdated within months.

There are only two admonitions worth passing on at this time. First, shop around to avoid paying list price. There are scores of manufacturers trying to make their mark in this growing market, so competitive pressures should drive prices down. The more aggressive manufacturers can be identified by reading the trade press and talking with people already active in the field.

Second, don't think a large studio stocked with several hundred thousand dollars worth of equipment is a mandatory first step toward getting an audio-visual program off the ground. Slides can be gathered with a $100 camera and some trips to the nearest film processor. And a $100 slide projector and $25 screen are the only other ingredients required for a slide show. Good movie footage can be taken by inexpensive cameras, while a $100 videotape recorder-

playback unit can get the job done for a television project.

There are numerous firms whose production facilities and talents are available for hire. Newcomers to the field needn't buy a lot of equipment that may become obsolete in very short order. Wait until there are several productions under your belt—and after you have identified key audiences and the means of reaching them—before developing an in-house production capability. And don't make any binding decisions until you've hired a person with a good technical background to serve as chief engineer.

DO'S AND DON'TS OF ELECTRONIC COMMUNICATIONS

• **Do** try to attend meetings of organizations such as International Television Association, International Tape Association, and National Association of Broadcasters. This is a growing field, so pooling of information can be helpful.

• **Do** opt for leasing rather than buying equipment as you start stocking your studio. There will be something of a "trial and error" aspect to your early years of operation, so it is best to avoid locking yourself into equipment.

• **Don't** use senior management's reactions to films, tapes, and other audio-visuals as indications of how the general public will react. Senior management and the average viewer do not have that much in common.

• **Don't** feel there are certain types of stories that can only be covered by print. There are many that might be better suited for print than for electronics, but, generally speaking, there is nothing that print covers that can't be included to some extent in an audio-visual program.

• **Do** time yourself when rehearsing slide shows. It's important to know if some slides are on the screen too long or too briefly.

• **Do** start and end slide shows with the lights on. This gives the speaker an opportunity to build credibility and close with it.

• **Do** check the noise level of your projector before a show. Some are noisy, so the projector should be placed to minimize distraction.

• **Do** include sound tracks when sending film clips to television stations. Most stations will prefer to do their own voice-overs, but a sound track can come in handy if there is no time to prepare new text.

• **Don't** put too many plugs into your films, film clips, tapes, slides, and so on. If a production starts out as a form of education and ends up as an advertisement, most of the audience will lose interest.

• **Don't** ask theater owners to pay for films. One of the reasons sponsored films do well and get large audiences is that they are free.

• **Do** try for special audiences for special films. General audiences aren't bad, but you get more bang for the buck by specifically zeroing in on key publics.

• **Don't** ignore airport cinemas when trying to have your film booked. People who fly often represent important audiences. (The same can be said for resort cinemas.)

FOR FURTHER EXPLORATION

1. You would like your company to introduce a television version of the house organ. Your senior managers are skeptical. What do you tell them to convince them of the merit of your proposal?

2. You are planning a slide show for your college, the purpose of which is to interest high school students in applying for admission. Come up with a list of twenty-five photographs.

3. You work for a local theatrical company that depends on contributions for most of its money. Come up with some general ideas for a film that will be used for fund raising.

4. You work for a manufacturer of bicycles and mopeds, and your firm has just produced a film on safety with these vehicles. Where would you want to distribute it?

5. What other uses do you envision for audio-visuals in the future that weren't mentioned in the text?

COMMUNITY RELATIONS

PICTURE this.

It is the annual meeting of the fictitious Ohio National Bank Corporation. As chairman of this $6-billion-asset, one-bank holding company, you are in the process of regaling shareholders and the press with the highlights of the corporation's gains during the previous calendar year.

Lest your audience deduce that Ohio National is an avaricious institution bent on maximizing profits to the exclusion of all other goals—and with no consideration for its many publics—you decide to close your remarks with a discourse on the holding company's role as a corporate citizen.

It's a large role, of which you are extremely proud. You talk about the job training program for teen-agers from the inner city. You explore the accomplishments of your loan program for minority entrepreneurs who would not be considered credit-worthy under normal banking procedures. You wax eloquent on the bank's leadership role in having the state's convention center constructed in your headquarters city, a decision that created twelve hundred jobs for area residents. And you modestly review the accomplishments of Ohio National Foundation, the holding company's philanthropic arm, which dispensed $2 million in grants to charitable organizations throughout the world.

The audience applauds politely at the end of your talk, you acknowledge this gesture of appreciation, then you announce it is time for questions from the floor.

Whereupon an eminent gadfly* leaps to his feet, is given a microphone, and sounds the initial query of the day.

"Mr. Chairman," he says, "I strongly object to your corporate citizenship program. We are a bank. We are not chartered to find jobs for the poor. Our function is not to lobby in the state legislature for a convention center. We should be striving for greater profits, not making risky loans to men and women who couldn't obtain credit at other banks. And we shouldn't be giving shareholders' hard-earned money to

charities in which they may have no interest. How dare you give our money away without our permission for activities that have nothing to do with banking? If you're not going to use that money for business development, why not give it back to us in the form of increased dividends?"

Okay, what do you tell him?

The fact of the matter is that businesses have become active in community relations not only because they should, but because they would be foolish not to do so. There are several justifications for an ambitious community relations program.

1. Organizations are affected by their relationships in the communities in which they operate—Better relationships assure a warmer reception to goods, services, and positions on issues. There aren't many better ways to establish positive relations than working side by side with community leaders in alleviating serious problems or donating personnel and monetary resources to the amelioration of society's ills.

In 1957 the Columbia University Graduate School of Business and the McKinney Foundation for Management Research conducted a symposium at which chief executive officers from ten large corporations discussed the responsibilities of directors. Their comments were summarized by Professor Courtney C. Brown, who wrote:

> The very survival of the corporation as a private, profit-making institution, in the interest of stockholders, was seen to depend upon its acceptance by society at large, and this in turn to depend upon how well the corporation serves broader interests than just the immediate welfare of the stockholders. In the words of one of the group, "acceptance of obligations to groups other than the stockholders is a part of the continuity of the corporation in the long-term interest of the stockholders, because if a corporation doesn't take on obligations of a citizen, it is quite likely not to remain a corporation in the long run."[1]

2. Businesses need thriving economies in order to sell goods and/or services in sufficient quantities to earn a profit—If the upper and middle classes of a

---

*A gadfly is a person who attends annual shareholder meetings to present the presiding officer with a litany of questions, many of them of a critical nature.

given community are leaving it in droves, the area's prognosis for economic growth is dismal. Unemployment and underemployment usually follow an exodus of many citizens, which, in turn, leads to serious problems for those organizations trying to sell to shrinking populations with economic troubles of their own. Attempting to reverse such trends is not just an act of altruism; it is a case study of self-preservation.

3. Businesses and nonprofit organizations are expected to participate in community affairs if for no other reason than that their competitors do so—It could become very difficult for Ohio National Bank to expand its customer base among its neighbors if it closes its eyes and ears to local appeals to which rival banking institutions are responding meaningfully. Quality of service and prices of loans aside, it is a fact of life that a customer will regard banks quite differently if one aids his or her favorite charity and the other doesn't, especially when it is the customer who makes the appeal.

Years ago, I was involved in a fund-raising drive at a school for hearing-impaired children. When a bank at which the school's parent association had kept its checking and savings accounts for several years refused to take a quarter-page ad in its dinner-dance journal (this was the association's first request for a contribution), the body's board of directors voted unanimously to take its accounts to a rival bank down the street.

A mild and perhaps unfair bit of blackmail by the parents association? Absolutely! But a cost of doing business for the bank? Also absolutely!

It isn't a nice way to raise funds, and it certainly should not be the proper rationale for making a gift, but it is nevertheless the way things are done.

As a result, there are some businesspeople who say to themselves, "If I'm willing to take a customer out for lunch and spend $50 in the process, why don't I spend that amount on a quarter-page dinner-journal ad instead? It will keep my waistline down, and the money will be put to better use."

4. Good community relations beget good government, labor, and customer relations—As we will see in

chapter eight, working in concert with government agencies and employees on a particular problem—or taking on the whole load by yourself and freeing government funds for other uses—is an excellent way to enhance government relations.

In addition to getting to know government officials better and opening doors for possible gain at a later date (nothing underhanded here—just an attempt to ensure that the business has an opportunity to be heard), the community involvement tangibly demonstrates an interest in community affairs.

5. Community relations expose businesses to individuals they might not otherwise get to know—All organizations pursue potential customers vigorously in the hope of converting them into existing customers. But what if these prospects are happy with the firms currently serving them and see no need to listen to new sales pitches? Chances are it will be difficult, if not impossible, to see them.

The situation is different, however, if you serve on a board of a charitable organization with one of your targets. Or on the same government-appointed committee. Or coach in the same Little League. Your hopes of getting together for lunch are considerably brighter.

6. On-premise community relations activities get potential customers used to being there—The community relations activities that can be presented on company turf will be discussed later on. The point worth mentioning here is that such events—exhibits, talks, bazaars, and so on—attract people who never visited the facilities before. These men and women may like what they see on the grounds or in the building and come back as customers at a later date.

7. Community relations allow organizations to learn more about key publics—We discussed the importance of bringing information on the outside world to management in chapter two. And we mentioned earlier in this chapter that community relations allow concerns to interact more with government, employees, and customers. It follows that a side benefit of this increased contact is a greater understanding of the strengths, attitudes, and needs of specific constituencies.

AS with other public relations activities, community relations start at the top. An organization can't offer meaningful responses to the needs of society if there is no management commitment to a role in external affairs. And management can't effectively encourage total or near-total staff involvement if it doesn't lead by example. Words of encouragement are effective, but they are exposed as shallow and ultimately meaningless when there is no plausible answer to the question "Why should I give my spare time to community needs when you (senior management) don't?"

There are, of course, more desirable motives for participating in external affairs activities than "my bosses do it, so I guess I better do it, too, if I want to advance in the organization." But when all else fails, this inducement has considerable appeal as an alternative to having an inactive staff.

HOW TO DEMONSTRATE
MANAGEMENT'S COMMITMENT

• Make it the topic of speeches by senior officials.

• Devote a portion of the annual report to the concern's role in community betterment.

• Have officers give talks to the staff on the benefits to the concern of community involvement.

• Make sure the external activities of senior management are adequately covered in internal publications.

• Let the media know what senior management is doing.

ROLES FOR MANAGEMENT TO PLAY
IN THE COMMUNITY

• Head fund-raising drives

• Speak out on issues

• Host seminars and conferences on community problems

• Assume executive positions in community organizations

• Testify at legislative hearings

THE PR DEPARTMENT'S ROLE

Hopefully, management will eagerly take on community responsibilities, with no prodding from its PR department. After all, no one likes a nag, and regardless of the virtue of the communicators' arguments, the welcome mat for them in executive corridors will start wearing thin if their appearances are too often accompanied by lectures.

However, one does occasionally hear of managements with head-in-the-sand or profits-first-and-the-public-be-damned attitudes. A treatment for such symptoms is large doses of talks on the rationale for community relations programs.

Whether management initiates ambitious community relations programs on its own or at the urging of its image counselors, the major roles of the PR department in the overall process are to:

• Shape and administer the programs

• Communicate information to management

• Communicate the concern's actions to its many publics

Shaping and administering programs will be discussed later in the chapter. And chapter two covered communicating observations to management, the importance of which cannot be overstated because an organization must have accurate and timely information on its publics' needs, perceptions, and expectations.

The whys and wherefores of disseminating information into the community appear throughout the book, but a few words must be inserted here on the science of extolling community relations activities. PR practitioners must trumpet news of their organization's public affairs role with a somewhat muted horn, because to do otherwise might raise suspicions about motives behind the involvement. Yes, we publicize the activities, but we don't want publics to think a three-column head in the local newspaper or a two-minute spot on the evening news are our primary objectives. So we exercise restraint. We don't call media attention to everything the organization or its people do in the community, we don't insist on a leading role in every venture, and we don't take pictures every time we make a contribution to a worthy charity.

Selectivity is the key word. Pick a small handful of programs that deserve a first-rate publicity effort and use very broad and general strokes in discussing the others.

SHAPING AND ADMINISTERING PROGRAMS

BUSINESSES, publics, and the events shaping community needs differ from locale to locale and year to year. Rather than blueprint a specific community relations program that may not be applicable to a majority of this book's readers, I will briefly describe different kinds of activities that can be adapted to specific problems at varying times and places. All can be offered by branch offices of an organization or can emanate from the headquarters site as part of a master program.

ON-PREMISE COMMUNITY RELATIONS

1. Plant tours and open houses—It's always nice to invite people to your facilities if for no other reason than it is a form of inexpensive advertising. If there is new and expensive equipment to show off, do so. Does your firm have an unusually good safety record? Talk about it. Is the production procedure marked by an innovative and visible technique? Put it on display.

In short, just about every organization has something on its premises worth exhibiting. This showpiece phenomenon needn't occupy the entire tour, but it should be the star attraction, designed to have the greatest lasting impression on viewers.

There are other advantages of tours and open houses. One is that they eliminate the mystery of products and services, making the visitors feel more familiar with them and more willing to try them out.

A second advantage is that opening your doors to the public shows off your staff, which should be among your key selling points. Em-

ployees are seen in their natural surroundings doing what they do best (or at the very least, fairly well). When you get right down to it, this is an advantageous way to present individuals.

2. Anniversary celebrations—Anniversary celebrations are effective because the hosts and the guests both gain. The former have attention called to their presence in the community for an extended period of time, and the latter get to attend parties, which are generally fun.

The celebrations aren't difficult to coordinate. They can be one-day affairs ranging in style from "c'mon down to our office for a doughnut and cup of coffee" to a lavish banquet. Or they can be for a week or more, during which time refreshments are served each day and prices are reduced. Or they can be marked by a generous gift to the community.

The rationale for such activities is that customers have been responsible for the organization's success over the past *x* number of years, and now the organization would like to say "Thank you."

3. Exhibits—If people aren't going to be drawn to an organization's premises by the lure of an open house, food, or reduced prices, an art object may get the job done. Failing a warm response to an art program, a display of photographs, products, tools, and so forth related to the concern's line of business could do the trick. Exhibits can also be of general interest, such as political cartoons, humor on other subjects, history, or crafts.

Another inducement is the prospect of seeing one's own work on display. Colleges, banks, department stores, hotels, and so on make it a point of canvassing local organizations to determine if they have works of art by members that they wish to exhibit.

The advantage of presenting such divertisements to the public is that it gives the artists exposure they might not otherwise obtain, the host organization earns the gratitude of the club or group providing the works, and it gets people used to visiting the premises.

4. Shows in parking lots or plazas—Organizations fortunate enough to own a large parking lot or be located on a spacious plaza have a perfect vehicle for staging attention-getting and crowd-pleasing events.

Among the activities that have been staged in parking lots have been fairs, safe-driving demonstrations, model auto races, band concerts, and political rallies.

Concerns hosting events on plazas (generally during lunchtime to attract neighborhood workers) have hired professionals for displays of animal acts, magic, folk dancing, gymnastics, and juggling. These performances generally draw large crowds, because even if mediocre, they are a diversion from normal lunch-hour activities.

5. Use of a concern's facilities by local organizations—Many community groups are relatively cash-short entities with nary an auditorium or conference room to their name. They generally meet in someone's home of a weekday evening and entertain mixed emotions about the size of each session's turnout. On the one hand, the organizations' officers want large crowds, because this would signify an interest in and a positive response to their efforts. On the other hand, they fear abundant turnouts, because where in blazes is everyone going to sit? There just aren't that many people with a living room sufficiently spacious for assemblages of twenty or more individuals. Even a crowd of fifteen might necessitate frantic calls to a neighbor for more bridge chairs.

Fortunately, there exists in every community the makings of a delightful and mutually satisfying match. On one side we have concerned and active citizens looking for a place to meet. On the other, we have corporations, colleges, and other institutional members of a community with numerous meeting and conference rooms that are rarely used on weekday evenings and weekends. Add to these ingredients the fact that the institutions are not averse to obtaining goodwill, and a solution to the respective parties' needs immediately suggests itself.

So the institutions allow local groups to use their facilities. They gain admiration and appreciation almost immediately, and their prospects of converting public affairs relationships to business relationships are enhanced.

6. Talks to area organizations—Every private- and public-sector organization has a considerable amount of expertise on its payroll, without which it could not exist. Why not show this expertise off and gain public support at the same time by letting talented and personable employees give on-premise talks or conduct clinics on their areas of specialization? These presentations can be given to community organizations or the public at large.

7. Community bulletin boards—Organizations that attract large numbers of area residents to their premises have won friends in their community by setting up community bulletin boards on which people disseminate information to their neighbors. These messages may warrant some monitoring to assure tastefulness, but other than some casual editing, there is very little work involved.

8. Tables for fund raising—Some concerns will also let community groups set up a table on which they can display promotional literature or cannisters for fund raising. This requires very little work, but it is usually greeted with a large amount of gratitude.

9. Offering products and services at reduced charges or for free—This doesn't want much explanation, because people and organizations are grateful for any breaks they can get in paying for needed goods or assistance. If Ohio National Bank can't, for example, assist a local health care center with a contribution or a corps of volunteers, it can still be of invaluable assistance by offering free checking, interest-free loans, excess office equipment and supplies, and payroll services.

10. Offering free consultations—In addition to reducing or eliminating charges, Ohio National can share its expertise. For example, its lawyers can counsel the health care center on a host of legal issues; its accountants and loan officers can help with its financial recordkeeping; its purchasing officers can advise on buying supplies; and its public relations, insurance, advertising, site planning, and data processing personnel can counsel on their specialties.

11. Charitable contributions—More will be written about philanthropy in chapter ten. Suffice it to say here that gifts for medical equipment, schoolbooks, art collections, research grants, and even Little League uniforms reap large dividends in goodwill.

It is important to note that while all of the foregoing acts of generosity and interest are, to varying degrees, well received, they should not be offered indiscriminately. Rather, they should be part of a coordinated community relations program so that each activity builds on the goodwill generated from a previous effort.

An isolated demonstration of care can win support for an organization, but it's the sustained and coordinated programs that chalk up the most gains in the long run.

Another important rule to remember is that in-house legal and insurance experts should be called in with alacrity to assure that no undue risks are taken. What happens if a visitor touches something he shouldn't during a plant tour and severely burns his hand? Or a painting on display is damaged by a careless browser? Or someone gets injured during a safe-driving exhibition in a parking lot?

I don't know the answers to these questions. And neither do most PR people whom I have met. But lawyers and insurance experts do have ready responses—which is why their advice should be sought during the formation of a community relations drive.

Still another rule is not to waste time debating the merits of having an event on- or off-premises. There are arguments for both alternatives. Those who prefer to operate on their own turf feel that on-premise functions get people used to visiting the concern's operations, and they give the sponsors more control over the people working on the events. Their colleagues who opt for holding the activities

elsewhere argue that doing so generates less legal and insurance headaches.

Fortunately, most people in public relations feel that *where* the event is held is secondary in importance. The pivotal issue, and the topic over which the arguments are worth the sweat and the tears, is getting an organization committed to alleviating community problems. Determining the sites for dealing with these problems are mere postscripts.

OFF-PREMISE COMMUNITY RELATIONS

There are some activities that can only take place off a concern's property. They fall into one of two categories: involvement in the programs of community organizations (such as sponsoring and coaching Little League teams, volunteer work at hospitals, teaching at local schools, and so on) and involvement in major issues confronting a community.

It is in the latter category that an organization can really make its presence felt, because an alleviation of major problems has a tremendously favorable impact on the quality of life in a community, city, state, or country. Some of the considerations with which public-spirited concerns may deal include the following:

1. Unemployment and underemployment—Corporations can initiate job training programs in which they take hard-core unemployables, provide them with basic skills, and give them full-time jobs upon the successful completion of their training. Or they can help them find other jobs by running a referral service. The way this can work is that the sponsoring organization collects data on all job applicants and disseminates this information along with their work preferences to other concerns within the community.

2. Urban decay—Private- and nonprofit-sector firms can help communities revitalize themselves by giving them contributions, free counseling, mortgage and home improvement loans, volunteer labor, and fund-raising assistance.

3. Care for the handicapped and aged—Typical community relations activities in this area are the maintenance of clinics, job training programs for the handicapped, financial support of medical research, volunteer work to help both groups, and reductions in prices and service charges for these constituencies.

4. Corporate disclosure—There is a tremendous amount of interest in having corporations disclose more information about their financial performance to regulatory agencies, analysts, and institutional and individual investors. Bank of America, the nation's largest bank, recently took a leadership role in this issue by preparing and disseminating a disclosure code that carefully spelled out what information it would make available to its publics, and which facts and figures would not be made available. The code clearly called for more disclosure and has since been copied by other private concerns.

Then there are issues that may arise at different times and in different communities. For example, Ohio National Bank was described at the outset of this chapter as having played an integral role in the decision to erect a convention center in its headquarters city. Other concerns may lead drives to rebuild a hospital, raise funds for a cash-short university, repair the damage brought on by a hurricane, or organize an anniversary celebration for the city in which they are based.

ATTAINING STAFF INVOLVEMENT

AS stated earlier, the activities described in the previous pages would have difficult times getting off the ground and generating meaningful impacts without management commitment and involvement.

Of lesser importance, but nevertheless vital to the overall effectiveness of an organization's community role, are the attitudes and behavior of the staff. Lower-echelon employees have less influence over area events than do their bosses, but the men and women who comprise the work force of an organization have to be considered valuable ingredients in community relations because of their overwhelming numbers.

Corporations can get around employee apathy by donating generous chunks of money and committing executive personnel to the needs of a community. But they will not be completely successful in earning a reputation as a concerned institutional citizen without staff support, because to too many people in the surrounding area, the men and women who provide services and interact with the public *are* the corporation. If these individuals don't demonstrate good citizenship, the concern's community efforts won't ring completely true.

Organizations can, however, induce staff involvement by motivating employees, helping them to become involved, and then recognizing them for their roles in local affairs. Motivating workers is probably the hardest of the three tasks, but it can be done if aided and abetted by measures that assist and reward staff volunteers.

The key thing for PR executives to do is show employees that management considers their involvement important and that it appreciates any attempts they make to improve the quality of life. This can't be a one-time effort. It must be an ongoing program that manifests itself in management talks to the staff, photos and texts in annual reports and house organs, and printed and spoken words to external audiences on the importance of a strong community role. The preparation of communications to outside publics should include prose on the need for such activities and the benefits they bring to all members of society.

Once management has succeeded in generating enthusiasm about a concern's efforts to improve the quality of life, it has to help the staff members convert their zeal into effective actions. One way is to provide them with know-how and skills.

For example, Ohio National Bank could have seminars for its employees on topics such as coaching youngsters in athletics, becoming active in politics, helping the aged, working with the physically impaired, and fund raising for charities.

The bank could also operate a volunteer

bureau for the staff. Volunteer bureaus work in the following manner. The bank sends a memorandum to all personnel asking if they would like to become active in community affairs. A form is enclosed, and those who are willing to donate some of their time to community organizations are invited to fill it out. They are also told to list the activities in which they would like to participate—athletics, education, the arts, home improvement, politics, and so forth—and to mention any special skills that they possess. At the same time, a letter is sent to nonprofit enterprises in the area asking them to inform Ohio National of their needs for volunteer workers.

With the staff forms on one side of a desk and letters from community organizations on the other, efforts are made to match individ-

uals to organizations. Volunteer-bureau personnel also counsel the volunteers when necessary and conduct follow-up investigations to assure that their matchmaking is working. This counsel and review are key ingredients in the undertaking, because staff members can soon realize that their interests differ from what they had written on their forms.

Another aspect of the counseling and reviewing process is the dissemination of information so that mistakes aren't repeated and staff members can learn from the successes of others. Some companies that have established volunteer bureaus enhance these efforts by producing periodic newsletters with how-to tips and success stories.

REWARDING STAFF INVOLVEMENT

HAVING found outlets for employees' desires to become useful citizens and helping them perform well, the next chore for community relations operatives is to ensure that the staff volunteers continue to donate their time and energies for others. This is where rewards enter the picture.

First, organizations reward staff members for their involvement by recognizing them. They run articles in house organs and other publications on the accomplishments of staff members. They send press releases about the active employees to the media. And they pay homage to the personnel's community work in speeches inside and outside the organization.

Second, they reward staff members by giving them things of tangible value. An annual dinner party for those men and women who have devoted themselves to community problems is one way of doing this. Another is to give prizes to those whose deeds are especially noteworthy.

There are numerous businesses today that have outstanding-citizen award programs. These annual events have a committee of senior officials review the work of staff members in politics, charity, and so on before they designate individuals who are deserving of special atten-

tion. This "attention" can consist of a savings bond, a bonus, an extra week's vacation, or a special gift.

An idea I've toyed with but have yet to market successfully is a compensating time-off program. This is based on the theory that if an organization wants its employees to donate some of their spare time to community activities, it should allow them to give company time, as well, to the same endeavors.

The program would work this way. Staff members who serve as volunteers in the community would be allowed to give a similar amount of company time—up to a maximum of two or three hours per week—to their volunteer activity. This would require checks and balances to assure that the employees are spending the extra time in the community activity—and that they will use the compensatory time for the same volunteer work they perform on their own time. But it would clearly demonstrate to the staff, as well as to the community at large, that management is sincere about its commitment to community activities and that it recognizes the importance of its employees' role in these efforts.

My own prejudiced view is that the compensating time idea is close to brilliant, but this reaction is not yet widely shared. I shall keep promoting the suggestion, however, and believe it is only a matter of time before it is accepted somewhere.

FOR FURTHER EXPLORATION

1. What could a college do to improve relations with home owners on the edge of the campus who are less than thrilled with noisy fraternity parties, students grabbing parking spaces, and tax dollars being used to support such goings-on?

2. How can a hospital take advantage of its staff's medical expertise to enhance its image in the community?

3. What kind of work-related exhibits could an insurance company sponsor?

4. What are the critical issues in your community and how could a local corporation play a key role in affecting positive resolutions?

5. How can a multinational organization export its good domestic corporate-citizenship programs abroad to countries in which its image is less than outstanding?

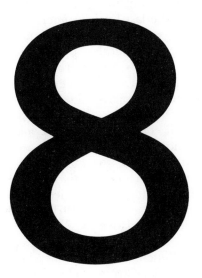

GOVERNMENT RELATIONS

GOVERNMENT relations is the art of working with the myriad of legislative and regulatory bodies that have influence over your organization. It takes place at the municipal, county, state, and federal levels. And if your organization does any kind of business abroad or has clientele overseas, it occurs at the international level as well.

WHY GOVERNMENT RELATIONS?

THE answer lies in the opening sentence of this chapter, or, more to the point, in the last five words of the definition.

Narrowing it down further, the critical word is *influence,* which can come in many different ways, from different angles, and with varying effects, ranging from minor to catastrophic.

Imagine the impact on an oil company's earnings if the government decides that research expenses for gas exploration can no longer be tax deductible. Or what would happen if the government said such research could get a tax credit of $3 for every $1 expended?

Or look how a state or federal legislative body could influence a college's future. For example, picture the effect on enrollment if the government no longer guaranteed college loans and/or stopped allowing tax deductions for contributions to alumni drives. And how positive would be the consequence of government-mandated free tuition at all universities?

In short, the many units of government have the power to impact heavily on whether and in what ways concerns operate and whether they operate at a profit or a loss. Public officials may not always be the most important individuals with which an organization interacts, but they are rarely far from the top of the list. Their potential for speeding up or slowing down the progress of private- and public-sector organizations dictates that they cannot be ignored. The stakes are simply too high.

And if these statements have failed to convince readers of the need to court government officials, there are still other justifications for generous government relations budgets.

1. Governments aren't going to disappear. They are here to stay and they are assuming larger roles—The general trend has been a closer monitoring by legislators and regulators of both the private and the public sectors. A more demanding consumer, a rise in investigative reporting (and the attendant spurt of articles catching private and public officials in unethical practices), and the growing interdependence of the diverse segments of society have combined to induce mounting government interest in a variety of endeavors.

Look at the legislative calendar in California as an indication of soaring government interest. A total of 6,836 bills were introduced in the state legislature in the 1978–79 year, almost twice the 3,756 bills introduced during the 1976–77 year.

2. Government relations programs have worked— Remember the point made in chapter three about the different ways people view an issue if they hear both sides of it instead of just one? Government personnel are no less effected by the principle of equal time. The need to hear both sides is of vital importance to them because failure to do so could cost them their jobs come election day.

New bills that could have deleterious effects on different organizations are introduced or conceived by legislators on an almost daily basis. More often than not, they are the result of prodding by constituents. If other legislators are similarly prodded, and no opposition is voiced by concerned parties, these bills have reasonably good chances of being passed without major revisions. If, however, the organizations that could be hurt by the legislation have government relations staffs monitoring current events, the opposing voices will be heard. If their arguments are sound, these new voices could prevail.

The head of a major bank's government relations office in Washington used to have an interesting way of lobbying for a raise prior to each annual salary review. He would itemize all the negative banking bills that had been suggested over the previous twelve months and then reveal what they would have taken from his institution's bottom line had they been passed in their original form.

Next, he would show what the bills currently on the books were costing his bank, highlighting, of course, the fact that many of the negative bills never even made it to the committee hearing stage as a result of his efforts. The difference between his first and second set of figures was always in excess of $10 million, so who, he reasoned, could begrudge him an increase of a piddling seven or eight thousand dollars?

He rarely got what he wanted, because the bank's assessment of his role in the demise of some of the more damaging legislation differed from his—and almost to the same degree that his two sets of figures differed. But his superiors did find his arguments interesting. And the point can be made that the difference between certain bills becoming law or fodder for a wastepaper basket is the difference between profit and loss for many years into the future.

3. The emergence of one-issue interest groups and the growing boisterousness of the average citizen dictate that different voices will always be heard in legislative corridors, so why not your organization's? More will be said about the impact of consumerism on government units in chapter nine. Suffice it to note at this point that there are more and more individuals and groups taking grievances to their local and national representatives. Institutions have to step up their own pace just to maintain equal time.

4. There are numerous opportunities for beneficial cooperation between government and the private and nonprofit sectors—Dealings between organizations and the governmental bodies that oversee their activities needn't be adversary all of the time. Or even half the time.

There are many societal ills that can benefit from a joint approach by governmental and nongovernmental entities. And there are quite a few examples that illustrate this point.

Look at the victories against illness that have been chalked up by combined research ventures, the work that has been done to bring some of the economically disadvantaged into the mainstream, the development and implementation of new learning tools now in use in schools throughout the country, or the cooperation among all sectors in times of war.

This cooperation clearly demonstrates that one and one can add up to three or more when key elements of society join forces to tackle a common problem. It has also convinced opinion leaders that there is much to be gained from a silencing of hostile rhetoric and a lessening of inflammatory posturing.

5. Both sides gain from joint efforts—The obvious advantages are that there is less duplication of effort, less dollar expenditures on the part of individual partners in group efforts, and improved relations as each side learns more about the other.

Additionally, a friendlier climate can lead to more sales of products and services to governmental agencies by cooperating private- and public-sector concerns and more financial support and votes for elected officials who work with nongovernmental entities toward a common goal.

6. John Q. Public wants more cooperation between the private and public sectors—The overwhelming endorsement of Proposition 13 in California in 1978 and the growing support for efforts to keep government spending down are clear indications that the average citizen would like to see legislators exercising fiscal restraint in coping with problems. John Q. Public would also like to see the problems removed, however, so a picking up of the slack by the private sector allows citizens to have their cake and eat it too.

WORKING WITH GOVERNMENTS

LET me immodestly assume my arguments on the preceding pages have convinced readers

there is value in having a government relations program; the next question is, should organiza-

79

tions establish offices in Washington and/or their state capital, or should they confine their government relations activities to active participation in trade association activities?

The advantages of having a concern go it on its own are the following:

• It doesn't have to compromise its position. Say, for example, you are in charge of government relations for a major airline, one of the dozen or so in the country. There is no way you are going to get the other lines to agree with you unanimously on every issue, so working through an association—either regional, statewide, or national—means that there will be some compromises along the way.

• It has complete control over the people doing the government relations work, because it is the source of their salaries and their promotions. Association employees, on the other hand, serve many masters and may therefore have less than a deep and abiding interest in seeing that the wishes of one organization become realities.

• It gets more credit when it makes a positive suggestion by itself as opposed to endorsing an industrywide proposal. Why, for example, should an airline want to lobby with competitors for a lowering of air fares when it can grab all the goodwill that accompanies such a position for itself?

• Lobbying as an independent agent allows a concern to refrain from sharing information with competitors it would rather keep to itself.

Working through an association has the following arguments in its favor:

• It is cheaper. Paying rent and salaries for a

Washington office can seem excessively expensive and possibly wasteful to shareholders who feel membership dues in an association can buy the same results at a much lower price.

• It avoids duplication of effort. Rather than have one dozen, one hundred, or one thousand firms make studies on the impact of a particular legislative proposal, each firm can share in the cost of a single, and probably more detailed, research project.

• An organization representing hundreds of institutions is likely to have better research facilities than do each of its members. Equally pertinent, it can use the experiences and specific informational resources of each of its members, as well as its own facilities.

• There is strength in numbers. Legislators and regulators are more likely to respond to a request from an association representing x number of institutions and votes than they are to a request from a single firm representing decidedly less voters.

• There is safety, as well as strength, in numbers. No one likes to be opposed to a measure that appears to have the support of the general population. If you are going to assume a negative stance, it is far better to do it as part of a multi-institutional effort.

The advantage of doing both—going it alone when you want to and joining with others when it seems appropriate—is simple: you enjoy the advantages of each one. So use your Washington or state capital office when it makes sense to do so and work through an association when strength or safety in numbers is required. And never think it is an either-or situation. Both alternatives have distinct advantages, and it is senseless to give any of them up.

WHAT A LOBBYING OR REPRESENTATIVE OFFICE DOES

FIRST, let's discuss the use of the term *lobbyist*. Watergate, stand-up comedians, authors of political novels, and some media representatives have given the word *lobbyist* an unsavory image. In response to this, lobbying operations are often called representative offices or simply the Washington office of XYZ Corporation.

Random House's American College Dictionary defines the verb *lobby* as "to frequent the lobby of a legislative chamber to influence the members" and "to solicit the votes of members of a legislative body in the lobby or elsewhere." Other dictionaries use similar wording to describe the term.

There is nothing singularly dishonorable about such endeavors, unless one wishes to assume they are generally performed through bribery and deceit, which is an erroneous assumption. Nor is wanting legislators to vote one way or another in and of itself despicable.

In short, lobbying is legitimate. The term *lobbyist* will therefore be used interchangeably with *government relations official* in the remainder of the text without any negative connotation.

Now, what does a lobbyist do? The following is an article that appeared in *Bank of America News* in 1977 describing the work of the bank's Washington office.

WASHINGTON OFFICE STAYS ON TOP OF MANY KEY ISSUES

Riddle: What do about 175 pieces of legislation, government reorganizations, personnel changes at regulatory agencies and the actions of the World Bank, Eximbank, IMF, Federal Reserve, Comptroller of the Currency, etc., have in common?

Answer: The somewhat divided, but nevertheless alert, attention of Bank of America's Washington office.

Based in the heart of the nation's capital for the past 50 years and staffed by six individuals, the Washington operation serves the entire bank by: (a) providing information on legislative, political, and regulatory developments which could affect the banking industry and (b) suggesting BankAmerica responses.

"I guess you could say we function as a business embassy," said Bob James, vice president and head of the office. "We represent the bank in discussions with Washington officials and serve as a source of information for them on banking in general and Bank of America in particular. We're also a source of information for all bank units on developments which could impact on our global activities.

"That does not mean, however, that we go around spying on meetings or looking for printed material we're not legally entitled to see. But it does mean that we'll attend public meetings and talk with elected and appointed officials as representatives of the bank."

Included among the specific functions of the office are following the flow of legislation (paying particular attention to bills affecting bank operations); developing and maintaining contacts at the Departments of Treasury, Commerce, Labor, etc.; working with regulatory bodies and international agencies; identifying business opportunities; serving as a liaison with foreign embassies, and cooperating with bankers associations and other groups on issues on which there is mutual agreement.

James oversees all these endeavors, Bill Nachbauer is the bank's legislative counsel, Mary Clare Fitzgerald "works across the board with an emphasis on legislation," Carolyn Willingham is the office's administrative assistant, Lillian Jolliffe serves as legislative assistant and Teresa Encinas is executive secretary.

"Given the large number of activities, we all have to be familiar with a very broad range of topics, shifting our attention almost daily to cover all the major banking and political issues of the day," James noted.

"Right now," he added, "a major thrust in Congress and the regulatory agencies seems to be an examination of the role of the larger international banking organizations and the possible domestic effects of international banking."

"This means that there are a lot of bills in various stages of development that are looking at the structure of financial institutions and related topics," Fitzgerald noted.

A perusal of the status report the office prepares on bills of interest to Bank of America substantiates her contention. Approximately 175 pieces of legislation—covering topics such as permissible activities of bank holding companies, consumer protection, housing, pensions, energy, disaster relief, boycotts and tax reform—are being watched by the bank.

The monitoring takes the form of sitting in on public hearings, making positions known through conversations and/or formal statements and following issues through the media.

"In many cases, we're aware of legislative proposals long before they are introduced," Mary Clare said.

She added that the monitoring activities continue after a bill is voted on because there's always the prospect of a new bill superceding it, or of it coming up for renewal.

For example, the bank consistently backs a comprehensive approach to the question of restructuring the existing banking climate in the country, as opposed to tackling "reforms" on a piecemeal basis each time Regulation Q comes up for renewal.

"A comprehensive approach to financial institution reform would hopefully rid the system of inequities such as the interest rate differential allowed for savings and loans on passbook savings accounts, and we relay this message, among others, during our daily interactions with various power bases in Washington," Fitzgerald said.

Other issues with which the office has involved itself over the years include the status of Edge Act banks, subsidiaries of bank holding companies and trust activities. James noted that he and his colleagues were particularly active in the political discussions which led to the granting of permission to banks to have more than one Edge Act bank in the United States and to put their travelers checks operations under a separate subsidiary.

Another issue which also involved the active participation of the office, he added, was the debate leading to the decision that the Glass-Steagall Act does not apply to overseas investment banking.

When not following legislation and maintaining contacts throughout the city, James and his colleagues remain alert to potential business opportunities for the bank. Contacts are maintained at the World Bank and Inter-American Bank, as well as area commercial banks, to see if there are co-financing or correspondent banking needs which can be met by Bank of America.

"What it all boils down to is that our reason for being is to serve the bank and its individual units as spokesmen and sources of information on a variety of topics. We hope all bank offices will feel free to call on us when they think we can be of assistance," James said.

Now let's discuss the specific duties of a capital-based government relations office.

1. Monitoring legislation and regulation—This has to be the key function of government relations people in Washington; Albany, New York; Sacramento, California; Trenton, New Jersey; and so forth, because capitals are where the legislative and regulatory action is. Decisions that could have serious—if not make-or-break—effects on organizations are being made within a mile or two of lobbyists' offices, so it is important that government relations specialists know when, where, why, and how they are arrived at; and then pass this information on to senior management. All it takes is dedication, patience,

alertness, good contacts, intelligence, and experience.

Fortunately, lobbyists have a lot of help.

First, there is the media, which is continuously reporting on legislative and regulatory happenings.

Then there is the *Congressional Record* and its counterparts at the state level, which serve as chronicles of legislative developments.

There are committee hearings and open sessions of the legislature.

There are also the breakfast, luncheon, dinner, cocktail party, and office grapevines containing the latest in rumor and fact. (Experience is very helpful when it comes to deciphering gossip, because the source and quality of the information can be better evaluated by a seasoned professional than by a newcomer to the capital.)

And there are the scores of active participants in the legislative and regulatory processes. Legislators, regulators, committee staffs, other lobbyists, and consultants all have mountains of information to share—if one knows how to sift through the data.

Lobbyists must therefore build a base of contacts with whom they can trade facts and figures. This is where patience and dedication come into play, because it takes time, hard work, and careful nurturing to establish friends in high, medium, and low places.

But lobbyists need not resort to sub rosa tactics to obtain their needed intelligence. They can—and do—make it known that they represent a particular organization or cause and that they are seeking information in its behalf.

In trying to establish contacts, one of the first places to start is the committee (or committees) that deal with the industry or sector represented by the lobbyist.

Take, for example, the Washington representatives for the airline industry. It would be mandatory that they know the members of the Senate and House Armed Services Committees; the Senate's Commerce, Science and Transportation Committee, and the House Public Works and Transportation Committee. They needn't become drinking or fishing buddies of the legislators, but they should know how they vote; why, who, and what influences them; and how they feel about their companies.

They should also know the members of the

committee staffs and the key aides to the legislators.

It is important to realize that senators and representatives serve on several committees and that they don't have as much time to devote to each one as they or their constituents would like. As a result, legislators rely on their staffs for guidance and often base votes solely on the recommendation of a trusted advisor. Knowing who the trusted advisors are and creating opportunities to exchange views with them are major goals of all lobbyists.

The regulatory agencies are also worth knowing. Those covering the airline industry include the Department of Transportation, Department of Defense, Civil Aeronautics Board, Interstate Commerce Commission, Department of Commerce, Environmental Protection Agency, and National Aeronautics and Space Administration.

After establishing relationships with key participants in the legislative and regulatory processes, lobbyists might want to focus on the Washington press corps. There is an awful lot of information one can obtain from talking with scribes. Equally important, developing press contacts is a key first step in getting arguments aired in the media.

Lobbyists will also want to know counterparts from allied organizations and trade associations in anticipation of the day when joint efforts are desirable. Furthermore, it is useful to know what information can be shared instead of purchased or compiled separately, as well as which tasks can be pooled to save money and avoid duplication of effort.

Additionally, there are the congressmen and their staffs who aren't on committees overseeing the lobbyists' companies. While most of the critical debates on bills take place in committees, it is the entire Senate and House that will deliver the final verdict. Communicating effectively with other senators and representatives could be worth a few votes in the final analysis.

In establishing relationships with these key individuals in and around Washington, government relations personnel are not unlike a new press relations director, whose initial activities were described in chapter four.

They will write letters to men and women they want to know, they'll arrange informal get-acquainted sessions, they'll hand-deliver printed materials, and they'll assiduously follow up on these tentative beginnings.

An important ingredient in the follow-up process is detailed record keeping. Card files should be built up, covering all discussions between the office and important personages in Washington. Embellishing this information should be data, where applicable, on past voting records, mutual friends, public statements and speeches, committee memberships, previous dealings with the firm and personal information such as schooling, family, and so on. Given the number of contacts a lobbyist must maintain, these files are invaluable as quickie refresher courses and in maintaining office continuity as new personnel come on board.

As an attendant function of getting to know the key players in Washington and other capitals, government relations officials should make it a practice to poll their organization's employees periodically to learn which staff members have close relationships with which public officials. Some may, perhaps, be related to an important senator. Others may have grown up with influential representatives. Still others may live in the same neighborhood, belong to the same fraternal organization or be a close personal friend of a powerful regulator. If so, it is possible they would be willing to speak with their contacts on behalf of the organization at a time when such a conversation will do a lot of good.

There is nothing unethical about this practice, because employees are told to fill out the forms *only* if they would be willing to represent the organization's cause. It is simply based on the principle that friends and relatives generally have an easier time gaining an audience with busy people than do strangers.

The only warning concerning this practice is that the volunteer spokespeople should be properly briefed on the issues so that they don't embarrass themselves or the organization they represent.

2. Creating opportunities to present an organization's views—Learning who the key movers and shakers are, and how they think or vote, is only part of the effort to influence legislation and regulations. A second, and equally important aspect, is effectively stating one's case. This can be done informally during a casual conversation or formally by testifying in a committee hearing.

The advantages of the casual conversation are that others needn't know it has taken place; there are certain things better said in private; and it is easier to arrange. Testifying before a committee gives the speaker a wider audience and serves as an indication to others that the views being espoused—and the espouser—are considered important by some pretty powerful people. Both methods should be employed when opportunities for them arise.

In attempting to arrange formal appearances for their senior management before congressional committees, lobbyists must convince legislators that their organization should be heard when bills are being considered. And they definitely have to monitor committee calendars to know when the opportunities to give testimony occur. Last but not least, they have to contribute to the formulation of the testimony by recommending text and anticipating the moods of the committee members. This means that if a question-and-answer session is to follow the testimony, the government relations staff should anticipate the points to be raised by the inquisitive legislators and suggest appropriate responses.

3. Assisting in the preparation of messages to the general public—Occasionally, one has to go over legislators' and regulators' heads and communicate directly to the general public. After all, if Congress or regulatory agencies are suggesting changes because the public wants them to rewrite current guidelines, why not get the average citizen to change his or her mind and remove or reverse the pressure on the officials?

Generally speaking, public-affairs-type messages to the public are prepared by public relations or advertising people back at the head office. But the government relations people should participate in copy-planning sessions, because they are closer to the legislative and regulatory processes and they have a better feel for the kind of verbiage that would be most persuasive.

4. Serving as a source of information to government officials and their staffs—One good way to assure an open-door policy from capital decision makers is to respond quickly and well when you are asked for information. Officials know they don't have all the answers and they are not above asking for help. Those who respond in a helpful fashion will tend to get asked more often than not—and probably hassled less often.

Lobbyists therefore do not operate under the theory that information dissemination is done only at their initiation. Indeed, the smart ones welcome requests for facts and figures because they recognize them as opportunities to be of service, to get points across while fielding questions, and to do a little information gathering of their own.

The *very* smart lobbyists not only welcome the requests, they actively solicit them. If, as an example, the Washington representative for an airline learns that the Armed Services Committee is considering legislation on jet noise, he or she might call the committee staff and volunteer to share the company's studies on the subject. This can be followed by an offer to fly company experts on noise control to Washington to meet with the staff or the committee.

5. Keeping the folks back at the head office informed on legislative and regulatory developments—Government relations work in Washington—or a state capital—deals with two kinds of information: (a) what has happened; and (b) what may happen in the future.

Keeping the head office updated can be done in several different ways:

• Written monthly updates on the status of all bills covering—or even remotely touching upon—the organization's operations. The bills mentioned in these reports needn't be only those that have been formally introduced. Those that are merely a rough idea of an ambitious legislator are also worth discussing.

• Periodic oral briefings for senior management. The advantage of these sessions is that they allow for questions, answers, and discussion.

• Chatty newsletters on what's happening at the regulatory agencies and in Congress. The text in these publications can cover pending changes in existing rules and bills, personnel moves, and descriptions of agencies' and committees' working habits and philosophies.

• Urgent phone calls to the head office. If something major breaks, *don't* wait for the next legislative report, scheduled briefing, or newsletter. Phone it in at once. There are times when yesterday's news is worthless and today's news is critical.

In summary, government relations officials, or lobbyists, are really public relations practitioners who serve as the eyes, ears, and mouth of the organization, but who limit their two-way flows of communication to legislative and regulatory matters. They should be trained communicators, with backgrounds in political science and/or law, if possible. They should also know their organization's operations and policies extremely well, because to many important people, they serve as the sole spokesperson for their concerns. They have important jobs.

SOME WORDS ABOUT ETHICS

As stated earlier, the word *lobbyist* has come to be regarded as less than complimentary in many circles. Unfortunately, the unsavory connotation is sometimes well earned.

There are Washington representatives who have used bribery or plied their trade with the help of expensive parties and experienced call girls. But most capital operatives pointedly reject these practices. For one, bribes, parties, and call girls don't bring desired results as often as one would think. For another, these results are not worth the loss in prestige that is the by-product of engaging in such practices.

My experience, and that of most observers of District of Columbia mores, is that the majority of lobbyists are men and women who discharge their duties in a professional and ethical manner. They gather information in the same way that journalists do: by reading publicly available reports and articles, by talking to contacts, and by attending meetings open to the public. And they disseminate their findings as journalists do: via printed and oral reports. There is no subterfuge involved in these practices, and most lobbyists have the respect of the people with whom they interface. Losing this respect is too high a price to pay for getting away with an unethical practice.

FOR FURTHER EXPLORATION

1. What are the legislative and regulatory issues currently holding center stage for followers of the energy industry? What can the industry do to make its opinions heard in Washington?

2. Which are the socioeconomic issues motivating legislators and regulators today? How does this affect various industries?

3. How can government and industry work together to solve the problem of unemployment and underemployment?

4. In the wake of Watergate, how would you defend the work of lobbyists?

5. You are public relations director of a public college. Name five topics you would like your president to discuss with congressional committees.

CONSUMER RELATIONS

IT all started with a disenchanted automobile driver.

The time was 1965, the driver was Ralph Nader, and the car was the ill-fated Corvair.

Nader decided the car was unsafe at any speed. As a matter of fact, he liked that phraseology so much he used it as the title of a book in which he encouraged the public "to make effective demands through the market-place and through government for a safe, non-polluting and efficient automobile that can be produced economically."[1]

Nader's book had an impact on the country in two extremely significant ways.

First, it redirected the attention of the public in the automobile safety controversy away from the skill of the driver to the merits of the vehicle. Was it possible that a large percentage of automobile fatalities could have been eliminated not by better driving but by better manufacturing procedures? The answers that came back from readers of the book or those that learned about it in casual conversations was a loud and resounding yes.

Second, the response to *Unsafe at Any Speed,* manifested in a sharp decline in Corvair sales and ultimately cessation of production, showed that sufficiently aroused consumers could have an impact on the marketplace. Could it be that if angry and disenchanted purchasers continued to unite and make their voices heard, there would be people and institutions listening to their complaints? Again, the answer was loud, clear, and affirmative.

Consumers, now cognizant of their power when properly incensed, started flexing their muscles. And one of the most powerful movements in American history was off and running.

The movement warmed up in the late sixties, reached full speed in the seventies, and shows no signs of abating. Environmental and consumer advocates have taken gigantic strides toward institutionalizing their concerns, swelling their ranks, and instilling fear in the hearts of those who incur their ire. In addition, new consumer organizations are forming on a near daily basis, and thousands of nonjoiners are acting without the benefit of group support. All feel there is much merit in voicing complaints and making demands.

Worse—from the standpoint of those on the receiving end of the complaints—city, state, and federal legislators have joined the bandwagon. They realized there are votes in consumerism, and this has led to a proliferation of laws and regulations on the manner in which goods and services are shaped, delivered, guaranteed, and acted upon when things go wrong.

That these rules and regulations contain direct and implied criticisms of the ways concerns operate is irksome to corporate America. That they often conflict with corporations' obligations to their shareholders is troublesome, as well. And that they portend more rules, regulations, and consumer actions generates a strong need for responses.

Hence consumer relations.

Business and nonprofit concerns alike have become increasingly aware of the importance of maintaining good relations with customer publics. They know that today's users of goods and services are concerned with quality as well as price and that brand loyalty is only as strong as the satisfaction following the most recent transaction.

Before explaining the intricacies of consumer relations, it is important to look at the socioeconomic factors behind the unrest of the buying public, because it wasn't Nader alone who triggered the movement. He was a vital catalyst, of course, but if he didn't come along, it would have been someone else tapping consumers' potential for monitoring corporate and noncorporate America.

The ingredients were there in the sixties and they are still with us today. They include the following.

1. Sophistication of consumers—What with inflation and other economic pressures, today's buyers are more concerned with getting value for their money than they were in the fifties and early sixties. They read consumer publications, they compare experiences with friends, and they study the lists of ingredients and other information on packages. If they don't like what they see or hear, they don't buy.

2. A general weakening of authority—People have become more critical of power figures and less willing to believe what they have to say. Richard Nixon gave his side of the Watergate story time and time again, yet the mood of the populace was such that he was forced to resign. Time was when the word of the president would have sufficed.

The same can be said of statements by other politicians and corporate and civic leaders. People are skeptical and not very easily deceived these days.

3. Rising expectations—We've sent people to the moon, made inroads against cancer, increased gas mileage in automobiles, and developed computer technology which has favorably impacted on just about every aspect of life. Why, then, consumers complain, can't we have products and services that live up to their claims?

4. Depersonalization of the marketplace—Remember the friendly neighborhood grocer? He sold food to your family for years, he greeted you with a smile, and he probably had a home not too far from yours. If he sold you bad food, you knew it was an accident and that he'd make it up to you with an apology and an exchange. If his prices rose sharply, you assumed it was because his costs increased just as dramatically. With years of good relationships behind him, it was going to take something pretty serious to evoke anger in his customers.

There aren't many friendly neighborhood grocers today. They have been replaced by supermarket chains and suburban shopping centers staffed with people who live in distant locations.

It's much easier to get mad at these individuals and institutions. They are cold, they aren't known to you, and, in the case of large supermarkets and department stores, they are perceived as financially well off.

Lack of good personal relationships generates a breeding ground for hostility and contempt.

5. Increased complexity of products—With so many technological developments behind us, it is no wonder that the workings of many consumer goods are beyond the understanding of numer-

ous individuals. People press the wrong button, fail to perform the appropriate maintenance, misread instructions, or use the product improperly. When the inner mechanisms eventually go awry, it is the manufacturer or seller who gets the blame.

6. Numerous examples of disreputable business behavior—It isn't considered improper to wax eloquent about the abuses of business and the need for extra supervision if several firms have been caught with their hands in the cookie jar. Several have been.

Reports of bribes overseas, court rulings on price fixing and deceptive advertising, massive product recalls, and purchasing scandals have been appearing in the media for years. It is therefore understandable that people would want the concerns they deal with to be closely watched.

7. Increased media attention—As more stories of institutional misbehavior crop up, more and more newspapers, magazines, and television stations designate reporters as consumer followers. And as more journalists are assigned to cover the topic, more shenanigans are uncovered and reported—by individuals who now feel they have receptive audiences at the media, and by the reporters themselves who feel they should justify their being in their new assignments.

8. The effectiveness of consumerism—Nader's victory over the Corvair is one case in point; there are others. For example, if we haven't done it ourselves, we all know of a friend or relative who wrote to a company complaining about a damaged product and got several free ones in return. And we've read of recalls, lawsuits, and other pro-consumer developments.

It isn't hard to drum up the energy to object to an alleged wrong when all one can lose is the time and the cost of a stamp or phone call. The potential gain is much greater than that.

GOALS OF CONSUMER RELATIONS

THERE are three broad goals of consumer relations and seven more sharply defined objectives. The initial three are the following.

1. To heighten management's interest in and response to consumers—Senior managers have the greatest ability to shape new policies within an organization. They *are* the company to many key publics, and their active participation has critically positive effects on the enthusiasm of others lower in the chain of command.

2. To advocate the consumer viewpoint—It cannot be emphasized enough that public relations (which, I believe, encompasses consumer relations) must maintain a two-way flow of communication. In taking information on consumers into the organization, it is mandatory that PR practitioners express this public's opinions to management.

It is equally vital that the communicators look at things from consumers' viewpoints so that they can anticipate questions and complaints before they are publicly voiced. This could eliminate problems while they're still in the formative stage.

3. To make recommendations—Identifying consumer concerns and anticipating those that will emerge later is only half the battle. Doing something about them is the key ingredient in satisfying customers. Company officials charged with representing consumers in executive corridors —and who are therefore considered the in-house experts on their whims and fancies—are the ones management looks to for ideas.

This leads to the more specific goals of consumer relations. They are the following.

1. To encourage all employees to get into the consumer relations act—A consumer relations program that doesn't include efforts to educate the staff about company products and services, the company itself, and the importance of treating customers well is doomed to failure. Employees must realize that discourteous or unprofessional behavior on their part reflects badly on the concern.

2. To guarantee that all statements made to consumers about price, value, service, repairs, and so on are truthful—Many consumer relations problems can be nipped in the bud by a careful explanation of goods or services before any cash changes hands. If this means that consumer affairs specialists should sit in on meetings of the advertising department or go over press releases

with a blue pencil, so be it. As badly as customers react to a poorly made product, their response to erroneous information is worse.

3. To ensure that all letters and calls are answered— It isn't easy to come up with a satisfactory answer every time out, but producing a response of some sort isn't that difficult. What a shame it would be, then, to thoroughly annoy already disgruntled individuals by not bothering to extend the courtesy of a reply—any reply.

4. To gain acceptance of an organization's products and services—Consumer relations officers are, allegedly, the in-house experts on how consumers think and react. It wouldn't hurt, therefore, to seek their counsel when new company offerings are being planned.

5. To disseminate information on products, services, and company philosophies—Consumer specialists must become involved in the preparation of instructions, packaging information, and press releases on new products. Their counsel is sorely needed to ensure that past mistakes aren't repeated and that clues to future customer reactions, as provided by letters and phone calls, are taken into account.

Since many consumer relations specialists have some public relations training it might also be wise to put that experience to use in heralding the firm's efforts to satisfy consumers. It is probable that some people will hestitate to complain—and will even assume the blame is theirs when they misunderstand directions—if the company in question has a reputation as a firm that treats its customers fairly.

6. To maintain contact with consumer groups— Consumerist organizations want a fair deal for the buying public. Consumer relations departments want to see their companies recognized as giving fair deals. With such potential for common ground, it would be silly for the two not to meet occasionally to compare notes. Consumer relations practitioners can learn about customer perceptions sooner than if they waited for letters and calls, and they would have an opportunity to convince major opinion leaders of the sincerity of their organizations' efforts. Assuming that consumer relations personnel are successful in the latter endeavor, they will have vehicles through which they can reach thousands of people.

7. *To maintain contact with other organizations and individuals who forward information to the buying* *public*—This would include educators (especially those teaching subjects directly related to the company), government officials, salespeople, retailers, and journalists.

CONSUMER RELATIONS ACTIVITIES

THE major activity at most consumer relations departments is responding to complaints and requests for information. Given the number of letters and phone calls arriving at a business each day, these departments are forced to—and should—turn out a considerable amount of literature.

According to a 1973 study of consumer affairs departments by the Conference Board, a nonprofit, independent business research organization, inquiries and complaints from consumers are a prime concern of nearly three-fourths of the 149 units studied.

The report noted that General Foods had received 118,000 letters in one year; Lever Brothers, 50,000; Scott Paper, 70,000; Campbell's Soup, 40,000; and Pillsbury, 30,000.[2]

Not all are complaints, however. Analysis of the 118,000 missives sent to General Foods showed, for example, that:

72,000 were requests for recipes, dietary data, and the like

4,000 were requests for nutritional information

2,000 were suggestions for new products

40,000 were complaints[3]

The last number indicates that for one reason or another, at least forty thousand people were momentarily miffed at General Foods. If some of this animosity were of long-term duration, the firm could have been seriously hurt.

Say ten thousand of the letter writers ceased buying GF products and spread their $3,000 to $5,000 in annual food purchases among rival firms. That could have been a large chunk off the company's gross sales. So it would have behooved General Foods to get a program underway that would have:

• Answered the complaints promptly and completely so that the customers would remain loyal to GF products.

• Studied the complaints to see if they pointed to internal deficiences that could be corrected. (One not only wants to retain the forty thousand letter writers as customers, one also wants to keep other clients who might become annoyed by the problem in the future.)

Knowing the reputation of General Foods, the firm most likely responded to the letters in a manner that allowed them to enhance their customer relations.

Let's move away from General Foods for a moment and look at how Chase Manhattan Bank deals with complaints.

I did a couple of brief stints years ago as substitute head of the consumer affairs unit when the manager was ill, and found it to be an impressive operation.

Here's how it worked.

All letters or phone calls to the bank that dealt with a complaint or request for information were sent to the consumer affairs unit, which is part of the corporate communications department.

The communications were immediately logged in, and an officer in the unit would determine to whom it should be sent for reply. General practice dictated that it would go to someone at the vice-presidential level; an officer in charge of a geographic division of branches if the problem dealt with retail banking (as most did); or an equally high-ranking individual in the corporate, trust, international, or institutional banking divisions.

A short note would go with the letter or written description of a phone call asking the recipient to respond to it within five working days and to send the consumer affairs unit two copies of the response.

The replies sent by the vice-presidents would usually follow one of three approaches. If they were in response to a request for information, the bank officer would either supply the necessary data or explain where it could be obtained. If they were responses to justifiable complaints, the authors would apologize and explain what steps were being taken to ensure that the incidents wouldn't occur again.

If, however, the person doing the complaining was in error, the bank official would attempt to show how the aggrieved consumer was wrong. In numerous instances it was simply a question of customers having erroneous expectations about a certain bank service or a misunderstanding of banking law.

It was, of course, always nicer when the customer rather than the bank was wrong, but an important advantage of a justifiable complaint is that it alerted us to a trouble spot we might not otherwise have known about.

The purpose of logging in each call or letter and asking for a copy of the reply is that the unit was able to know when an answer wasn't mailed within five working days. If a check mark didn't appear in the response column by the deadline date, a second reminder would go out with a copy to the appropriate supervisor.

Besides making sure that replies were sent out, the unit also prepared monthly and annual reports on the performance of individual divisions and the bank as a whole. When necessary, it recommended remedial action. For example, shortly after it was noted that the tone of various dunning letters was deemed abrasive by customers, the department had the text reworded.

The unit also sent out questionnaires asking customers to rate the quality of service at different branches. The returns were analyzed and potential problems were eliminated before they induced a rash of new complaints.

There are other ways to handle customer objections, but they really don't differ much from Chase's or General Foods' or most other companies' procedures. The common elements in all successful programs are the following:

- Clearly established guidelines as to who receives the complaints
- Time limits for responding to complaints
- Detailed record keeping
- Communication with the appropriate department regarding the complaint
- Analysis of complaints
- Follow-up procedures
- Recommendations to improve products and services

Most consumer affairs units are sufficiently staffed to handle the flow of incoming letters and calls in an orderly fashion. But complaints don't arrive in steady flows, and there are occasions when it appears the floodgates have been torn from their hinges. If it is impossible to answer all consumer communications within a reasonable period of time, it becomes necessary to flag those requiring especially prompt replies. I don't like the principle that "The loudest wheel gets greased first," but I'm afraid it carries considerable weight when you are dealing with angry customers. One has to be concerned about how irate people will react, so they are generally given priority over placid letter writers. Then long-standing customers receive attention; they have remained loyal to the firm for a long time, so they deserve special treatment, whenever possible. Next on the list are big customers. They may not have been doing business with the firm for very long, but they hold the promise of many important deals down the road. So don't keep them waiting too long for a reply. Sadly, this leaves all others until last. One doesn't like having anyone wait for the courtesy of a response, but if you are forced to make a choice, this catch-all category of consumers represents the smallest potential problem.

One other point about inquiries and complaints: firms don't have to wait for them; they can actively solicit consumer comments.

There are two ways to do this. The first is through advertising and public relations. Many companies have announced that they are anxious to respond to customers who may be having problems with a product or service and that they have established an office specifically to deal with questions and complaints. Some of these companies also publicize their consumer specialists by preparing press releases on their activities.

The second method is to make it easier for consumers to get their messages to company headquarters. An efficient and popular way to do this is to set up a toll-free, hotline number that can be called twenty-four hours per day. Some companies use a recording device, while others have a person at the end of the line to field the calls.

The advantage of the latter approach is that the recipients of the calls can take advantage of the opportunity to speak with customers by asking questions. They might want to know how other company products are received, why the customer chose the product in question, how he or she feels about various distribution outlets, and what is the overall impression of the firm.

It is a good idea to encourage calls and letters, but the venture is fraught with potential dangers.

Chief among them is an inability to perform. Inviting comments and failing to respond—or not having enough phone lines so that callers only get busy signals—negates many worthwhile efforts.

Another problem is that the person receiving the complaints could become combative and turn slightly annoyed customers into raging bulls.

Organizations that attempt to improve customer relations by soliciting comments had better make accurate predictions about the number and temper of incoming calls and letters so that they can properly staff the activity.

EDUCATING CONSUMERS

THE amusing thing about consumer education activities is that those concerns that carry it to the furthest extreme are warmly regarded as generous and caring do-gooders. It's possible they *are* exemplary citizens, but one shouldn't assume that solely on the basis of consumer education.

More than anything else, consumer education is good business. It eliminates unnecessary questions, it promotes the use of products and services, and it helps customers get more out of the goods, thus whetting their appetites for other offerings by the firm.

The logical starting point for getting facts and figures to potential buyers is the place where the sales are to be made. Not all companies can take advantage of this, however, because not every concern has its own retail outlets. Many share counter space with dozens of other businesses in a given store.

Those that do own or control their retail outlets have a leg up in the race for consumer education blue ribbons. They include banks, automobile manufacturers, gasoline companies, and fast-food chains.

It is not unusual to go into a gas station, car showroom, fast-food establishment, or bank branch and see booklets on the effective use of available products and services. Some of these outlets also have literature on broader subjects, such as how to prepare food, how to drive safely, how to care for cars, and what the economic outlook means to the average family.

Similar booklets can also be prepared by firms that don't have their own stores. Marketing managers might be able to persuade executives of retail outlets in which their handiwork is sold to permit them to display literature on countertops. If their powers of persuasion aren't effective, the booklets can be mailed to potential customers.

The next place to convey information is on the products themselves. Data on the package should tell how the product can be used and what is in it. And the instructions inside must eliminate all doubts about proper use.

One normally doesn't like to insult customers' intelligence, but instruction sheets are items in which oversimplification makes sense. Why go to the trouble of writing instructions and then wondering if readers will understand them? Write them in such a way that there can be no doubt. Then follow that effort up with other materials. Consumer education can't rely on one piece of copy; it has to be a continuous process to be successful. In addition to booklets, package information, and instructions, companies have run seminars, joined with educational institutions in sponsoring courses for consumers, introduced point-of-sale demonstrations, and produced films. A few have even designed box games that educate players about particular products, services, and/or industries.

Numerous companies also prepare consumer information in different languages. They realize that although many people speak more than one language, they do their best reading in their native tongue.

Students of consumer relations who would like to read of outstanding educational programs or activities should get a copy of the Conference Board's study entitled "The Consumer Affairs Department: Organization and Functions." They can also write to Public Relations Society of America, 845 Third Avenue, New York, New York 10022 (the same address as the Conference Board) and ask for information on consumer programs that have won Silver Anvil Awards.

ORGANIZING FOR CONSUMER RELATIONS

THERE are two categories of organizational structure that should be of interest to readers of this book: (a) those that have consumer relations as a part of public relations, corporate communications, or external affairs; and (b) those that don't.

At the present time, there are more consumer relations departments operating outside the public relations arm than within it. This is because senior managements, which are often the initial recipients of letters and calls, want to monitor the activity themselves and/or they want immediate action. Having the consumer relations director report to management as opposed to having two or three layers between them can definitely speed response time.

Where a company is very large and spread out over a huge geographic area, it is often necessary to have departmental consumer units as well as a centralized one. The advantage of a dual system is that it has the benefit of expertise at the local level as well as the overall knowledge domiciled at a head office operation.

Regardless of where they are placed in the organization, an important thing to note about consumer relations units is that they are growing in number. When the Society of Consumer Affairs Professionals in Business (SOCAP) was formed in 1973, it had 100 members. Five years later it had 1,012 members, representing 850 firms.

According to a 1978 SOCAP survey, the average age of the consumer affairs units was twelve years, and the average staff had eight professionals. And 68 percent of the reporting firms predicted they would grow by 1983.[4]

Also important to the study of consumer relations is an awareness of the ingredients that go into a successful department no matter where it is located in the overall structure and to whom it reports. The consumer relations units that have built up good track records over the years can boast of the following:

• Ready access to information

• Positioning within the organization that shows that management cares

• Good communications skills

• Good record keeping and an ability to quantify findings

• Willingness to make recommendations

• Monitoring to see that standards of performance are maintained

• Staffing with people who have a good overview of the organization

Consumer relations may appear easy to the uninitiated, but a closer look reveals considerable challenges. There are a number of developments taking place inside and outside of each company, and all warrant close attention. It is only when consumer affairs representatives get on top of these events that they can begin the task of effectively deciphering messages from the public and doing something about them.

ADDITIONAL DO'S AND DON'TS
OF CONSUMER RELATIONS

• **Do** insist on having access to management.

• **Don't** say you can't accede to a customer's request because "the auditor won't approve." There has to be a better reason than that.

• **Do** date everything that comes into the office. It's important to know how long the consumer has been waiting for a response.

• **Do** save all your records. You never know when they will come in handy during a lawsuit.

• **Do** save time by using form letters, but **don't** have them look like form letters.

• **Do** take corrective action so that the same grievance won't be filed again. (It is human to err, divine to forgive, and ridiculous to do nothing about correctible deficiencies that have been pointed out to you.)

• **Don't** promise that corrective action will be taken if you aren't sure something can be done.

• **Don't** be afraid to tell consumers when they are wrong. That's part of consumer education.

• **Don't** respond in kind to insults.

• **Don't** use humor in replying to an angry letter writer. It is all right to joke occasionally in face-to-face conversations, because the other person can see your expression and know that you are trying to be funny. However, putting a light remark in writing may not accomplish the desired result, because it is possible the reader will not interpret it as a light remark.

• **Do** get the telephone operators and mail room personnel in the organization on your side so that they know to funnel all complaints and queries to your office. The letters and calls are going to end up at your desk anyway, so sooner is better than later.

• **Do** study the media to identify the publications and broadcast programs aimed at consumers. We don't establish consumer relations departments in order to obtain free publicity, but as long as some print space and air time are devoted to consumerism, we would be foolish not to look for opportunities to have our specialists quoted from time to time.

FOR FURTHER EXPLORATION

---

1. Name three issues of current concern to consumers and discuss how you would attempt to handle them as a consumer affairs executive.

2. You head the consumer affairs unit and one of your associates has just completed a report showing that the company's Rochester branch has had thirty-five complaints about rude salespeople in the past two months. Something has to be done about this, so you decide to draft a letter to the branch manager for your president's signature. Draft it.

3. Your company manufactures camping equipment. Compile a list of five consumer education booklets that you can distribute for display at retail outlets.

4. You head consumer relations for a major department store chain, and you have three pro-

fessionals reporting to you. Prepare an organization chart for the unit.

5. You are a consumer who likes to be treated with courtesy and respect. What, specifically, would you want from an airline company in terms of customer relations?

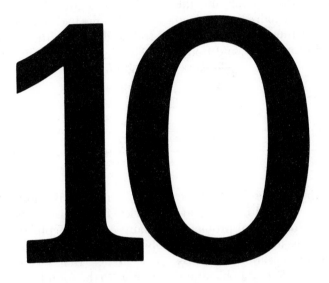

PHILANTHROPY: GIVING AND GETTING CONTRIBUTIONS

PHILANTHROPY, one of the more visible elements of public relations, is also one of the more expensive functions.

Fortunately, its accomplishments are also more tangible than those attributed to other PR units, so one is generally on solid ground in rationalizing the generous financial outlays. In addition, these tangible accomplishments are extremely worthwhile.

There are poor, sick, physically handicapped, uneducated, and undereducated people throughout the world. Schools and the arts need support. Scores of children go to sleep hungry each night. And victims of natural disasters such as earthquakes, tornadoes, and floods need assistance fast.

Private- and public-sector organizations are responding to these and other needs with record amounts of contributions. According to the American Association of Fund-Raising Counsel, corporations and foundations gave $4.16 billion to charitable organizations in 1978, up from $3.71 billion the previous year.[1]

The major recipient areas of the corporate largesse, in descending order of volume of support, were health and welfare, education, culture and art, civic activities, and the catch-all "other" category. The corresponding list for the foundations had the education field at the top, followed by health, sciences and technology, welfare, humanities, international activities, and religion.

WHY GIVE?

THE major reason for giving is the severity of the needs. There are grave health, educational, international, cultural, and sociological problems challenging the best minds in the profit and nonprofit arenas. Those organizations with disposable funds available have a moral obligation to address themselves to the imbalances in our society.

Other reasons may not be as commendable, but they are no less influential on numerous entities. For example, because many businesses respond to external problems by making contributions, some organizations, which may be cool to the idea of sharing their wealth, also establish philanthropic arms lest they be censured in the marketplace. And some that have responded poorly in the past start giving more generously if for no other motive than to "keep up with the Joneses."

In the best of all possible worlds, corporations will make charitable contributions solely out of altruism. In the real world, the words of Mae West, "Goodness had nothing to do with it, dearie," apply to philanthropy more often than they should. Many firms give solely because they feel not giving is bad business.

I took a twelve-month leave of absence from my public relations job at Chase Manhattan several years ago to serve as director of development for The Deafness Research Founda-tion. One of my most vivid impressions as a novice fund raiser was the interest shown by many corporate philanthropists in the contributions of competing firms.

When first asked for a list of corporate donors to the foundation, I was somewhat reluctant to comply out of fear that potential contributors would say, "Oh, you already have a lot of corporate support; you don't need ours too."

I was wrong. The majority of the people who asked to see the list became more interested in The Deafness Research Foundation if their competitors were among the donors or if they thought the list was impressive. Those whose industries were not heavily represented or who thought we should have had more corporate contributors showed a marked inclination to direct their kindness elsewhere.

As a matter of fact, one executive, who was the first in his industry to be courted by me, suggested I give him a call after I had completed my rounds among his competition.

"If most of them give, we'll make a contribution too," he promised.

In fairness to corporations not included in the Fortune 500, there is some justification for a "them first, then me" approach. A thorough evaluation of a proposal for support takes time and personnel. If the philanthropic component of a small concern lacks these qualities, its officers are likely to say, "Well, General Motors, U.S. Steel, I.T.T., and Mobil Oil support this organization, and they wouldn't do so if they hadn't checked it out carefully. If it's good enough for them, it's good enough for us."

Also in fairness to "me too" corporate philanthropists, they are probably matched in number by fund raisers who try to take advantage of competitive pressures when seeking funds. I remember an interesting phone conversation I had during my days on the other side of the philanthropic desk, when I served as secretary to Bank of America's contribution committee in the eastern United States. The call came from a customer of the bank who wanted to make a fund-raising proposal to me over lunch. I suggested he submit his proposal in letter form, because we thought it inappropriate to be taken out by prospective recipients of grants. I added that we would be happy to review his request but that I couldn't guarantee a positive response, since the matter would have to be reviewed by the entire committee.

"You mean you can't ease the request through even though I'm a customer?" he asked in a surprised tone of voice.

I tried to explain why such a policy would be contradictory to the bank's contributions philosophy, but I didn't get too far. He hung up on me midway through my third sentence.

Another customer once wrote to his account officer and asked if she would like to contribute to a fund named after his father (who was alive and kicking at the time). The account officer told me she wasn't interested and my fellow contributions committee members echoed her sentiments, so I wrote a polite letter of regret. In a sarcastic response to my note, the customer observed that it was too bad that the nation's largest bank couldn't contribute to the fund when several smaller financial institutions found it in their hearts to acquiesce.

Guess which bank he didn't call first when he had some banking business to transact? Which is why competitive pressures are reasons (albeit not very altruistic ones) for giving.

Another rationale—one that is far more commendable—is that a healthier, better educated, and problem-free society creates a better environment in which to sell goods and services. If there are officers, shareholders, gadflies, and other individuals in our midst who declare that the business, and only business, of corporations is to make money, we can retort with the following:

• If we find a cure for deafness or blindness, there will be more people who are potential buyers of stereo equipment, books, and so on.

• If we can rebuild a slum area, we'll have another neighborhood in which to sell our wares.

• If we contribute to area colleges, we'll have a larger pool of educated people from which we can recruit our future managers.

• If we can enhance the cultural environment, we will attract more people to the area, keep our employees happy, and improve the business climate through increased tourism.

Still another reason for corporations and foundations to give money to charitable organizations is that it is expected of them; not only by people who use various forms of pressure to solicit gifts but by the public at large. There are numerous problems that can't be alleviated without large expenditures of money, and there are many institutional entities with disposable funds. The average citizen views this as a comfortable fit and often expresses disappointment, disbelief, and disgust when needs and dollars can't be matched.

HOW THE PRIVATE SECTOR IS ORGANIZED TO MAKE CONTRIBUTIONS

BUSINESSES can give money to charities directly or through a foundation that they have created. There really is not much difference between the two in terms of tax advantages or size of gifts.

Some companies will, however, choose to form a foundation, because it is thought in some circles that a gift from the Jones Steel Foundation sounds more impressive than a contribution from the Jones Steel Company. Additionally, a foundation is a separate entity, and its employees are said to have some distance from those of the company. If Jones Steel is enmeshed in a dispute that may reflect badly on the company, people working at its foundation are less likely to suffer an image loss than the individuals who work for the company.

The advantage of giving through the company, as opposed to its foundation, is that there are less government reporting requirements. Generally speaking, a foundation that dispenses as much money each year as the philanthropic arm of a company's PR department will have more employees because of the paperwork demands.

In addition to giving through foundations or directly, corporations and nonprofit-sector concerns can join forces with employees in helping to meet the funding needs of charities. The vehicle for doing this is the matching gift. The way it works is that an employee makes a contribution to an eligible charity (some firms may limit the program to academic institutions, hospitals, cultural centers, and so on) and the company matches it on a 50-percent, 100-percent, or 200-percent basis.

Generally speaking—and I emphasize the word *generally* because many organizations have their own distinct style of doing things—the in-house contributions function is overseen by a committee of senior executives, whereas the administrative work is handled by a unit of lesser-ranking officials and nonofficials. This latter unit more often than not is part of the public relations empire, but it can be a separate operation or wing of another department, perhaps legal or personnel.

The head of the unit providing the administrative support serves as secretary and possibly voting member of the contributions committee, which meets monthly, bimonthly, or quarterly.

All contributions requests that come into the organization end up on the desk of the secretary to the committee, who, we shall assume for the sake of avoiding repetitive uses of *he or she,* is female.

These solicitations may arrive with scribbled notes from the president or chairman saying, "Let's look into this," "This seems inappropriate," or something along those lines. Or they may land in her in-box after stopping at the desks of five other officials first. But sooner or later they reach her.

When they do, she's faced with several options. If the requests are form letters that didn't even bother enclosing background material or addressing them to a particular individual, she may deposit them in her wastebasket.

If they are from reputable organizations and she knows for one reason or another that the committee will reject them (due to an established policy or because they have been rejected earlier in the year), she will have someone on her staff send out a form rejection letter that looks as if it had been individually typed.

Sometimes the letters are requests for memberships, not contributions. She forwards these to the individual or individuals who would decide on the membership and drops a note to the applicant stating that an answer will be forthcoming shortly.

The majority of the letters in her in-box are legitimate applications with reasonable expectations of serious consideration. Notice I say "consideration," not "a gift." This is because the great number of requests coming in to most fund-dispensing organizations dictates that the odds against receiving a contribution are exceptionally high.

Let us pretend that the woman we've been discussing works for a large organization. This means she has two or three professionals working with her, each of whom specializes in one or more philanthropic areas—for example, health, education, the arts, international understanding, and so on.

She takes the requests that have completed the perilous journey from her in-box to the pile that will receive further consideration, and she doles them out to her staff so that each person gets the applications in his or her own areas of specialty. The contributions secretary may even keep a few for herself to review.

She and her colleagues then prepare reports on each applicant, using the material that accompanied the letter as sources of information. It is not unusual that a phone call or two will have to be made to the charity in order to obtain additional data.

After reviewing the reports and possibly talking with people inside and outside the company who have dealt with the organization in question, the secretary makes a recommendation to the contributions committee. The recommendation is usually either "support" or "decline"—and in some companies the secretary will also suggest the amount of the gift.

In assessing each applicant and seeking additional facts and figures, the contributions committee secretary and her staff will want to get the following information:

1. Is the organization tax-exempt?—If the organization has a 501 (c) (3) Internal Revenue Service rating, it is permitted to accept contributions without having to pay taxes on them as income, and the donor is allowed to claim a tax exemption. If the organization doesn't have the rating, its chances of obtaining financial support are seriously weakened.

2. Is it a new operation or is it an already established one?—Some philanthropists don't like to fund de novo organizations because many of them never get off the ground, no matter how desirable their goals or qualified their personnel. Gifts to such organizations cover start-up costs such as supplies, publicity, recruiting, and so on and are rarely used for the stated goals. If the operation folds before ever reaching the point where it can offer its particular services, its sponsors may feel awfully foolish.

Conversely, there are philanthropic units that make gifts to new organizations as a matter of policy. They may prefer to shun established charities because these operations are already receiving significant support.

3. Who made the request and how important is he or she to us?—Let's not be naive. If two equally deserving charities make an appeal and one is headed by the chairman of a firm that has been doing business with the committee's corporation for years whereas the other is headed by perfect strangers, the former has a decided edge.

The contributions committee, composed of men and women who buy from and sell to the heads of many major charities, are not unmindful of the occasional pressures that accompany a solicitation for funds. They may not like these pressures and they may decide not to bow to them, but they still like to know with whom they are dealing.

4. What is the geographic scope of the organization?—With so many deserving charities vying for a slice of the philanthropic pie, it doesn't make sense for a global corporation to confine its giving to organizations serving people in a small area surrounding corporate headquarters. Nor is it smart for a Kansas-based manufacturer of children's furniture sold only in neighboring environs to spead its charitable dollars all over the world.

5. What has been the applicant's past history with the company?—Most contributions committees want to know if they have supported or rejected the applicant in the past and why. They would also like to know what has occurred since the previous decision was made to warrant a continuance of support or a reversal of a decision to reject aid.

If contributions have been given to the charity in the past, committee members will often ask if the company has benefited from the services provided by the applicant. For example, one of the more frequently sounded questions during the evaluation of a grant request from an academic institution is "How many of the school's graduates have come to work for us?"

6. Where does the organization's support come from?—Committees are interested in this aspect of the applicant's operations for several reasons. First, if the organization is overly dependent on a small handful of donors, it is vulnerable to collapse if some of these sources suddenly decide to discontinue their support.

Second, it is possible that many of the institutional donors have excellent track records in picking deserving charities. If, however, the corporations and foundations listed among the charity's backers are infamous for picking organizations that are of little value to the communities they claim to serve, it makes sense to decline the request.

Third—and this goes back to the point raised earlier in the chapter—it's good to know if the competition is supporting the charity. If so, a refusal by the committee to follow suit could make the company noticeable by its absence from the donor list.

7. What has the organization been doing lately?—It would be helpful to know if the charity is involved in any noteworthy projects, if it has been the object of media attention—and, if so, has the publicity been favorable or unfavorable?—and if it is involved in any lawsuits that would preclude its ability to meet financial obligations.

8. Who are its officers and directors?—One can get a good fix on an organization simply by learning about the men and women who give it direction. If they are disreputable or incompetent characters, a decision to reject the application comes much easier. If they are people of vision and ability, the request warrants further consideration.

9. What are its purposes and its record in reaching its goals?—Regardless of the quality of the charity's personnel, its scope, and its past accomplishments, it isn't likely to get support if the potential donor doesn't think its purposes are commendable. By the same token, the soliciting organization must be able to convince potential backers that it can accomplish its goals. Showing recent case studies is an effective way of making this point.

10. What percentage of its financial resources is spent on program goals?—Commendable goals and impressive performance can go a long way toward meeting fund-raising goals, but some potential donors may still be turned off if they feel the dollars they contribute will be used to raise other dollars rather than meet program objectives. A key question in the deliberation process has to be, Where and how will our money be spent? If it appears that more than 30 or 35 percent of the moneys collected are to be used for administrative and/or fund-raising expenses, such a revelation can have a cooling effect on the interest of the contributions committee.

11. How does the charity intend to keep donors appraised of its activities?—No one likes to give money to an organization, receive a thank-you note, and then be forgotten. They like—or should like—to be kept up-to-date on the charity's progress after the gift has been received. So they'll want to know if annual reports and/or progress reports containing meaningful information will be forthcoming.

In a 1980 *Business Week* article on charitable giving, Harold B. Adams, executive director of the Minnesota Charities Review Council, a private nonprofit organization that screens charity appeals in the state, was quoted as saying, "I guess my approach to disclosure has always been, 'Don't give unless they give.' "[2]

12. Is it the best organization in its field that we can support?—The donor will not get maximum mileage out of its gifts if it assists good organizations and ignores excellent ones. Having become convinced that the goals of the applicant are commendable, the potential donor should also be convinced that better avenues of realizing such goals aren't available.

With the answers to the preceding questions—and any others that come to mind—the committee members make their decisions. The committee secretary then notifies the applicants of the final verdict, and that, plus some detailed record keeping on all requests and outcomes, is the way corporations handle the philanthropic process.

At the risk of sounding like an overly critical second-guesser, I would like to point out some of the problems I see in such a system.

First, it is too reactive. With few exceptions, the organizations that are considered for grants are the organizations that contact the institutional donor first. There may be charities that are far more deserving of assistance but that don't get support because they didn't ask for it. I'd like to see philanthropies go on the offense more and try to identify these worthy charities. Unfortunately, there aren't enough philanthropists willing to ask the twelfth question listed above.

Second, I think philanthropy is handled badly when decisions have to be made on charities that operate in distant locations. People in overseas or field offices of the philanthropic unit's parent company are rarely briefed on the organization's grant policies or the art of screening applications. As a result, they are given small budgets to operate with and end up making gifts to the schools their children attend or the pet charities of their golfing partners. The major decisions on out-of-state (or country) grants are made at corporate headquarters, which wouldn't be bad if the people there had a feel for the local conditions, mores, and socioeconomic climate. But they don't.

Third, business considerations often play too large a role in the review of applications. I don't know what the answer is to this dilemma, because grants to the charities headed by large customers still help the needy and are easy to defend. Nevertheless, it seems that if altruism were the sole motivating factor, grants might contribute more to enchancing the quality of life.

Fourth, as generous as many private concerns have been, there is room for considerable improvement in business-sector giving. A. W. Clausen, president of Bank of America, noted in a 1979 speech to the National Chamber Foundation and the California Chamber of Commerce that only about one-fourth of the 1.5 million corporations in the United States make cash contributions. And nearly one-half of all corporate philanthropic gifts came from fewer than 1,000 companies.

HOW TO MAKE THE SYSTEM BETTER

THE following are suggestions for getting better mileage out of each philanthropic dollar.

1. Pick an area of concentration—Unless you work for the Ford Foundation, the Rockefeller Foundation, or an equally bountiful organization, it is important to realize that the limitations of your budget mean that you can't favorably affect all the problems of the world.

But you can make a dent or two if you elect to concentrate. Many foundations and corporations have chosen to go this route because they want to make an impact and they realize that a shotgun approach just can't allow their presence to be felt.

An added benefit to the concentrated approach is that rejection letters are less likely to antagonize the anxious applicants. Fund raisers dislike getting turned down by foundations or corporations that support operations similar to their own, because they think theirs is the most worthy or one of the most worthy in their field. If, however, they get a letter from a potential donor explaining that although it feels that the charity is deserving of support, it (the donor) has decided to focus its attention on one area (such as education or the arts) and therefore won't be able to make a contribution at this time, it is a different story. Recipients of such messages may not like the response, but they can't be too angry, because it makes sense for some philanthropies to concentrate on one problem at a time.

2. Be consistent—Don't reject an applicant for one reason while supporting another guilty of the same charge. Fund raisers have been known to compare notes, and it would be embarrassing to have it revealed that different standards were applied to different charities.

3. Respond to all legitimate queries—Fund-raising organizations that take the trouble to find out the names of the people they should approach for funds are deserving of a response. It isn't that time-consuming, because most institutional philanthropies have form letters that can be used to reply to applicants. Failing to expend the piddling amount of time and money to exercise this minor courtesy is silly given the loss of stature and respect that can follow.

On the other hand, there is nothing wrong with ignoring form letters that are sent indiscriminately to hundreds of potential donors with a "to whom it may concern" salutation.

4. Don't make grants simply because the budget calls for a certain amount of expenditures each year—There was a time when professional fund raisers would attempt to ascertain when corporations and foundations were approaching the end of their fiscal years. They would then time their requests to arrive in the eleventh or twelfth month of the cycle, the theory being that some establishments are tightfisted the first ten months of the year, then loosen their purse strings in order to meet spending goals. Philan-

103

thropic organizations that become more generous at year-end are foolish because this leads to inconsistency and faulty judgments. One should try to maintain the same high standards throughout the year.

If it appears that an institutional donor will not expend the budgeted amount by the end of the twelve-month cycle, the alternatives to a lowering of standards are the following:

• To hold the money for another time

• To increase the size of the gifts to organizations that merit assistance

• To seize the offensive and look for charities that should be supported

5. Don't be afraid to withdraw support from an organization that has received gifts in the past from the committee but that no longer maintains the same high standards—Breaking a string of successive affirmative responses does not imply that the donor is inconsistent; it could signify an awareness that the charity's performance has declined or that other organizations have emerged that are far more deserving of financial assistance. The reason for the reversal of a trend is immaterial. The important point is that support in the past shouldn't guarantee support in the future. Each year's request is a new ball game, and you call 'em as you see 'em.

6. Don't forget about a charity after you have sent it your check—Regardless of the amount, the money that is sent to a charity is money that could be put to good use elsewhere. Make sure it is being spent the way the applicant said it would be spent. Ask to see reports updating new activities. And study the field in which the charitable organization endeavors so that you understand the depth of the need and you learn about what other charitable organizations are accomplishing.

THE OTHER SIDE OF THE COIN—SOLICITING FUNDS

ASKED to describe the secret of his organization's success, a noted fund raiser once said, "It all boils down to who asks whom."

In other words, find out who in your organization knows whom on the board or contributions committee at the prospective donors and then have the request come from your person to theirs.

There is sound reasoning behind this simplistic approach. Most institutional donors get far more requests than they can possibly meet. They can't even properly evaluate all the solicitations they receive. Solicitations that are presented by a friend therefore have to be given a slight edge over those written by strangers. At the very least, they will be given some consideration. This consideration may only come from the contact to whom the appeal was made, but at least it is a hearing of one sort or another.

This means that after getting a charity adequately staffed and funded to commence operations, a key priority of any organization dependent on outside support is to flesh out its board and senior management so that the fund-raising apparatus can work at maximum effectiveness.

FINDING GOOD BOARD MEMBERS

There are other functions board members can and should perform, but we should initially focus on their roles as fund raisers. In looking for potential directors, a good question to ask is, Where do we want our major contributions to come from, or where do we think they will come from? The answers should tell us where to begin our search, because we need to gain entry into the chosen areas to make successful appeals.

But we shouldn't stop in the designated areas because, unless our charity is meeting an exceedingly esoteric need, we will want broad support in addition to the generous gifts from our initial targets. For example, it isn't a bad idea to have most industry sectors represented, as well as the sports and entertainment fields, labor, minorities, and the aged. There is a lot of untapped money represented by these sectors, and a charity has a much better chance of receiving some of it if doors can be opened for it by individuals who know their leaders, speak their language, and have their respect.

Once we have identified the constituencies we want represented on our board, we have to

104

identify the appropriate liaisons. One way is to seek out men and women who would be personally motivated to join the cause. For example, if we are raising money for medical research on birth defects, we would look for important individuals who were born with a physical handicap or who have relatives with congenital disabilities. These people have lived with the problem, they can discuss it intelligently, and they have valid reasons for wanting to see it eliminated. Their personal involvement also makes it understandable to others why they would be seeking to raise funds, and their appeals will be met with more tolerance and less resentment and skepticism.

A good source of help in the board membership hunt is the slate of men and women currently serving as directors. It is very likely that their involvement with the problem over the years has exposed them to other individuals who travel in the same circles and are equally well connected.

Another way to come up with candidates is to look over the roster of major donors. They have demonstrated by the size and/or the longevity of their support that they are concerned about the birth defects the organization is trying to eliminate. It is possible they may be willing to give their time and influence, as well as their money, to obtaining more funds for research.

It is important to note, however, that fund raising is not the only function expected of directors. There are other activities to be performed, so a lack of contacts or six-figure income need not be a bar to board membership. Some directors can provide legal counsel. Others can assist in public relations, invest excess funds, or advise on the day-to-day administration of the office. And still others can offer guidance in long-range planning, insurance, auditing, purchasing, and recruiting and managing volunteers.

If the organization had to go outside the boardroom and pay for these services, it would drain large sums from the budget. Getting professional advice gratis is almost the same as receiving a generous gift.

HOW LARGE SHOULD A BOARD BE?

The apocryphal story of Abraham Lincoln being asked, "How long should a man's legs be?" comes to mind. He allegedly answered, "Long enough to reach the ground." The equally appropriate response to the question about board size is, "Large enough to get the job done."

There are fund-raising charities that place ceilings on the number of directors that can serve at any one time, but I question the need for such a practice. What does one do if a valued contributor with numerous other skills to offer asks to be on the board? Do you wait for a current director to die, resign, or be removed? If so, why? What is so sacred about a ceiling?

According to the National Information Bureau, the organizations listed below had the following number of directors or trustees in the early seventies:

American Heart Association	127
American Lung Association	121
American Cerebral Palsy Associations, Inc.	121
American Cancer Society	114
The National Association for Mental Health	86
National Society for the Prevention of Blindness	75
The Arthritis Foundation	59
Leukemia Society of America	52
American Diabetes Association	50
National Multiple Sclerosis Society	48
National Cystic Fibrosis Research Foundation	38
National Association for Retarded Children	37
Recording for the Blind	31

FUND-RAISING PROCEDURES

RATHER than condense thoughts culled from discussions with development experts and from other books on the subject (see Bibliography), I think it would be more meaningful to describe and comment on the fund-raising practices at The Deafness Research Foundation (DRF) when I was there from the summer of 1973 to the summer of 1974. From my conversations with people in the field, I can say they were not atypical.

There were two categories of targets at DRF: existing donors and potential donors.

The DRF staff kept card files on all existing donors and divided them into four subcategories: those who gave in the first quarter of the preceding year, those who gave in the second quarter, and so on and so forth. In addition to listing each gift on the cards—and when it came in—we also indicated whether the donor had a contact at the foundation who was instrumental in calling his, her, or its attention to DRF.

Prior to the beginning of each quarter, we would pull all the cards of the people who sent a contribution in the three-month period from the preceding year. We would then prepare a solicitation letter for the chairperson's signature reminding the donor that the anniversary of their last gift was approaching. Enclosed was whatever addenda we thought pertinent (annual report, newspaper clippings, news of the research we were funding, and so on).

We wouldn't send the letters out right away, however. First, we would ask the contacts listed on the cards if:

• They wanted to make the request themselves
• They would rather we merely mentioned their names in the letter
• They preferred we simply send them a carbon copy of the letter
• We give the request no special treatment

As gifts arrived in our office, thank-you letters would be sent out and the donor cards returned to the files. Those individuals and institutions who did not respond to the appeal sent out at the beginning of the quarter would get a follow-up request at the end of the three-month cycle.

As a general rule, contributions of less than $25 were acknowledged by a preprinted card and receipt. Those who gave $25 to $99 received a form letter that was individually typed, and those who gave $100 or more received a personal note from the chairperson.

Regardless of the size of the gift, if it arrived in the office accompanied by a letter that asked for information or made a point worth acknowledging, an original response was mailed out in return.

GOING AFTER PROSPECTIVE DONORS

Here's where the novices to fund raising get separated from the professionals. It's fun if you succeed, disaster if you don't, and a serious business all of the time.

We all know there are unidentified potential contributors out there—and that they can be found. How quickly and accurately depends in large part on the quality of the research.

In short, the better the research, the better the prospects and the more frequently they are found. And the better the fund-raising operation and the more dedicated and wired in to potential donors the directors are, the greater the amount of money collected at the end of the fiscal year.

So much for the obvious statements, let us see how it is done.

RESEARCH

There is a wondrous aid to all fund raisers called the Foundation Center. Based at 888 Seventh Avenue in New York City, this oasis of information contains a library open to all seekers of funds. And for those to whom a trip to New York is neither easy nor desirable, it produces an informative directory on grant-making foundations.

The directory is the starting point for all prospect-finding ventures. It lists hundreds of foundations, their officers, and their areas of interest (for example, health, education, the handicapped, science, and so on).

Fund raisers use the directory to identify targets. Then they rely on the center, newspapers, other libraries, and other sources of information to seek additional data on their prospects, such as who the actual recipients of their gifts are, how much money they give each year, how often their decisions are made, and how they can be approached.

Other sources of leads for me at DRF, in addition to the wealth of facts available through the Foundation Center, were our own directors, the media, contributors, recipients of the research grants we made throughout the country, and individuals active in programs to help the deaf.

That the media are valuable is obvious because they report on a variety of topics, any one of which can provide valuable clues. By reading newspapers and watching the news on television, I learned which foundations were ceasing operations and therefore distributing their funds at record paces, of wealthy individuals who had incidences of deafness in their families, of the growing interest in deafness by Lions Clubs, of the concern over noise pollution by labor unions, and of the number of social clubs serving the hearing impaired.

Directors and major contributors were able to point me in the direction of the individuals who shared their concern about deafness and, equally important, who were as wealthy and important as our key supporters.

And recipients of our grants and those helping to educate and train the hearing handicapped exchanged information with me on prospective donors.

One can't, however, expect too much cooperation from men and women working for other organizations attempting to serve the same constituency. While we were all partners in terms of our ultimate goals, we often competed for the same philanthropic dollar.

COURTING PROSPECTS

After we identified likely candidates, we would seek the assistance of our directors in making a solicitation. Once every two months, I would identify all the corporations and foundations I planned to approach over the next sixty days. I would list the organizations, along with the names of their directors or trustees, and then send copies to our directors with the understanding that they should alert me if they knew any of the individuals on the sheets well enough to approach them in DRF's behalf. It was also understood that they would also identify the men and women they knew well enough to write a letter of introduction for me or arrange to have me call on.

Based on the responses of our directors, I would:

• Send the targets a form letter asking for the opportunity to meet them and explain our needs

• Write a letter mentioning that I was doing so at the suggestion of ___(one of our directors),___ then ask for an appointment

• Join one of our board members in making a presentation

• Sit back with my fingers crossed as the director made the presentation alone

Initial letters to a prospective donor would rarely ask for a gift. Instead, I would ask for the opportunity to explain what DRF was doing and what its financial needs were.

I preferred to have a conversation first, so I could ascertain if the target had any special interests in deafness to which a specific proposal of support could be shaped. We were funding a variety of different research projects, so there was always the possibility the potential donor might want to have his, or her, or its name permanently associated with a breakthrough in a given area.

Those who did not want to spend the time chatting with us were still considered prospects because there was the realistic hope they would read between the lines and know that the major purpose of the correspondence was to solicit funds. Quite a few of them ignored our request for a meeting but sent a check anyway.

TOOLS OF FUND RAISING

1. The Proposal—The purpose of a proposal is to tell the prospective donor exactly what will be done with his, her, or its money. It is generally written for institutional donors who are capable of making a contribution large enough to fund a particular project.

These efforts spell out in detail what the goals of a specific project are, how the charitable organization will attempt to meet the goals, and what the benefits of realization will be to the individuals served by the organization. Proposals also contain biographical data on the people running the project, a plan on how the donor will be kept informed of the progress along the way, and detailed information on the charity itself.

2. Speakers Bureaus—There are numerous service organizations, women's clubs, civic organizations, and religious groups looking for speakers at their various functions. Since they also make charitable contributions from time to time, opportunistic seekers of funds would be wise to brush up on their oratorical skills and look for opportunities to serve as a luncheon or after-dinner speaker. They also should look for opportunities to send other people who can represent the organization—directors, heads of local chapters, recipients of help from the organization—into the community to spread the word about its capabilities.

3. Use of Chapters and Volunteers—Retirees, housewives who would like respites from their daily routines, and other people with time on their hands constitute a large array of potential volunteers capable of providing skills of varying value.

The following list, taken from the 1979 annual report of the American Association of Fund-Raising Counsel, shows just how large this array can be.

Organization	Volunteers
U.S. Committee for UNICEF	3,500,000
American Heart Association	2,731,342
American Cancer Society	2,469,700
Muscular Dystrophy Association	1,820,025
United Cerebral Palsy Association	1,650,000
The American National Red Cross	1,382,749
National Council—Boy Scouts of America	1,186,303
American Lung Association	1,000,000
National Association for Retarded Citizens	1,000,000
The National Easter Seal Society for Crippled Children and Adults	900,000
National Multiple Sclerosis Society	850,000
National Council of YMCA	757,727
Girl Scouts of the USA	570,000

The popularity of chapters is equally impressive. They serve as fund-raising arms that take information to and money from people not easily reached by the central office of a national charity. To be sure, there are occasional headaches in dealing with power-crazy or headstrong chapter offices, but their widespread use by major fund-raising organizations throughout the country serves as a solid argument in their favor.

4. Publicity and Advertising—Individuals and institutions can't support what they have never heard of. Publicity and advertising not only alert prospects to the needs a charitable organization is attempting to alleviate, they pave the way for development personnel by creating a receptive environment for their appeals.

5. Luncheons, Dinners, and Special Events—Some people dislike these activities because a large portion of the money raised goes to pay for rubber chicken, lukewarm peas, waiters, busboys, liquor, and bartenders. Nevertheless, special events attract people who may not otherwise be interested in a charity's work. And they create numerous allied fund-raising vehicles.

When I was president of the parents' association at the New York League for the Hard of Hearing in the mid-seventies, we held a dinner dance at which we charged $50 per couple. This didn't even pay for the food and drinks. But we raised $25,000 from the raffle, $10,000 from advertisements in the dinner program, and $5,000 from gifts in lieu of tickets.

That wasn't a bad night's work.

6. Telethons—Television specials and benefits have raised thousands of dollars. But they should not be attempted unless the charity behind the event has a large corps of volunteers to handle the necessary details.

7. Deferred Giving—At the risk of appearing morbid, you can't take it with you. Charities have, as a result, become aggressive in promoting bequests, trusts, and other forms of deferred giving with their current donors and have found it not at all unusual to receive gifts in excess of four figures from people whose annual contributions rarely exceeded $50. Others, who didn't give at all in their lifetimes, became excessively generous when writing wills.

108

8. Memorial Giving—Contributions instead of holiday greetings or flowers after a death are actively promoted by charities as a more meaningful way to be remembered by friends, acquaintances, and loved ones. Cards suggesting that gifts be sent to a particular charity in lieu of flowers, greetings, congratulations, and so on can be distributed to funeral homes, chapter offices, donors, service clubs, and a host of other places.

UNICEF, for example, has raised thousands of dollars each year with a card that says something along the lines of "Seasons Greetings. A contribution has been made to UNICEF in your name by _____."

ADDITIONAL DO'S AND DON'TS OF FUND RAISING

• **Do** have an excellent record-keeping system. Know how much each donor has given and when, keep correspondence, record who in your organization knows which donor and prospect, and add notes on pertinent conversations to your logs on donors. When in doubt about keeping or throwing out some information, keep it. And while you're at it, make a copy and cross-reference it somewhere.

• **Do** acknowledge rejections. Many of the people and organizations to whom you write for funds will not take the trouble to respond in any shape or form, so a letter stating a decline of your proposal is at least an acknowledgment of your effort. Build on that little advance by thanking the author for the consideration and expressing the hope that next year's request will elicit an affirmative response.

• **Do** keep donors updated. You want their support again, so it is vitally important that they be told of the accomplishments made possible because of the generosity of contributors.

• **Don't** complain about a rejection. That will almost guarantee a rejection the next time around or, more likely, no response. We're all big boys and girls. Listening to someone say no, or reading it in a letter is not sufficient justification for whining and complaining.

• **Don't** invite people out to lunch so that you can make a pitch. You want to convince them of your organization's needs; dropping $35 to $70 for lunch fails to make the point. Besides, the invitee might respond to your invitation by saying, "I won't go out to eat with you, so you can count my refusal as a $50 gift."

• **Don't** ignore the people you are trying to help

(the blind, deaf, retarded, sick, undereducated, and so on). They probably won't have the wherewithal to contribute to a fund-raising drive, but they can give of their time and energy.

• **Don't** spend the major portion of your time seeking the $10 and $20 gift. There are always a small handful of individuals and institutions who do—or can—account for the lion's share of the money collected. Real and potential sources of six-figure gifts deserve special care and treatment.

• But **don't** ignore individuals while courting institutional donors. Individuals gave $32.80 billion to charitable causes in 1979, as compared with the $4.16 billion that came from foundations and corporations. While many individual gifts are of the $20 variety, some reach six figures.

• **Don't** sneer at gifts of $20 or less. Gifts of three, four, and five figures are certainly much better, but the small contributions do add up. Fund raisers who feel $25 or even $50 is the dividing line between meaningful donations and a waste of time are being foolish. There are thousands of individuals who make contributions in small amounts, and they are worth pursuing. In addition, some of these small donors could become large donors in the future.

• **Do** take advantage of the public service obligations of local radio and television stations. They are obliged to devote a certain number of hours of air time to public service announcements each year. Get a message ready and find out which stations can use it.

• **Do** make sure your key staff members and

chapter presidents are skilled in public speaking. If necessary, enroll them in public speaking courses. There are numerous speaking engagements to be filled each year, and many charities parlay this fact into new contributions.

• **Do** try to keep your fund-raising letters to one page. It's not realistic to assume that people who know little or nothing about your organization will be willing to spend more than a minute or two on your letter.

FOR FURTHER EXPLORATION

1. You are the head of your corporation's foundation and you have decided to zero in on one area rather than make contributions on an across-the-board basis. Name five areas you would concentrate on and explain your reasons for picking each one.

2. Design a matching-gift program and draft a memorandum that will be sent to the staff explaining how it will work.

3. Write a letter to foundations and corporations asking for an appointment to explain your organization's operations and needs.

4. You've had a very meaningful conversation with the head of a large foundation who told you he's interested in your organization's efforts to provide day care centers for the children of Indian mothers in Prescott, Arizona. Prepare an outline for a proposal to him for a six-figure gift.

5. How would you use local chapters if you were head of a national fund-raising organization that attempts to help alcoholics?

11

INVESTOR RELATIONS

INVESTOR relations consists of maintaining effective communications with stockholders and prospective stockholders, the professional investment fraternity, the financial press, and other financial audiences. From a broader point of view, it involves communication and interaction between a corporation and all those groups and individuals whose attitudes and actions can have a meaningful impact on the organization's earnings and price per share.

Before launching into a treatise on the whys and hows of investor relations, words on the why of reading this chapter are critically in order.

All the public relations courses I have taught have been marked by one common phenomenon: The lecture on investor relations had the worst attendance. Beginners in the field are simply not interested in the subject. Blessed with a schedule of the lectures at the outset of each semester, and being of the opinion that cutting a class or two isn't necessarily fatal, they looked to the investor relations discussion as a midterm respite—or early- or late-term breaks when I tried juggling the schedule to see if that would positively affect the turnout.

This was a mistake on the part of the students. Yes, dealing with annual reports, proxy statements, balance sheets, and stock analysts can seem dreadfully confusing and/or dull to some people. But there are three important facts about such labors of which newcomers must be aware.

One, there are a lot of financial public relations jobs nowadays.

Two, the number is growing as corporations become more and more aware of the needs for (a) better communications with investor publics; and (b) larger investor publics.

Look at a recent classified-advertising section from the Sunday *New York Times.* Note the number of financial PR jobs that are listed. Then look at issues five or ten years into the past. You will note there are more financial PR jobs listed today and that the percentage of communications openings that require some financial know-how are also on the rise.

Three, investor relations jobs tend to be among the higher-paying spots in a corporate communications department. This isn't hard to

understand. Investor relations practitioners deal with a company's most important publics.

Those needing an indication that corporations at least perceive their investor publics to be among their most important audiences need only glance at a random sampling of annual report budgets, then compare them to those of other corporate publications. Telling a firm's financial story is one of the most important challenges facing a business's PR department.

A complete listing of all the publics that merit more than the fleeting attention of investor relations personnel would have to include the following:

1. Stockholders

2. Potential stockholders

3. Financial press

4. Analysts

5. Trust departments

6. Pension fund managers

7. Statistical services

8. Rating services

9. Investment counselors

10. Stockbrokers

11. Banks

12. Investment companies

13. Employees

14. Regulatory bodies

15. Legislators on committees covering the company's industry

16. Financial vice-presidents and treasurers

17. Business educators

18. Purchasing agents

19. Mutual funds and other institutional investors

20. Executive recruiters

THE most important and obvious answer to the question Why investor relations? is the preceding list. There are some very important people in each of the twenty classifications. Any activity designed to obtain and maintain their goodwill is a worthwhile endeavor. The planning and execution of investor relations activities shows these important publics that the organization cares about them. The demonstration of interest alone is a very worthwhile course of action. Other reasons include the following:

1. Corporations need capital—Almost any current textbook or essay by a noted observer of financial markets will cite capital formation as one of the pressing needs of our economy. Industry needs funds to construct new plants, test new products, enter new markets, hire and train personnel, and contribute to overall economic growth.

2. Generally speaking, the companies that have large stores of information available to the public have an easier time getting their stocks and bonds sold than do those that dole out facts and figures in a parsimonious fashion—If people are going to plunk down large portions of their savings on corporate paper, they will be more inclined to do so if the corporation is known to them. The familiar always feels safer than the unknown.

At the same time, better-known companies tend to have more satisfying price-earnings ratios, and the value of their shares holds up better against bad news than do those of lesser-known firms. This is because the former companies have histories of communicating with their many publics and are therefore perceived as relatively stable organizations. They are thought to be capable of withstanding a poor earnings quarter, an unsuccessful marketing effort, or almost any other dire economic development.

If, however, a firm is an unknown quantity, its ability to cope with unpleasant economic news is suspect. Where there is doubt, there is likely to be a selling of shares at the first sign of trouble.

3. Those corporations in constant touch with investor publics have a better understanding of their informational needs—A key question in any communications effort is, Will we be giving our audience what they want or need to know? The answer comes more easily if we have talked to external publics and listened to their questions.

This is what investor relations practitioners do; they maintain contact with key publics and pay careful attention to the informational needs of each group.

4. Good investor relations decreases the chances of a successful takeover attempt—Takeover attempts generally meet with success if the shareholders are unhappy with their investments. Conversely, they face difficult, if not impossible, struggles if the owners are happy with the way things are going. After all, why would investors sell shares and turn management over to outsiders if they are pleased with the firm's performance and envision continued strong earnings well into the future?

5. The abundance of government regulations mandates the need for a talented investor relations team to churn out the required information—A perusal of the informational demands made on publicly held corporations by legislative and regulatory bodies is all that is needed to rationalize the time, dollars, and man-hours spent on putting the facts and figures together. There is the annual report, the quarterly report, proxy material, and the 8-K, 9-K, and 10-K forms, as well as a host of other materials, which must be prepared because the government wants them prepared. The Securities and Exchange Commission even dictates how earnings releases and other major stories are to be disseminated by PR departments. And there is always the prospect that additional publications will be required in the future, so investor relations officers are constantly trying to anticipate the informational needs of key publics and meet them before new guidelines are shoved down their throats.

6. Today's investing public is becoming increasingly sophisticated—Remember the movie *The Solid Gold Cadillac* with Judy Holliday and Paul Douglas? Ms. Holliday played a nice but slightly dumb blonde who is given a job with a large corporation. She is named director of stockholder relations by an unscrupulous management team that wants to keep her out of the way by placing her in what they consider an unimportant position. The irrepressible Ms. Holliday manages to stay busy, however, by exchanging chatty letters, phone calls, and visits with shareholders—primarily sweet, old ladies—and quickly develops an army of loyal supporters. She puts this army to good use when she helps Mr. Douglas regain control of the company at the annual meeting.

Although Judy and Paul live happily married ever after, the pertinent point for our purposes is that such empire building is unlikely now because today's investors aren't won over by a friendly phone call or recipe for apple pie. While they will appreciate a warm exchange of small talk, what they really want is detailed information explaining how the company is per-

forming and how it is strengthening itself for the future.

According to the New York Stock Exchange, 70 percent of the shares traded on the exchange each day are purchased or sold by institutional investors, whereas individuals account for only 30 percent of the shares.

The growing number of sophisticated and important middlemen in the transfer of stock ownership augurs well for printers and other outside vendors who assist corporations in the preparation and dissemination of financial information.

7. Institutional investors and analysts don't merely require information; they desperately need it—It isn't easy making six- and seven-figure investment decisions with other people's money. It takes very detailed knowledge to perform this function well. As a result, many influential market shapers do not sit back waiting for information to come to them; they get on the phone and seek it out with penetrating questions and little patience for anything short of a quick and detailed response.

How investment relations officers handle these queries goes a long way toward shaping the company's image in the marketplace.

GOALS OF INVESTOR RELATIONS

THE goals of investor relations are the following:

1. To increase the number and geographic spread of shareholders—Having a large number of shareholders physically scattered throughout the world makes it difficult for a takeover attempt to succeed and reduces a corporation's vulnerability to regional economic problems.

2. To strengthen shareholder loyalty to the stock and to the company's goods and services—Investor relations people should never lose sight of the fact that shareholders are especially motivated to help a company succeed and that they should be anxious to do what they can to enhance the bottom-line performance. The following is a list of activities for shareholders interested in assist-

ing the organizations in which they have invested their money:

• Using the company's goods or services
• Encouraging friends to do the same
• Recommending the stock to others
• Passing on leads about new business opportunities to the company
• Staying on top of company affairs by attending the annual meeting, reading company literature, and studying the external environment and its effects on the organization
• Writing letters to editors supporting company positions
• Supporting political candidates who are friendly to the company and its industry

114

Other investor relations goals include the following:

3. Obtaining support of analysts and other middlemen.

4. Creating favorable climates for acquisitions and negative ones for takeovers.

5. Improving the climate for business development.

6. Meeting government regulations.

7. Reducing legislative and regulatory control.

8. Enhancing the climate for executive recruitment.

WORKING WITH SHAREHOLDERS AND ANALYSTS

THE people who own—or may own—shares and the individuals whose opinions influence the buy-and-sell decisions of thousands are the primary investor relations publics. They will, therefore, be the major topics of interest in the remainder of this chapter.

SHAREHOLDERS

Shareholders are the owners of the company. Consequently they expect to be treated with respect, an eagerness to please, and, if you will, a modicum of servility. Some are unconcerned about deference, it is numbers that interest them. They expect to see their investments appreciate in value and they'd like generous dividends in the meantime.

But regardless of their attitudes toward servility or monetary gain, they don't want to be ignored. The men and women who own pieces of the company want to feel that their corporation is desirous of keeping them in the shareholder family, that management is more than willing to share pertinent information with them, and that it is receptive to the ideas and comments that they submit.

Efforts to show a willingness to communicate can begin immediately after an individual buys shares in a company. A form letter should go out over the chairman's or president's signature to welcome the new investor to the shareholder family. This letter should express gratitude for the indication of faith in the concern's management, and it should provide some recent facts and figures that will make its readers feel they have, in fact, exercised wisdom and insight in purchasing their shares.

For example, the author can refer to the last quarterly earnings report, assuming that the numbers were impressive. Or the letter can discuss expansion plans, some current research projects that have reasonable expectations of success, or favorable comments about the organization by a noted analyst or financial writer.

This correspondence should also state clearly that the firm welcomes a two-way flow of communication between management and stockholders. This means that stockholders will get specific publications (samples of which are enclosed) and that they should feel encouraged to share thoughts with senior executives (with the name of the person to whom comments should be directed also included in the text).

One definite no-no in writing welcoming letters to new shareholders is a comment along the lines of "we are sure you will be happy you became a member of our shareholder family" or "we're certain your investment will be a profitable one." Such prose is to be avoided because the writer *can't* be sure the relationship will be a pleasant one. There are simply too many factors over which the company has no control that can send the price of each share spiraling downward.

It is bad enough to see an investment turn sour; it is doubly annoying when such a catastrophe occurs following shallow promises of success.

Included in the informational flow to investors are the annual and quarterly reports, proxy materials, reprints of major speeches, and special letters to announce major happenings.

Since the good welcoming letter invites opinions, the preparation of prompt, friendly, and informative replies is another activity conducive to good shareholder relations. It is not a difficult activity. Someone on the investor relations staff is charged with the responsibility of fielding stockholders' comments, getting replies out (many of which can be form letters), and monitoring incoming letters and calls so that trends, problems, success stories, and so on can be identified and acted upon quickly.

Another way to show concern about shareholders' attitudes and perceptions is to conduct opinion surveys from time to time and/or distribute questionnaires to get demographic data about the men and women who have purchased the company's stock.

Most people like to have their opinions sought. It is flattering and it gives shareholders a good indication of which issues are occupying management's time. In addition, most people like talking about themselves and their opinions, so they welcome the opportunity to answer questions.

Others like asking them, which is why the annual meeting serves as such a valuable barometer of stockholder opinion. These sessions, usually held at corporate headquarters, feature a question-and-answer period that can last upward of three hours. Some of the queries are rude and insulting, others are merely silly. But many are legitimate misgivings voiced by serious individuals and are indicative of the feelings of shareholders who are unable to attend the meeting.

All should be answered courteously, and no one should walk away thinking that management is keeping pertinent information from investors. If the questioner seeks data that cannot be revealed for competitive or legal reasons, the person chairing the meeting should explain why there can be no answer.

There are some chairpeople who are reluctant to field questions from the floor because it is impossible to have a solid grasp on all the subjects that are likely to be raised. The PR department, if it handles its responsibilities in a professional manner, has probably prepared a list of possible questions and suggested answers, but there is no way every query can be antici-

pated in advance. Some will definitely catch the presiding officer by surprise.

Many executives will attempt to answer such inquiries anyway, and occasionally they do a bad job of it. As a result, an emerging trend at annual meetings is to have senior officers of the corporation seated in the front of the room so that the chairperson can call on them when a topic touches their area of specialization. This makes much more sense than trying to have a one-person show. The audience gets better responses, and the person at the podium is spared the embarrassment of discussing a topic in which he or she is only broadly versed.

The Institutional Investor—Most people think of individual shareholders when discussing stockholder relations. But keeping Mom and Pop Investor happy is only half the battle—sometimes much less than half in terms of numbers. At least as much time and attention must be given to the institutional investor; the men, women, and organizations representing thousands of people as they make buy-and-sell decisions.

The rationale for considering the wants and needs of institutional investors in a diligent manner is similar to the justification for giving institutional philanthropists priority over the individuals who contribute $25 or thereabouts each year. The institutional entities simply carry more weight and more votes than do individuals.

Furthermore, the small investors aren't as likely to support management positions with their handful of votes as are large stockholders with generous blocks of company shares.

A study of shareholder behavior over the years will most assuredly show that the large investor tends to support management positions more frequently and fervently than the small investor. This is understandable. The institutional investor, for the most part, is cut from the same cloth as members of management. Almost all have business or legal backgrounds and thus tend to view issues from the same vantage points and with similar biases.

The little old lady in tennis shoes, the young couple investing some of their wedding gifts, or other small investors do not share common experiences with captains of industry.

116

This makes it easier for them to support dissident groups on resolutions concerning investments in South Africa, more disclosure, transfers of power from the board to shareholders, and so on.

All this aside, the fact that institutional investors tend to buy in large blocks has another advantage to the corporation. It is much easier to sell one person many shares than many persons a few shares each.

Two other traits of institutional investors that also gladden the hearts of management teams are that major buyers are inclined to invest for the long term, as opposed to the short term, and they generally buy against declining markets. Both penchants are conducive to stability in the price of the stock, as opposed to volatility and unpredictability.

Finally, the purchase of large blocks of stock by an institutional investor serves as a loud and visible stamp of approval in the marketplace. The people making investment decisions for pension funds, trust departments, mutual funds, and insurance companies bring an amount of expertise to their labors that is several cuts above what most individuals have at their command. This expertise tends to produce follow-the-leader reactions.

ANALYSTS

Analysts have to rank alongside shareholders—both large and small—as important investor relations audiences because they have so much potential for influencing the price of companies' shares.

This potential derives from the fact that analysts dissect publicly held corporations for brokerage houses and other entities and report their findings to millions of stock market followers. Their analyses can be disseminated in newsletters, speeches, special reports, or other forms of communication, but regardless of their format, they carry much weight.

Why? Because analysts are exceedingly knowledgeable men and women who narrowly devote their time to the workings of a specific industry or, in some cases, the operations of only a handful of companies within one indus-try. Armed with all the public information they can get their hands on, analysts get to know corporations as well as do the management teams they are constantly reviewing. Sometimes their grasp of a company's performance is even more detailed than that of the firm's managers, because the analysts benefit from an understanding of the competition as well.

Analysts know the numbers and the meaning of the numbers. And they know what the numbers were (and meant) in the past. This allows them to spot trends not visible to the layman's eye and gives them a running start in predicting the future. Since future direction is what investors are most concerned about, the ability to interpret financial figures is very important.

So, too, is the need for an investor relations unit that can get their company's stories to analysts in as favorable a light as possible.

These stories must, however, be conveyed with no frills, no exaggerations, and no lies. Analysts will see through puffery quickly, and any attempts at camouflage will result in a double loss: the loss in prestige that accompanies poor performance and the loss in analysts' respect. The latter setback will result in a reluctance by analysts to believe future company communications.

Conversely, a willingness to own up to poor performance and to spell out clearly why it happened and what steps are being taken to reverse downward-earnings trends can gain the respect of analysts. It won't induce favorable write-ups, because analysts have to call the numbers as they see them, but it might minimize a negative report by focusing on corrective measures. At the very least, it will create a receptive atmosphere for future attempts to explain a company's outlook.

Obviously, then, the best way to earn an analyst's respect and goodwill is to maintain a steady and honest flow of communication. But more than that is required if a company wishes to stand out as an accurate and responsible source of data.

One way is to ensure that the people responsible for communicating with analysts are capable of talking on the same level as the men and women doing the analytical studies. Com-

117

munication skills alone just won't get the job done. Novices interested in a career in investor relations must become exceedingly knowledgeable about the industry they work in, as well as about accounting, finance, disclosure laws, and possible new disclosure laws. Above all that, they must know their company backward and forward. Armed with this information, new investor relations functionaries are then—and only then—ready to go forth and meet analysts.

Courting these outside experts is very similar to establishing relationships with media representatives. Investor relations practitioners find out who the analysts are who cover their industries, where they are, and what they have said or written over the past several years. They then write letters introducing themselves, they follow these up with calls suggesting a meeting, and they strive to provide the facts and figures that will meet all of the analysts' legitimate information needs.

But that's not all. Investor relations officers also want analysts to meet members of their senior management team, so they try to arrange informal get-togethers for company officials and the financial experts. They also find out when local and national analyst organizations hold meetings, then they ask for opportunities to make formal presentations.

The important thing is to generate a steady dialogue between analysts and the company. If the men and women who make the all-important buy-and-sell recommendations feel that the company is willing—and able—to answer questions honestly and accurately, they will be more than willing to get management's side when writing about poor earnings performances or a dismal outlook.

Again, the greatest investor relations program in the world won't get analysts to recommend a stock if the facts and figures point to declining earnings per share. But it can keep doors open so that corporations are able to explain and possibly minimize the effects of disappointing numbers.

DO'S AND DON'TS OF ANALYST RELATIONS

• **Don't** guess. If you don't know the answer to a question, say you will try to get it.

• **Don't** gripe because an analyst's report recommends the stock of a competing firm. All you can do is to ask for an opportunity to present facts and figures showing that your organization's stock is also worth buying.

• **Do** get on the mailing lists for analysts' reports. Not only should you want to know what they are saying about your industry and the firms in it, but you should also try to identify what facts seem to impress these experts the most.

• **Do** put analysts on your mailing lists of important speeches and press releases. The analysts aren't only interested in your firm's financial figures; they want to know *everything* that could affect its performance. Reorganizations, involvement in community activities, statements on key issues, physical expansions, and so on are all capable of impacting on earnings.

• **Don't** clam up when the news is bad. You must be consistent in your willingness to provide information.

• **Don't** just give out numbers; explain them. There has to be one or several reasons why earnings move in one direction or the other—or not at all. Spell them out.

• **Don't** exaggerate. The professionals know what is and isn't significant. For example, a dividend increase after twenty years of no changes in the payout rate is not an indication of excessive largesse.

• **Don't** violate customer confidentiality. While you should be willing to cooperate with analysts, you have to draw the line somewhere in terms of what you will or will not provide. Questions about various customers generally fall on the side of the line requiring silence.

• **Don't** surprise people with your earnings report. If analysts are shocked by a sudden spurt or drop in earnings, it is because you, not they, haven't been doing the proper amount of homework. The information pointing to a burst or a plunge should have been included in the material previously sent to analysts.

• **Do** present analysts with both the micro- and the macro-views of your organization. They should have the overall picture and the detailed views of the components making up your corporation.

FOR FURTHER EXPLORATION

1. List five investor relations publics and two adjectives you would like each of them to use in describing your firm. This should convince you that different publics have different desires.

2. Pretend you're an automobile stock analyst. You are meeting with the president of Ford Motor Company in two days. Make up a list of ten questions that should be raised during the interview.

3. Write a welcome letter to a new individual (not institutional) shareholder.

4. We have discussed the many reasons for paying special attention to institutional investors. What are the reasons for courting the proverbial "little old lady in tennis shoes," who will only buy five or ten shares in the company?

5. How would you maintain a steady flow of written communications with individual shareholders?

12

ANNUAL REPORTS

THE annual report is the most important, most widely read, and most expensive publication produced by a public relations department. Its importance can't be overstated because it performs so many different functions for so many different publics.

To employees, shareholders, and potential shareholders it provides a broad overview on where the organization (corporation or public-sector concern) has been, where it will be going, and why.

To the sophisticated institutional investor and stock analyst, it is a source of financial facts and figures that holds just about every important phase of a corporation up to public scrutiny.

To potential employees it is a one-stop guide to the information needed to determine if the concern is the kind of organization where one would like to work.

And to everyone else it is the first publication they would think of reading to learn quickly about an organization they previously knew little or nothing about.

In his book *Financial Public Relations,* Oscar Beveridge wrote, "When an annual report is developed to its full effectiveness, it is the greatest sales tool, persuader, good will builder and educational device in management's public relations kit."[1]

It is, therefore, no wonder that the reports are given the generous budgets and scheduling that they currently enjoy. Unlike house organs, marketing publications, speeches, and articles—which are written, edited, and printed in one month's time or less—the annual report has come to be a six-, nine-, or even twelve-month job at most publicly held corporations.

There are reasons for the budgets, scheduling, manpower allocations, and hysteria that accompany annual-report production.

First, as stated earlier, it's *the* publication for telling so many publics what the organization is all about—past, present, and future.

Second, it is exceedingly difficult to produce a tome that meets the needs of so many diverse groups. Some of the readers are expert in law, accounting, and the industry or sector in which the concern operates, whereas others wouldn't recognize a balance sheet if they tripped over it. And many others belong to the different shadings in between the two extremes.

Third, all publicly held corporations and most nonprofit operations produce annual reports, mostly in March or April. Competing for attention with a publication that must meet government regulations (which results in a certain amount of uniformity) challenges the creativity—and sometimes defeats it—of some very creative people.

Fourth, deadline pressures can be very tight, even though some of the work on the report starts a year early. Choreographing the gathering of year-end financial figures, government-mandated data, and other pertinent facts and figures that the concern itself wishes to share with its publics requires organizational ability, leadership, and toughness.

Fifth, there is the mounting interest of the Securities and Exchange Commission in what annual reports should and should not say. There are those who feel that this interest makes the SEC a more demanding "editorial board" than senior management.

PRODUCING THE ANNUAL REPORT

BECAUSE it is the most important publication a company produces, it logically follows that the vehicle is also the greatest source of headaches and ulcers.

The following, taken from a paper entitled "Rules of Life in Annual Report Season" that was handed out at a 1978 Public Relations Society of America/New York University seminar on shareholder publications, accurately captures

the aggravation one contends with when supervising the preparation of an annual report.

Murphy's Law: If anything can go wrong, it will.

O'Toole's Commentary on Murphy's Law: Murphy was an optimist.

Howe's Law: Every man has a layout that will not work.

Etorre's Observation: The other company's job moves faster at the printer.

Law of Selective Gravity: An object will fall so as to do the most damage to your printing plates.

Jenning's Corollary: The chance of your milk shake falling on the conference table is directly proportional to the number of irreplaceable photos on the table at the same time.

Brady's Law of Photography: If you have a large selection of photos of the president, his wife won't like any of them.

Karsh's Corollary: If the president's wife likes only one photo, you will lose it on the day it's due to go to the printer.

The Fundamental Law of Deadlines: It was due yesterday.

(As an addendum to this list, I have to share with readers the skimpy memory of a cartoon I saw several years ago. The drawing showed a man poised on the balcony of a skyscraper contemplating a suicidal leap. An executive, obviously the chief executive officer, is leaning out the window and saying something along the lines of "But Wilson, *someone* has to do the annual report.")

Having established that work on an annual report is not for someone with a weak stomach, let's roll up our sleeves and look at how the publications are put together.

PLANNING—THE FIRST STEP

The importance of planning to any venture was discussed in chapter two. The points discussed on pages 12–13 are especially applicable to annual-report work because those responsible for the vehicle must know where they want to go, how, with whom, and with how much money. The importance of this publication and the need to have it ready on the allotted date dictate that there be no time lost to last-minute changes in the game plan. So the schedule and strategy devised six months before production date must be followed as closely as possible throughout the exercise. Which means that the plan must be a good one.

An initial step in the annual-report planning process is to determine what we want to say—including what thoughts we want our readers to have about the organization after one reading. Do we want them to think of our organization as aggressive or as conservative? Do we want to focus on plans for the future or on current performance? Will our people, products, services, or technology receive the most attention? Should we feature our corporate citizenship or our diversification program?

There are several questions worth asking to facilitate the process of identifying possible themes. They are the following:

- What is our concern's personality?
- What is its reputation?
- What are our strengths and weaknesses?
- Which of our publics are most important to us this year and what do we want to tell them?
- What were the most important steps taken to increase earnings in the future?
- What is happening outside the organization that will influence our ability to accomplish our stated goals?
- How is our research coming along?
- How have we improved our image in the communities in which we operate?
- What was our greatest accomplishment last year?
- How much do we want to spend?

(You've heard of showstoppers. This last question is the planning stopper. Until it is raised, bold plans can be made to have the report do everything up to and including whistling "Dixie" as it is opened. After the query is voiced, reality sets in, and more reasonable goals are examined.)

After deciding what we want to say, we have to talk about how and by whom. This means that planners have to consider tactics and personnel, too. Included among the topics up for consideration in this phase of the planning process are printing procedures, scheduling, writing and photography assignments, and distribution.

The most important consideration is scheduling because this affords the least room for flexibility. Almost any kind of printing, writing, photography, and design will get the job done, but the SEC says that the report must be distributed ninety days after year-end figures have been compiled. Failure to meet this deadline will result in fines and embarrassment.

SCHEDULING

In mapping out a schedule, annual-report masterminds must realize that there are several steps in the overall endeavor—and all of them take time. They are

• Planning the report
• Assigning work and gathering material
• Producing copy, photographs, charts, and other artwork
• Clearing the material and making necessary adjustments
• Production
• Distribution

What makes this scheduling especially perilous is the fact that all of the phases are subject to delays, many of them through no fault of the people in charge of the report.

For example, we've set up a meeting to go over goals and strategy and the chief executive officer is suddenly called out of town. Or, after producing copy and artwork on our profitable experience in a foreign country, the government is overthrown by an ultranationalist who introduces measures that make it impossible for us to do business in the country.

Or there is a machinery breakdown at the printshop. Or a lengthy strike by postal employees is started two days before the mailing of finished copies is to begin.

There really aren't too many antidotes to these dilemmas (hysteria doesn't count). The best approach is simply to create a schedule that allows more than sufficient time for each phase, so that unforeseen emergencies aren't fatal.

Additionally, senior management must be convinced of the importance of sticking to the schedule. As the last people to sign off on the text, it is imperative that they do so promptly—and that they offer suggestions for new approaches or the demise of old ones earlier rather than later in the cycle.

BUDGETING

One approach to budgeting is to decide what we want to do, then spend what it takes to realize these goals. Another way is to determine at the outset what we can spend and shop around for printers, designers, and so forth who will give us the desired services at the desired prices.

A third is to engage in "cycle spending." If we had an expensive-looking report last year, let's not get too fancy this year, because our shareholders may object to our spending so much on a publication that many people only glance at. Conversely, if last year's version was done in black and white on cheap or average stock, we can afford to get fancy this year lest shareholders think we don't care about communicating with them and others label us overly tightfisted.

There are two other things worth remembering about budgets.

1. There are only a few limits to what a printed report can do. We can, if we're so disposed, have a prettier, more colorful, better designed, and fancier-looking report than our competitors. All it takes is more money. If, however, we can't work with a topless budget, we're going to have to forsake our grandiose visions and give up a little in terms of design, color, stock, embossing, and other such decorative items.

2. Corporate annual reports generally average between $1.00 and $1.50 per copy, assuming the readership is in excess of 25,000. Smaller circulations will raise per-copy costs a bit, because one of the largest printing expenditures is typesetting, which doesn't change much as you go up or down in number of copies produced.

THE CONTENT

THE COVER

According to a New York Stock Exchange study, the average shareholder owns shares in about three and a half companies. So he or she will receive three or four annual reports, most at approximately the same time, in addition to any others that might be looked at for one reason or another. Since the average investor also gets other mail demanding some attention and has free time reserved for television, bowling, playing with the children, reading, and so on, competition for attention is pretty rough. A good cover is an important element in attracting attention, if for no other reason than that it is almost always the first—and sometimes the only—thing that's seen.

One can elicit considerable notice with a photo of a bikini-clad Farrah Fawcett, an adorable child, or a striking sunset. But if the picture has nothing to do with the organization producing the report, readers will wonder why instead of carefully reading the text.

Worse, readers may feel tricked. They picked up the report because something on the cover caught their eye only to discover soon that there is no justification for the attention-getting picture. Tricked readers are annoyed readers. Who needs that?

Additionally, trickery is unnecessary because it is not that difficult to have an arresting cover photo that ties in to what is discussed on the inside pages. A beautiful skyline is permissible if it shows a city in which the organization has an office. A picturesque foreign scene is appropriate if it was taken in a country in which the concern operates or has just opened a new plant. Shots of a hospital staff in action, a Little League game, children in a day care center, or local government at work are perfectly all right if the organization has been active in community affairs and wishes to discuss its role.

In short, there are so many topics annual report editors can choose from in seeking exciting picture ideas that the use of extraneous objects (no matter how attractive Farrah Fawcett is) makes no sense whatsoever.

THE TABLE OF CONTENTS

There are many who will wonder why this is worthy of discussion. After all, they may opine, it's only a short list of items and page numbers; what's the big deal?

The big deal is that many annual-report editors have had vigorous debates with senior managements and among themselves over the need for such lists.

There is the argument, in one camp, that says that readers are busy people and need an aid to find the information of greatest interest to them. Why not, proponents of the pro-table-of-contents school ask, provide the aid lest readers give up their search and chuck the report in the nearest wastepaper basket?

Those on the other side of the debate retort: Let's not ask why not, let's ask why. After all, these people say, the report isn't so lengthy that specific items can't be found easily. More to the point, if a reader has to thumb through the pages looking for a particular set of facts and figures, he or she may come upon other data we consider important enough to include in the text. Let 'em browse.

I say don't play games with readers, and they won't play games with you. If the report is more than twenty pages in length, use a table of contents. I don't believe that the number of people who would stop to read material they weren't looking for would be greater than the number of people who resent the absence of a table of contents.

THE LETTER TO THE SHAREHOLDERS

This is important for three reasons. One, it is the first lengthy body of text that the readers see. Two, it is signed by the chairman and president. Three, it is where knowledgeable readers look if they want a quick overview of the organization's progress during the last fiscal year.

In his book on financial public relations, Oscar Beveridge wrote that the letter should discuss the first few questions an intelligent shareholder would ask were he or she to spend a few minutes with the chief executive.[2]

I would think those key "first few questions" would come from a list similar to the following:

• What kind of a year did the company have?

• Were you satisfied with the results?

• What are the major external factors impacting on our earnings? (Don't ignore external factors such as shifts in government attitudes, recessions abroad, wars, and so on. Few, if any, organizations operate in a vacuum.)

• What is the outlook for future growth?

• What were some of the major internal developments (new products, acquisitions, personnel reorganization, and so on) that took place last year?

In shaping answers to these questions, annual-report editors must see that the letters are written in language all audiences will understand. If necessary, aim for the lowest common denominator, because sophisticated analysts, business editors, and others know that the financial information in the back of the report has been prepared to answer most of their questions. The proverbial little old lady in tennis shoes wouldn't even attempt to understand the complicated financial data, but she will attack the letter.

THE FINANCIAL HIGHLIGHTS

This section, which usually appears on the inside front cover, the first page, or immediately after the chairman's letter, gives a capsule listing of the firm's financial highlights in the past year. It itemizes figures for categories such as assets, sales, income before taxes, net income, dividends declared, and shareholder equity. And it always makes the numbers more meaningful by comparing them with the corresponding totals for the previous year.

Why the previous year? To show the direction in which the firm is moving.

THE MAIN BODY OF TEXT

There are small annual reports that allow the chairman's letter to serve as the sole body of text outside of the financial sections. Most year-end publications, however, do have a larger section of text for the lay shareholder. It can be presented in one of two fashions.

1. A straightforward departmental review—The organization is divided into major operating units, and each is the subject of a page or more in the annual report so that its performance can be summarized. The text is similar to the chairman's letter in that it attempts to explain what an average shareholder would want to know about it in a brief conversation. In addition to presenting sections covering the key divisions and the catch-all category of subsidiary operations, the authors can devote some pages to research, manpower development, and/or corporate citizenship.

2. A theme approach—Rather than give a simple review of the overall operation and its specific units—or perhaps in addition to such a review—some annual reports will zero in on a particular theme and highlight it as a large article or a series of smaller pieces.

For example, a bank once devoted a report to the numerous services it performs in a small, but representative, town in California. Separate articles covered topics such as loans to the small businessman, consumer counseling, participation in community affairs, municipal bond activity, assistance to large corporations, and aid to farmers. The overall impression left with readers was that the bank is a vital catalyst in the town's economic well-being and a force that beneficially touches upon the lives of almost every resident.

A manufacturer, in an effort to show its interest in designing new products, devoted the bulk of its annual report one year to its research department. The text and artwork covered the expansion of laboratories, the recruitment and training of researchers, the firm's research findings over the years, and some current projects (handled in a justifiably unspecific manner to discourage duplication by competitors).

Other possible themes are

• The company as a corporate citizen
• A history of the company (generally on the fiftieth, one hundredth, or two hundredth anniversary)
• The leadership role played by the company in a business, social, or economic issue
• The company's geographic scope
• The story behind an unusually successful new product or service
• Outstanding employees
• A cross-section of customers

The only caveats to the theme-issue idea are that each one should focus on a large, as opposed to an insignificant, part of the concern's operation, should reflect well on the organization without being weighted down with adjectives, and should not be repeated for a long time—say at least ten years.

THE CORE FINANCIAL STATEMENTS

Here's where management stops worrying about individual shareholders, the general public, employees, and would-be employees, and concentrates instead on members of the financial community, the men and women capable of dissecting the numbers and determining how strong or weak the company really is. These are the individuals who believe that an annual report shows two pictures of a corporation: the one suggested by a fast look at numbers and the one suggested by a careful analysis of the figures. They weigh one against the other and come up with a concept that may be completely at odds with what a layman might see.

The data for this section are compiled by the organization's accountants, so there is little PR people can do other than scream that the material should have been submitted closer to the deadline date. The communicators can, if they maintain good contacts in the financial community, also suggest topics for inclusion in this section.

In addition to core financial statements, which cover esoteric topics such as a consolidated statement of income, balance sheets, statements of condition, statements of changes in financial condition, notes to financial statements, and so on, there is the management review of financial operations and supplementary financial information. In the former section, management discusses the financial data and attempts to show how it interrelates. The authors generally review earnings trends and explain how the various components either enhance or impair earnings.

Communicators needn't worry about their failure to thoroughly fathom the numbers as the material comes from the accountants. But they should have a broad understanding of the financial data so that they can explain them to the average shareholder. Additionally, it pays to know the language of the accountants and lawyers so that you won't feel completely intimidated when debating annual report content.

SOME ADDITIONAL THOUGHTS ON CONTENT

1. Think future—Shareholders can't undo the actions that led them to buy securities in the first place, but they can sever relations by selling or enhance them by purchasing more stock. A good report therefore gives helpful clues as to where the company is going.

2. Think publics—Identify the groups with which management should be most concerned—and conceive the messages that must be sent to them. But don't forget that other constituencies will be reading the text, too.

3. Think external—There are too many things going on outside the corporation that can influence stock price. Unless readers know how the organization reacts—or plans to react—to external events, they haven't learned much about it.

SOME THOUGHTS ON TYPOGRAPHY

There are two important words on typography, one a concern of the Securities and Exchange Commission and the other a concern of editors (or, at least, it should be). The former is readability and the latter is scannability.

The SEC, not unmindful of the fact that many shareholders are in their sixties, seventies, or beyond, has mandated that annual-report editors think of senior citizens—and all those who have less than perfect eyesight—when selecting type, ink, color combinations, and so forth. For example, an SEC edict declares that body type must be at least 10-point type so that letters are large enough to be seen without difficulty.

This line is 10-point type.

This line is 9-point type.

This line is 8-point type.

Many PR directors fear that more rules may be forthcoming, so they concern themselves with things such as whether the colors of the ink and the paper are sufficiently contrasted. Blue ink on light blue stock or black on gray—two popular fads of recent vintage—may soon fade from the scene.

Some report editors also disapprove of the idea of doing pages in reverse (the words appear in a light color against a dark stock) because this can induce the same kind of eyestrain that results from lengthy encounters with large bodies of small type. I suspect that where reverse printing is used in the future, the type size will be 12-point or larger, the color contrast will be especially pronounced, and the message will be fairly brief.

Scannability refers to the ease or difficulty one encounters in trying to glance over an annual report briefly. Can one skim and get a feel for what the company is, what it does, and how well it does it? If so, the report is scannable.

Why would editors want readers to browse? Because in many cases the alternative to browsing is not reading the text at all. One can't forget that there are more annual reports being produced now than in the past and more non-reading attractions competing for people's time. Getting the average reader to scan is regarded as a noteworthy accomplishment in some circles.

One way to help the scanning effort is to use story headlines rather than bullet heads. This means that if a food company has a separate section on its breakfast foods division, the headline "Breakfast Division Enjoys 18% Earnings Rise Thanks To Four New Cereals and Instant Pancake Mix" is a lot more meaningful than "The Breakfast Division."

Another way to enhance scannability is to employ colorful and bold bar graphs showing the differences between the previous year and earlier twelve-month periods.

DISTRIBUTION

IMAGINE all the work, planning, and aggravation that goes into the creation of an annual report. Then picture, if you will, the look of agony on the face of the PR director who has met every production deadline only to discover that the reports won't be distributed on time due to an unforeseen mailing problem.

Once the shock and pain wear off, the communications executive will huddle with colleagues to ensure that there will be no distribution problems the next time around. (They will also do what they can to minimize the current difficulty, but their planning for next year should be of greater importance to each reader of this book.)

For starters, the PR people will allow more time for distribution.* The report *must* be sent to certain groups—regulatory bodies, analysts, financial press, and shareholders—immediately after production, and it should be distributed to other publics shortly thereafter.

In order to meet this requirement, the annual-report planners must:

• Know in advance how the report will be sent to each public—that is, by messenger, first-class mail, bulk mail, and so on.

• Know which post offices and outside mailing houses will be used for each mailing.

• Order envelopes to arrive six weeks in advance so that they can be addressed and grouped according to category—and make sure the reports fit into the envelopes. (It has happened that envelopes usually used for mailing magazines were ordered in large quantities for unorthodox-sized reports. They didn't fit.)

• Brief the printer carefully—both verbally and in writing—as to where the annual reports go after production.

• Know the local post offices. Some are best with letters, others are good with packages, and others are consistently good or bad with everything.

• Know how long the adhesive on labels will last. Some are good for only a week or two.

---

*This is a useful principle for most stages of annual-report production. But don't start *too* early, because you—or others—may run out of gas. You also have to accept the fact that the calendar year doesn't end before December 31 and a good portion of the text can't be finalized until the numbers are in. Interest and enthusiasm should be at their peak during the last month of the fiscal year and the first three of the next.

ADDITIONAL DO'S AND DON'TS
OF ANNUAL REPORT PRODUCTION

• **Do** your best editing early, because changes cost more with each succeeding step in the production cycle. **Do** accept the fact that there will come a time when it doesn't pay to make some changes unless they are of an emergency nature. Certain editors have decreed that they eventually must ask themselves and others, "Will the company go bankrupt if I don't make this change?" If the answer is negative, the alteration is not made. (This is often looked upon as a regrettably wise philosophy if the query is raised as a $350,000 annual report is on its way to the post office.)

• **Don't** let nonwriters compose copy. It makes sense to ask lawyers, accountants, and line personnel to check the facts on text dealing with their areas of specialization, but it isn't sensible to let them determine how the prose is to be shaped. That's the PR department's area of expertise.

• **Do,** however, touch base with the lawyers to ensure that the required information is included in the report and that no governmental rules have been ignored.

• **Do** include footnotes explaining any changes in the way financial information is reported. This means, for example, if the company has been using the LIFO (last in, first out) method of accounting and it suddenly switches to FIFO (first in, first out), this fact should be explained in a footnote.

• **Do** let people who have yet to see the text read it as you get closer to final approval. Individuals who have been editing the text on a near-daily basis may tend to anticipate words, whereas those looking at it with fresh eyes won't. It isn't a bad idea to consider using outside professional proofreaders.

• **Don't** look to your annual report to sell products. That's not a bad secondary goal, but it can't overshadow the need to tell readers what kind of a year the company has had and what kind of a year it will have.

• **Don't** always use formal portraits of your president and chairman (as well as directors, other members of senior management, and so on). Not only are the head shots boring, their continuous use reveals a distinct lack of imagination on the part of the PR department. Show your senior officers in an informal pose from time to time.

• **Don't** select a printer—or any other vendor—solely on the basis of a low bid. Talk to people who have used the vendor, visit its shop, and ask to see samples of its work. It could be that the reason for a very low asking price is that the bidder uses inferior materials or cheap and unreliable help.

• **Do** be very specific in writing bids. In looking for a printer, for example, specify what type faces you want, what kind of paper, deadline schedules, number of pages and issues, inks, and so forth.

• **Don't** let bad news go unexplained. There are some annual-report editors who will include the fact that earnings are down (simply because they have to), then never mention it again in the hope that no one will notice. This is wrong. Readers must be told why earnings are shrinking and what is being done to reverse the trend. There are numerous instances in which the company can legitimately attribute a poor performance to events beyond its control. Readers should be made aware of this fact. If, however, the company was at fault, shareholders and other interested publics must be told what is being done to make the future look brighter than the past.

• **Do** study other annual reports, especially those of your competitors. It's not very likely that all the good ideas will emanate from one corporation. The more reports you look at, the greater the volume of suggestions you can come up with for next year's production.

• **Do** keep management informed every step of the way. Senior officials hate surprises, and editors aren't very thrilled when an idea gets shot down at the last minute.

• **Do** show your layout to senior management in a booklet format rather than on separate pages. This gives the executives a better idea of how the items will relate to each other.

• **Don't** be afraid to ask the printer for overruns of certain sections. You may want to use them for other purposes.

• **Do** get an early feel for what the statistics will say so that you'll know if the year was a good one or not.

• **Do** simultaneous clearing of copy rather than using a linear approach that has officers clear copy one at a time starting from the bottom up.

• **Do** figure on printing two or three copies of the annual report for each person owning shares in the company. You'll need the extra copies for use with other publics throughout the year.

• **Do** look at last year's annual report to see if any specific goals were announced. If they were included in the text and have been met, this fact should be highlighted in the upcoming report. Many readers look at previous reports to see what promises were made.

• **Don't** ever forget that annual reports must be in the mail ninety days after the end of the fiscal year.

FOR FURTHER EXPLORATION

1. Get a current annual report from a Fortune 500 company. Then write to the firm asking for an annual report that is at least ten years old. Compare the financial sections and explain how they differ.

2. You are public relations director for a publicly held manufacturer of bicycles and mopeds. Come up with a list of ten topics around which a theme annual report can be designed.

3. You are public relations director of a publicly held tire manufacturer. Draw up a ten-month production schedule for its annual report.

4. Take an annual report and decide what you would have done with it if the budget had been increased 50 percent.

5. Critique five annual reports.

13

INTERNAL COMMUNICATIONS

THE following is a letter written to *Dun's Review* in early 1979 by Lee L. Morgan, chairman of Caterpillar Tractor Company, after the firm was named one of the five best managed companies of 1978 by the magazine.

> Dun's favorable appraisal of our company is a recognition that will be shared with all employees through our internal communications. Your writer was a most knowledgeable and perceptive interviewer, and the article captured the qualities we believe are the key to Caterpillar's growth and success.
>
> Working with your highly respected organization has been a rewarding experience for all of us at Caterpillar.[1]

Notice with whom the man is most anxious to share the news. Mr. Morgan's purpose in passing the news to the staff was to show that the company recognized that its successes and honors are the results of the employees' efforts. However, internal communicators might also argue that another, and equally valid, motive for telling employees is to take advantage of their potential as goodwill ambassadors.

And why not?

Caterpillar has approximately 90,000 employees. Say about half of the staff is married. That adds up to 135,000 potential spokespeople for the company, spokespeople who can tell upward of 500,000 individuals about the honor bestowed on the firm.

It also adds up to a major reason why institutional entities—both profit and nonprofit—spend time and money to keep employees informed about noteworthy happenings.

If the men and women who work for an organization aren't going to tell its story in the circles in which they travel, who will? But they can't talk about their concern's strengths, accomplishments, and policies if they don't know what they are.

Not only does a firm lose opportunities to have important messages carried to large audiences when it fails to share information with its employees, it also can embarrass its people and do harm to its image by keeping intelligence under lock and key.

Pretend that you work for an organization that has been in the news for the past month because it was accused—unfairly—of preparing false and misleading advertisements. You go to a well-attended cocktail party, where a guest who knows of your business affiliation asks you what's the real story.

Both you and your organization are going to appear pretty stupid if you retort, "All I know is what I read in the papers." Yet there's really not much more you can say if your company hasn't discussed the issue in the house organ or through some other vehicle. If, on the other hand, management openly talked about the charges with its employees and showed how the ads are *not* false and misleading, it would have hundreds of advocates capable of conveying this information to others.

This is therefore a rationale for the establishment and continuous care and feeding of internal communications departments. There are, however, other reasons why the subject deserves attention.

1. Informed workers are better workers—For one thing, employees know where their work fits in vis-à-vis other functions in the organization. For another, they know why. For a third, information gives them the tools to succeed.

If their work makes sense to them, there will be less time lost to questions. And it is likely that a helpful idea or two might spring forth from the brain of a knowledgeable worker.

2. Informed workers are happier workers—Most organizations are beset with false rumors, many of the grass-is-always-greener-on-the-other-side variety. Some staff members feel that employees in other units are putting in less time, get more pay, and/or are promoted faster. Still others believe that the company is reserving too low a percentage of its assets for salaries and benefits. And others may have morale problems because they don't perceive the company as an industry leader or because they harbor any one of a dozen other possible misconceptions. A steady flow of information can put false rumors to rest, instill pride, and make employees feel they are being treated well.

3. Informed workers have an easier time shaping career goals—It is exceedingly difficult for staff members to plan for their next assignment or to identify possible career paths if they don't know what other people in the organization do or if they are unaware of other departments that can make use of their skills.

On the other hand, it is reasonably easy to shape realistic plans for advancing up the corporate ladder if one understands each department's needs, importance, and outlook for growth. Since it isn't terribly difficult to arm ambitious staff members with such information, it is well worth a corporation's time to set the communication gears in motion so that career planning can take place.

An additional benefit to helping employees plan for their future is that it gives supervisors insights into their subordinates' judgment and ambition. It also provides clues to the types of training programs required by employees.

4. Internal communications is one of a PR department's more visible activities—A bad performance in the art of disseminating information to employees reflects poorly on the PR department and makes it difficult to get cooperation and support on other endeavors.

Take the house organ, for instance. It goes to all members of the official and clerical staffs, many of whom show it to their spouses. It is sent to retired employees and some members of the media. And as a professional courtesy, it goes to editors of internal publications at other concerns, as well as to some legislators and regulators. It is even likely that the house organ is left lying around in reception areas where customers, suppliers, and other visitors may see it.

With the exception of the annual and quarterly reports, there is no publication produced by the public relations department that gets as great a readership as the house organ. That makes for a strong incentive to turn out quality products.

5. Internal communications is a typical starting point for beginners—If given the choice between hav-

ing a subordinate's errors exposed to the outside world and keeping them within the family, the public relations director will most likely choose the latter alternative. Since errors tend to be committed more by newcomers than by seasoned veterans, it follows that the house organ will serve as an initial starting-off point in a neophyte's indoctrination into the communications art.

Not only is the company newspaper or magazine a popular place to start one's career, it is an excellent one as well. Assistant editors on a house organ will, within the space of a year, be exposed to just about every department within the organization. There are few other jobs that can provide rookies with such an all-seeing vantage point, opportunities to use so many communications skills, and contact with senior and middle management.

6. Internal communications is a growing field, so there will probably be more jobs for newcomers—There are several reasons for an anticipated rise in the number of job openings in the years to come. First, there is the government's interest in the need to clearly spell out employee benefits to all staff members. Current legislation calls for more information, disseminated more frequently. This creates manpower needs.

Second, there are the technological developments in print and electronic communications. They make it much easier to produce facts and figures, and this increases management's willingness to introduce new communications vehicles and hire people to staff them.

A third reason is employees' growing thirst for knowledge about their organizations and jobs. Workers are no longer content to read about births, betrothals, and bowling. They want meaningful news; they want it frequent; and they want it well written.

TOOLS OF INTERNAL COMMUNICATIONS

THE HOUSE ORGAN

This is the most popular method of getting information to personnel, and the cornerstone of any internal communications program. House

organs can be produced in newsletter, tabloid, or magazine form; they can be issued weekly, biweekly, monthly, bimonthly, or quarterly. They can also be put out by the internal communications people in the public relations department or by the personnel department. The norm is a monthly tabloid that is the responsibility of the public relations department, but it is not a very dominant norm. More will be said about this vehicle in the next chapter.

THE MANAGEMENT PUBLICATION

There is a new trend in internal communications. It is a by-product of a school of thought that sees little rationale for communicating the same information to a seventeen-year-old high-school dropout keypunch operator and a forty-year-old graduate of the Harvard School of Business. To do so, this school's theorists lament, is to severely miss the mark with readers who represent either end of the educational spectrum.

Rather than bore one segment of the audience or confuse another, it has been suggested that the house organ be aimed primarily at nonofficial employees and that management publications be introduced to meet the informational needs of officers.

Neither group need be barred from reading both publications. Indeed, house organs are usually sent to all employees, and management magazines are sent to all clerical staff members who ask for them. But there should be no doubt as to the intended audience for each journal.

Included in the subject matter for management publications at private-sector concerns are market information (which firms are making what kinds of deals, which customers are looking for what kinds of services, which competitors are bidding most aggressively for new business, and what's happening in regard to legislation and regulation) and data on how the company is organizing itself to take advantage of developments in the marketplace (for example, formation of new departments, case studies of successful deals, explanations of new services, and so on).

Publications at nonprofit organizations could center on current trends in the field—what's happening in higher education, hospital administration, the arts, and so on—or on the work of key personnel. For example, college faculty newsletters that focus on the research and writing activities of the academic staff are carefully read by lecturers, instructors, and professors.

In addition, management publications in both the private and the public sectors contain how-to articles on broad topics such as "How to Cope with Stress," "How to Manage Your Time," "How to Motivate Employees," "How to Recruit Outstanding People," and "How to Make Effective Presentations."

The management publication is one of the fastest-growing vehicles in internal communications.

DEPARTMENTAL PUBLICATIONS

Departmental publications also represent an emerging trend, especially at Fortune 500 firms, multicampus universities, and other organizations with diverse elements operating under the same umbrella.

It is becoming increasingly difficult for large organizations to touch all bases with an eight-page monthly tabloid. Employees in locations other than the head office—or even those in the head office who work for departments not normally in the limelight—feel disenfranchised when they rarely see their names or those of anyone they know in the company magazine. This disenfranchisement is accompanied by a near total lack of interest, which can soon give way to bitterness.

If, however, there is a publication that concentrates solely on a given department or field office, the morale will be given a decidedly positive shot in the arm.

EMPLOYEE ANNUAL REPORTS

Year-end reports, which are representative of another growing internal communications trend, serve two purposes. They demonstrate management's appreciation of its people's efforts and they contain the data that show employees are well taken care of.

Included among the information usually found in such reports are benefits figures, features on employees' contributions to profits, discussion of the staff role in the community, and news of employee club activities.

LETTERS TO THE HOME

The advantage of letters is that they go directly to the person named on the envelope—and they're likely to be read by the family, too.

Communicating to employees in their home conveys a warmth and closeness that isn't always generated by other forms of internal communications. Additionally, if an organization has established the precedent of writing to the home—usually about benefits or to extend holiday greetings—union organizers can't complain about unfair labor practices when letters are sent home during a unionization drive. If, however, all previous written communications had been disseminated at the office, the union could file a grievance with the National Labor Relations Board.

BENEFITS BOOKLETS AND TRAINING MANUALS

These items are important because all staff members want to know what their benefits are, and they believe that failure to follow manual text could result in dismissal. In addition, these vehicles are read early in employees' careers, when lasting impressions are being formed.

Unfortunately, the booklets and manuals are too often the work of personnel department officials untrained in communications. The enlightened organization recognizes that the best communicators are in public relations and therefore calls on them for help. This means that each public relations director must see to it that the best communicators *are* in his or her employ.

NEWS BULLETINS

Every now and then—say about four or five times a year—a development of such magnitude occurs that it would be ridiculous to delay an announcement to the staff until the next issue of the house organ.

Rather than wait, the news is reproduced in a one- or two-page memo and sent to all employees at their work stations. If a loudspeaker system is in working order, that vehicle is used too.

Items important enough to be communicated to major publics with dispatch are important enough to be shared with employees.

MESSAGES IN PAY ENVELOPES

Most personnel experts will agree that there are only a few facts that universally apply to all employees regardless of the country, state, county, or town in which they work. One such fact—which, aptly enough, applies to the subject heading of this paragraph—is, Sooner or later every worker who is physically capable of doing so will open his or her pay envelope and glance at the contents.

As a result, pay envelope enclosures have a fairly high readership. Attention to future enclosures can, however, drop sharply if the messages are of little import or the vehicle is used too frequently.

BULLETIN BOARD NOTICES

Bulletin boards are useful internal communications tools if they are strategically well placed.

The wall next to the waiting line in the company cafeteria, the walls of elevators, and the walls outside rest rooms are three desirable locations. It is not at all unlikely to see posters about health rules, company functions, and new products embellishing such areas—or to see groups of employees looking at them as they congregate for one reason or another.

Bulletin boards can also be used to disseminate information about a concern's performance or to display newspaper and magazine coverage of the organization's activities.

ORAL COMMUNICATIONS

Let us not forget the spoken word—delivered formally, informally, in anger, or in friendly bantor. There are numerous occasions when the best way to get information across to staff members is to say it rather than write it. Oral messages are more direct, easier to transmit and generally easier to tailor to the needs and comprehension level of the intended audience.

The forms of oral communication include

• Staff meetings
• One-to-one encounters with the department head
• Training classes
• Formal talks to large groups
• Bull sessions

ELECTRONIC COMMUNICATIONS

As stated in chapter six, this is a rapidly growing segment of internal communications. And with good reason. A majority of today's employees grew up with television as their major form of entertainment and major source of news. Men and women of the "age of the boob tube" are used to getting information quickly through an electronic medium, finding it more entertaining and easier to understand than printed messages.

If they prefer to get their news through television or radio when they are at home, it is safe to assume that their preferences would apply at work as well.

Those organizations that recognize the logic of the preceding statement—and that have the financial freedom to act upon it—have:

• Set up loudspeaker systems for important announcements
• Introduced a closed-circuit television version of their house organ, while keeping the printed version as well
• Produced films or tapes for staff members at non–head office locations
• Supplemented training manuals and benefits booklets with film, tape, or slide show presentations.

THE CHALLENGES OF INTERNAL COMMUNICATIONS

Given the compelling reasons for maintaining a vigorous and contemporary internal communications program, it is not as difficult as it used to be to hire good people and obtain realistic budgets. Were one to conduct a study on the topic, the findings would surely reveal an upswing in private- and public-sector expenditures for communicating with employees.

Nevertheless, and notwithstanding the loosening of purse strings, the influx of more and better-trained communicators, and the technological developments that allow news to be disseminated faster and in a greater number of ways, achieving internal communications goals isn't that easy. Some practitioners even complain it has become more difficult.

Chalk this up to a host of socioeconomic factors.

First, people move around more than they used to. The average family changes addresses every five years. And the breadwinners in it don't stay in the same job as long as their parents did—primarily because today's working generation is not motivated by a post-depression mentality, which induced many people to take jobs and hold on for dear life. This loosens ties between workers and their employers. What happens at the workplace just isn't as important to today's employees as it was to their parents.

Second, there are more two-income families. If neither job is the only one in the family, it can't hold the interest that the sole source of disposable funds induces.

Third, there are more divertisements available to today's working population. We watch television, we see shows, we jog, we read books, we get together with friends, we travel, and we sit debating which of many other activities could just as easily occupy our time. Discussing a work problem may be on the list, but it probably does not occupy a very high position.

Fourth, we have more time for play because we have less children. The birthrate has declined from 3.8 children per average woman during the peak of the 1946–60 baby boom to 1.8 children today. There is less reason to save and more time to spend excess funds.

Hedonism may not be the national pastime, but there is a much greater desire than ever before to enjoy the fruits of one's labors and to place one's job in a nine-to-five time slot only. A job is the ticket to a good life, but it is not a way of life to most people. Instead, the normal pattern seems to say, Let's seek employment to earn a decent living, but let's not get hysterical about it.

What, then, do internal communications experts do to compete against outside distractions at a time when the workplace is diminishing in importance to today's employee?

One solution is to produce materials that give personnel what they want. But how will sex, sports, humor, gossip, and horoscope information make people better workers? Facts and figures about jobs, external market conditions, and how-to tips could result in greater productivity, but how many people will actively seek out such data when their time can be spent on a book, television program, bowling, and so forth?

Finding the happy blend of what employees want and what they need to know is the greatest challenge facing internal communicators. Before listing the items workers want included in company media—and passing judgment on the relative merits of each one—there is a rule that needs stating: Make it job related. If employees desire to read about sex, sports, humor, gossip, and horoscopes, there are plenty of publications that can satisfy their needs—and that have the budgets and staffs to exceed the meager output of a house-organ crew.

More important, information not related to the workings of an organization shouldn't be in its publications, which are paid for by the organization and produced for the education of its employees. Extraneous material just doesn't belong.

The following is a list of items employees like to read about that are company related:

1. The three B's—babies, betrothals, and bowling

2. Employee club activities other than bowling

3. Salary policies

4. Benefits news

5. Staff promotions

6. Safety and health

7. Discounts on organizational products and services

8. Opportunities for advancement

9. Features on fellow employees

10. Classified ads

11. Deaths, retirements, service anniversaries

Starting with the top of the list, I'm not crazy about the three B's and feel that any publication that treats them as major items is doing its company a disservice. Most people get married, most married couples produce offspring, and many people go bowling. So why get excited about it? These items are only worthy of mention in small organizations where everyone knows everyone else and personal notices are of interest to all. But they don't deserve to be treated as lead stories. A brief mention in the rear of the vehicle will more than suffice.

No mention at all is the proper approach for publications with more than one thousand readers. Reading about the betrothal of two perfect strangers matches the excitement of watching grass grow.

Employee club activities are of interest because the athletic teams represent the entire organization, and the social events are open to all. But, again, they are not the stuff of which page ones are made.

Items 3 through 11 definitely belong in house organs regardless of the circulation size. And some, particularly salary and benefit news and features on staff members, can be lead articles.

Classified ads, deaths, retirements, and service anniversaries surely won't be page-one items, but they do deserve to be in the publication because of the significant interest they attract. As a matter of fact, even though there are members of senior management who question the necessity of classified ads, studies have shown that the listing of items for sale or rent is one of the most popular house-organ features.

Now let's look at the information management would like to present to its employees.

1. The workings of each department—It's important for workers to know what other departments do and why so that their own assignments make more sense to them. Instead of mindlessly checking and stamping papers all day, for example, an employee knows how and why the papers came to his or her desk and what's going to happen to them next. It's better for morale to see how one's work fits into the overall process, and it stimulates ideas.

2. News of the industry or field—None of us work in a vacuum, so what happens outside the company's gates can have a serious impact on all employees. Stories on developments in the industry or field, new manufacturing procedures, public perceptions of the company's area of interest, and legislative and regulatory trends also make employees feel more a part of the team, stimulate thinking, and generate ideas.

3. Goals of the organization—What the organization wants to accomplish and how it intends to achieve its goals could spur people on to greater efforts, especially if they see how their assignments contribute to the overall endeavor. This information also allows them to set goals of their own and to have greater feelings of pride and accomplishment when tasks are successfully completed.

4. New products and services, major reorganizations, or any other developments that will help the organization do a better job—If for no other reason, these developments are important because they affect the day-to-day work of many staff members. The desired results may be difficult to achieve if employees aren't informed and enthusiastic participants.

In addition, moves made by an organization to strengthen itself should induce pride and confidence in employees because they'll feel that the organization will be more successful. Programs that could have a positive effect on their pocketbooks will be well received if communicated properly.

5. Negative news about the concern—As was pointed out by the hypothetical situation described at the outset of this chapter, employees who can't voice the company position on negative stories embarrass themselves and their organizations. Moreover, opportunities to have negative opinions reversed are wasted.

Another compelling reason to discuss unpleasant situations in company publications is that doing so is an excellent route to credibility. How can editors pretend they are producing pertinent news about their organizations when negative issues that have been prominently aired in the media somehow don't find their way into the pages of the house organ? If employees can't see the company's side of a well-known topic in the publication specifically aimed at them, they will be inclined to question the vehi-

cle's thoroughness and their management's integrity.

6. Company performance—Employees should know how their organization is doing because:

• People may ask them
• A bad performance could encourage them to try harder
• A good performance will make them feel that their efforts have been worthwhile

There are two Cole rules about progress or earnings stories in company publications.

One, put it in language the average staff member will understand (see pages 186–187 in chapter seventeen).

Two, be consistent. Don't put stories about good earnings on page 1 while burying bad earnings under the soccer scores on page 8.

7. The concern's activities in the community—As was discussed in chapter seven, coverage of the concern's community involvement gives tacit approval of such activities and encourages staff members also to participate in programs to enhance the quality of life. If personnel are disinclined to participate, they at least know of their organization's role in community affairs.

8. Examples of successful work performances—Many educators will state that giving students a list of rules pointing to desired performance isn't as meaningful or easy to take as case studies showing how things have been done. Stories are more interesting to read than rules—and they're even more palatable when told from the viewpoints of people known to the readers and in contexts that are recognizable by them.

The following is a lead article from a 1976 issue of *Bank of America News.* This piece attempted to use the case study approach in showing bankers that even though corporate loan demand was down at that time, there were numerous things lending officers could do to solidify the bank's image with corporate clients.

The names of the individuals and companies involved have been changed out of respect for the bankers' and the clients' wishes for anonymity.

Writing in the last issue of the management newsletter, area general manager Tim Dorey called for greater business and personal development activities in the face of slack loan demand.

"There is much to be done if one is resourceful," Mr. Dorey wrote, adding that account officers should be increasing their call programs and adding to their knowledge of bank services and areas of specialization. The following four case studies describe resourceful and diligent efforts which can help the bank with all customers.

REVERSING A NEGATIVE IMAGE

Bill King's assignment to the Jones Steel account in 1974 took place shortly after the bank declined a request by the Philadelphia-based company to participate in a new revolving credit.

Bank of America didn't take part in the loan agreement because of tight money conditions, but several financial institutions chose to exercise restraint elsewhere.

As a result, the loan was made by a syndicate of other banks and B of A was clearly relegated to a minor—and almost non-existent—role in Jones's financial picture. "Furthermore, Jones seriously doubted our intentions and perhaps our capability," King noted.

Two years later, B of A is one of Jones's top banks in terms of momentum, and the potential for new business with the company is several hundred percent better than it was in 1974.

The major catalysts in this transformation, according to King, are calls, more calls, banking services specifically tailored to Jones's needs and the involvement of senior bank management.

"The road back certainly wasn't an overnight journey," Bill recalled at his office at the New York CSO, "but it shows that persistence and innovation can turn an account relationship around."

The bank officer averages eight visits a year to Jones's offices to know the company's staff better, discuss their needs and explore Bank of America's ability to serve them.

"I make it a point to see several financial officers on each visit. Some talks will be lengthy, others may be brief, but all have a good exchange of information.

More important, they convey the impression that B of A cares," Bill said.

Among the Jones executives that King sees frequently are the assistant treasurers, treasurer, manager of money and banking, and manager of financial planning and analysis. In addition, the vice president of finance is visited at least once a year.

Most of Bill's calls are one-man visits but he's alert to opportunities to bring other bank personnel when the needs arise. For example, Tim Dorey and Henry Rodd have accompanied him to reinforce the bank's stated desire to expand the relationship and overcome the doubt that resulted from the 1974 credit refusal. And Dave Perry and Eric Harris have joined him in discussions when expertise on foreign exchange and economic developments was required.

"One of our most effective meetings with Jones was a working session in Philadelphia in which the company's vice chairman and financial management team presented their plans for the future to a bank team consisting of Tim Dorey, Henry Rodd, Eric Harris, Mike Smith and myself. Jones was very pleased with our senior management's willingness to become involved in its future," Bill noted.

Four months later the bank made a proposal to Jones to agent a large revolving credit for domestic purposes.

"Jones's management was impressed by our plan because they felt we had ably identified their needs and innovatively structured an arrangement which met each one. They eventually decided, however, that the economic situation made it more feasible to go to the equity market, but they indicated that our proposal demonstrated a capability for innovativeness not shared by their New York banks," Bill said.

Two additional indications of the bank's return to favor are the facts that:

1. Although Jones reduced its commitments by $58 million in 1976, the company's line with B of A was increased by $5 million.

2. The bank has been asked to analyze and recommend the financial structure for a $300 million pulp plant in Brazil.

King is currently working with Mike Johnson of the New York Edge's Eximbank project finance group on this.

Looking back on his efforts over the past two years, Bill noted that there are three lessons to be learned from it.

1. You can make progress when loan demand is bad. Calls can generate much good will and insight.

2. Insight into the company's style of business, which is a reflection of individual effort to learn about the customer, can provide the basis for innovatively structured credits.

3. Innovatively structured credits specifically tailored to a company's needs, as opposed to standardized and rigid arrangements, are very impressive to customers.

GETTING ON TOP OF AN INDUSTRY

What does a person do when he or she is assigned responsibility for accounts in an industry in which he or she has had little experience?

In the case of Len Rall, an assistant vice president at the CSO, one pounds the pavement in culling information from every available source, burns the midnight oil analyzing the information and devotes days to planning and marketing.

Rall, who joined the bank in late 1975 after serving as a national accounts officer with a major New York bank, was assigned trucking in the CSO's manufacturing and transportation section after an orientation period in New York and California.

Because his immediate task was to learn about the industry as completely and rapidly as possible, Len spent the next nine months obtaining information from the following sources:

—In-house centers such as the economics department and libraries in San Francisco, New York CSO and BAIMCO. ("Talking with the industry specialists at BAIMCO and account officers on the West Coast gave me an insight into how the industry was financed. This also enabled me to read industry studies, trade publications and brokerage reports.")

—The government. Len labels the Interstate Commerce Commission and Department of Transportation major sources of information, noting that entry, operations, pricing, rates of return and the ability to borrow are often regulated by the former. ("I've visited these agencies and spent time in their records departments. I even obtained an ICC telephone directory.")

—Security analysts. ("Analysts covering the industry are excellent sources of information on what is happening today. I attend their meetings and make it a point of getting on their mailing lists.")

—Colleges. ("Harvard, Wharton and other leading business schools have professors of logistics and physical distribution. I've talked to them and read their publications.")

—Trade associations. ("We are members of the National Accounting and Finance Council of the American Trucking Association and the North Carolina Motor Carrier Association.")

—Competition. ("I've visited account officers at the leading banks for the trucking industry. It's interesting to note that the chairman of FNB-Boston and president of Citibank both handled trucking accounts at their respective banks.")

—The industry itself. In addition to talking with finance officers in the industry, Len visited truck and trailer manufacturing plants and toured terminal facilities of trucking companies in the South. ("Talking with finance officers is expected of bankers, but it's also important to meet with people on the manufacturing side and learn how they feel about the equipment we finance.")

The bulk of the information gathering process behind him—"It never ends though, it's an ongoing process"—Len established market objectives and then set up a preliminary market research analysis. This analysis isolated 30 trucking companies in the eastern third of the United States and evaluated each by 12 criteria, covering their financial condition, outlook, legal history and other key factors.

"This allowed me to give each company a desirability ranking, and start on my call program," Len said.

Looking back on his efforts, Rall called the results "particularly rewarding considering the poor loan demand at this time. I've called on a large number of middle market companies which had never been visited by Bank of America and have had requests for much new business."

He attributed his progress thus far to the early identification of good prospects and cooperation of other units of the bank, particularly B.A. Leasing.

Len also cited teamwork with New York Edge officials and made special reference to joint efforts with Jim Smith, Leslie Forrest and Mel Sarno in calling on one of the major firms in the trucking industry.

"We've made good contacts in the industry and with public and private organizations that are directly involved with trucking. Projections indicate that the carrier segment of the industry will double by 1990. B of A will be, I hope, a major factor in financing this growth," he said.

COURTING CUSTOMERS FROM AFAR

When it comes to calling on customers, Harry Tan and other account personnel in the New York Edge's geographic division are not your typical bank lending officers.

Unlike their colleagues at the CSO who are a walk, subway ride or short plane trip away from customers, Tan and his New York Edge co-workers often provide services from distances of several thousand miles.

Hence the need for ingenuity.

Tan, an assistant cashier in the EMEA division, recently employed the requisite amount of ingenuity—and hustle, legwork and timing—to introduce New York Edge cattle import financing to Iran and identify leads for similar loans well into the future.

Tan's exercise in resourceful banking began earlier this year when he was going over Iran's fifth five-year economic plan and noticed an emphasis on agricultural development.

"I have a friend in the air charter sales department of an air cargo company so I visited him to talk about the movement of agricultural products in and out of Iran," Tan recalled.

"My contact told me there had been numerous airplane loads of cattle shipments to Iran, so I decided to see if there were any opportunities for the New York Edge to become involved by helping the exporters or importers."

Harry then initiated a series of discussions with the bank's representative office in Teheran and with U.S. cattle shippers. He learned that the Iranian government, anxious to spur cattle imports, was subsidizing the air freight costs.

He also learned that there was a three-month gap between delivery and payment because of government paperwork.

With shippers preferring sight payments rather than waiting up to 90 days, Tan felt there was a definite need for bank assistance.

"We proposed that Bank of America New York finance the air freight cost of cattle shipments by lending directly to Iranian importers. The importers would then pay the U.S. exporters at sight and we would be repaid in three months," he said.

Working with the representative office in Teheran, as well as shippers in the Eastern United States in order to learn about prospects, Tan was recently able to conclude six transactions (for two customers).

"There is no doubt that more arrangements will be worked out in the future. Dairy cattle are in increasing demand in Iran, and U.S. shippers, appreciative of the fact that our involvement means quicker payments, are letting us know of orders in which we can participate," Tan noted.

"I'd like to add that James White in the Teheran representative office was extremely helpful. He identified prospects and represented the New York Edge in discussions with Iranian customers.

"Incidentally, he told us that Bank of America New York was the first bank to implement this type of financing, and that the Iranian Government was extremely grateful for our help."

STARTING FROM SCRATCH

"The key to any account relationship is service. We provided more service and better service than our competitors, and, as a consequence, we are now Aranow Corporation's lead bank," said Phil Adams.

Adams, a vice president in the CSO's chemical paper section, was describing a relationship which, in a period of three years, went from dormancy to one marked by a full range of banking services in the United States and Europe.

According to Adams, the Tarrytown, N.Y.–based firm was using several New York banks for lending and foreign exchange services when he was assigned the account in March of 1973. Worse, the company was pleased with the performances of its banks and was not inclined to switch institutions.

This did not, however, deter the aggressive young banker. Adams embarked on an ambitious calling program which has since resulted in the following B of A services for Aranow:

• A revolving credit in conjunction with the Office of Foreign Direct Investment in 1974.

• A domestic line of credit in 1974.

• Off-shore credits under a multicurrency line in 1975.

• Working capital loans to Aranow's European subsidiaries in 1975 and '76.

• Foreign exchange in 1973, '74, '75 and '76.

• Investment of surplus cash into Euro-deposits through the New York Edge in 1974, '75 and '76.

• Bridge loans to consolidate the firm's short-term debt before the signing of two term syndicate loans agented by B of A in 1976.

141

"Winning an account boils down to good service, the first element of which is an ambitious and well-attuned call program," Adams said.

The CSO official visited Aranow's treasurer and other members of the financial management team about twice every 90 days to learn as much as he could about the company. Perceiving a need for foreign exchange information, Phil began calling the treasurer every day to report on currency price changes.

"I eventually provided the company with copies of the New York Edge's foreign exchange printout forms so that my contacts at Aranow could fill in the appropriate blanks with the information I telephoned them each day," he recalled.

Adams added that he also provided information on taxes, collections, exposure planning and related matters—especially during the rapidly fluctuating foreign exchange markets of 1973–74.

"The more I learned about the firm, the better able I was to anticipate its problems and recommend solutions," he said.

One of Phil's more productive fact-finding ventures was a trip he made to Europe in 1974 with Aranow's treasurer.

"I had been planning to call on certain customers in Europe anyway, but I deliberately scheduled my visit to coincide with that of the Aranow officer."

His scheduling flexibility paid off because he was introduced to the management of Aranow's European subsidiaries and was thus able to show how his homework had made him more knowledgeable about the firm's operations than any other banker.

"Our bank became somewhat more identifiable to Aranow's European officers as a result. This directly translated into more European business for us," he said.

Other key components of good banking service, according to Adams, are competitive pricing, knowledge of the full range of the bank's services, an ability and willingness to socialize with business contacts ("I attended the wedding of Aranow's assistant treasurer"), longevity of the officer's tenure with the account and an ability to listen.

"The latter point is very important because there is no limit to what you can learn by listening to customers. I think there's a direct relationship between the ability to listen—as opposed to just hearing—and the quality of the questions you ask."

THE USE OF HUMOR

SEVERAL of the topics listed in the preceding pages are definitely lacking in socko appeal to employees—especially given the alternate uses they can make of their time. Nevertheless, some of the people will read the articles anyway because they recognize the value of such information, even though it may not be easy or enjoyable.

Humor can help. Everyone likes to laugh, and there are few other devices that can generate a warm feeling for a publication as a good chuckle.

This doesn't mean that humor has to be inserted in stories dealing with topics such as earnings, new products, speeches, or departmental shake-ups. But it can be employed in the house organ to very effective use nonetheless.

Two devices employed at *Bank of America News* that went over well during my reign as editor were "candid camera" centerfold spreads and the occasional use of gag answers in multiple-choice quizzes on banking.

For the former vehicle, my staff and I would look at photographs and contact sheets* from the previous year or so and pick the shots for which we could write gag captions. Some of the lines we came up with were only slightly amusing, but the fact that they embellished photographs of people known to most of the readers made them somewhat more entertaining.

For example, there was a picture of one of the bank's top economists giving a luncheon address to a group composed primarily of Japanese bankers. The caption read, "I want to thank all of you for coming to my bar mitzvah."

---

*A contact sheet is a sheet of paper on which all the negatives from a roll of film are shown in their actual size. This enables editors to quickly see what was taken and then make selections.

Another shot showed a man and a woman lying on adjacent tabletops in the company cafeteria as they donated blood during an employee drive. The caption read, "We have to stop meeting like this; I fainted twice yesterday."

Then there was the picture of a senior—and male—officer of the bank sitting at the end of a bench with four females at the annual picnic. One of the women is talking to him. The caption read, "Pardon me, sir, didn't anyone tell you this is the waiting line for the ladies' room?"

We inserted humor in the quizzes because some people are nervous about taking tests, even in the privacy of their home. Additionally, whether they liked the jokes or not, staff members were inclined to read all the questions and answers because they were looking for more attempts at humor. Some examples of punch lines in the quizzes are the following.

The McFadden Act prevents banks from engaging in

A. Investment banking
B. Premarital sex
C. Offshore lending
D. Interstate branching

One privilege extended to foreign banks in this country but not to domestic banks is

A. The ability to accept deposits from subsidiaries of overseas-based corporations

B. The right to engage in mortgage banking
C. The right to have branches in more than one state
D. Permission to be closed on Sophia Loren's birthday

A banker's promissory note is

A. A written promise by an unmarried banker to kiss on the first date
B. A pledge to hold securities in safekeeping for a customer
C. A guarantee to redeem the full value of a municipal bond
D. A promise to pay a specific amount of money to some person at a given time

The reason Bank of America established an office in New York City was to

A. Allow the bank to make loans to corporations based in New York
B. Enlarge the bank's branch network
C. Bring the bank's services and personnel closer to is customers in the eastern United States
D. Increase the bank's chances of getting tickets to New York Ranger hockey games

HOUSE-ORGAN GOALS

DESPITE the fact that some of the items on the previous pages have gotten laughs, there is still considerable debate over the use of humor in company publications. There will always be communicators who question whether premarital sex, ladies' rooms, and Sophia Loren are fitting subjects for house organs—or any other type of internal communications.

On the other hand, most private- and nonprofit-sector managers will agree on the merit of the following goals:

• To keep employees informed about the

organization—its goals, its performance, its products and services, and the external developments influencing its progress.

• To help them to become better workers—by informing them about the company and its industry or sector, by spelling out what desired performances consist of, by showing how their work ties in with that of other departments, and by giving them the information they need to establish career goals.

• To show employees that management cares about communicating with them—by discussing important information regardless of whether it is favorable or negative.

• To convince employees that the organization is a good place to work—and that it is an industry leader or is making progress toward that end, that it has good people, and that it recognizes good people by rewarding them.

FOR FURTHER EXPLORATION

1. Produce a table of contents for an employee annual report.

2. You are director of internal communications for Jones Motor Company. The company announces plans for a new sports car that gets fifty miles to the gallon. Explain how you would handle the news for (a) the house organ; and (b) the management magazine.

3. Read a year-end earnings story in your local paper's financial section. Try to rewrite it for employees of that concern.

4. Explain how you would set up a system that would get major news to each employee (in writing) within an hour.

5. Give reasons for and against having departmental publications.

14

PRODUCING A HOUSE ORGAN

SINCE so many newcomers to public relations will spend a portion of their formative years working on a private- or public-sector house organ, a chapter on the preparation of such vehicles is necessary.

So, too, are some words on why neophytes should take a house organ starting assignment over another entry-level position—salary and personality of bosses at both opportunities being equal.

The major reason is that house organ work exposes practitioners to every phase of the organization and allows them to employ a variety of editorial skills. Second, since most of the readership is in-house, an editor is more willing to let a newcomer flap his or her wings than would be a news bureau manager or head of the speech-writing department.

Third, house organ personnel get to build up scrapbooks of articles and photographs. If they can't put their experience to better use at their current places of employment, they at least have clippings to show potential employers. An absence of something to put into a scrapbook can have a deleterious effect on job hunting.

WHAT GOES INTO A HOUSE ORGAN

THERE are three categories of copy that fill the pages of internal publications. They are

• News stories

• Feature stories

• Items of record such as promotions, deaths, retirements, and classified ads

Let us pretend we work for the house organ of the Jones Motor Company, the enlightened automobile manufacturer we discussed in chapter three. The following would be typical items in the three categories just mentioned.

News stories

• Jones Motor Company's inauguration of a job training program

• The granting of a $250,000 gift by Jones' philanthropic unit

• The naming of two new executive vice-presidents

• The addition of six new exterior colors to next year's line

• Jones soccer team's clinching of first place in the industrial league

• Jones president's joining a team of in-house economists to study car-buying habits in Europe

• The introduction of a U.S. Senate bill calling for better mileage

Feature stories

• An explanation of how the purchasing department works

• A staff member who trains professional boxers in his spare time

• Five staff members who have learned sign language to communicate over noise on the production line

Items of record

• Promotions

• Obituaries

• Classified ads

• Retirements

• Inquiring photographer

• Employee club news

NOW that we have an idea of the kind of copy that will go into our sixteen-page, 8½-by-11-inch monthly magazine, let us plan and produce an issue.

The first step is setting deadlines.

It is mandatory that deadlines be set so that staff members know when stories and photos are due and the date beyond which nothing short of a super-major story will be accepted. Staffers have to be reminded continually of the importance of deadlines, because failure to meet them not only gets the current issue off to a bad start, it puts ensuing publications off schedule, too. If the deadline misses are numerous and long enough, it could be months before the schedule gets back on the right track.

Assuming that the first of the month falls on a Monday and that delivery of the publication is due around the thirtieth, a schedule for a monthly publication could look like this:

for the next month's issue can be doled out on the fifteenth, and news and photo gathering can begin very shortly thereafter—like five minutes later.

It is also worth noting that there is some "fat" built into the schedule to allow for excessive changes, last-minute cancellation of stories, or stop-the-presses additions to the final product.

For example, look at the scheduling for the page proofs. According to the agenda, the page proofs arrive on the seventeenth, are read, and are returned the next day. But they can just as easily go back to the printer on the same day, assuming that the printer delivers them before lunch. And if there isn't an excessive amount of changes, deletions, or additions, there won't be any need for second page proofs. The editor can ask that the printer take the corrected first page proofs and go right into blueprint.

Copy to editor	Fri., Oct. 5
Copy to printer	Mon. and Tues., Oct. 8–9
Galleys to editor	Wed., Oct. 10
Proofread galleys to printer	Thurs., Oct. 11
Corrected galleys to editor	Fri., Oct. 12
Do makeup and send to printer	Mon., Oct. 15
Page proofs to editor	Wed., Oct. 17
Proofread pages to printer	Thurs., Oct. 18
Second page proofs to editor	Fr., Oct. 19
Proofread second page proofs to printer	Mon., Oct. 22
Blueprint to editor	Wed., Oct. 24
Okay	Thurs., Oct. 25
Delivery	Mon., Oct. 29

Some people may scan this schedule and conclude that with delivery falling on the twenty-ninth or thereabouts and copy for the next issue due to the editor around the fifth of the following month, that only leaves one week for news gathering and writing.

They would be wrong.

Once the pages are laid out on makeup day, the remaining activities rarely consume more than half a day's time. Story assignments

KEEPING PEOPLE ON SCHEDULE

One very effective method is to let all staff members know that the ability to meet deadlines will be an important factor in their annual reviews. This must be done because regardless of individuals' ability as internal communicators, failure to stay on schedule for a monthly publication renders them of little use.

On the other hand, one can't always blame

the staff for the delays. There are occasions when production is slowed or even reversed by an edict from someone other than the editor or assistant editor.

Let's face it; as powerful as editors like to think they are, they don't have complete control over their printed "babies." Those who work out of a head office location generally report to a director of public relations, who, in turn, is a subordinate of the director of corporate communications or director of external relations—or someone with a similar title. These officers can and often do exercise the powers that go with their titles by suggesting new stories and asking (they're not really asking, they're telling!) that others be deleted.

They don't do it to flaunt their power; they do it because they are often privy to information not known to editors, and this information strongly suggests that changes be made in the plans for an upcoming issue.

There is, fortunately, a way to minimize the disturbing effects of their editorial control. Simply stated, it is keeping PR executives informed of what you are doing so that their suggested changes will come early rather than late in the production cycle.

Many organizations have adopted the idea of having editors distribute a story list and a page-one memorandum to their superiors before copy goes to the printer. The story list itemizes the articles that are to appear, and the page-one memo spells out what will be the lead text and photographs.

If the higher echelons object to what is included in either of these two memos, their opinions can be voiced long before changes become difficult to make. It is considerably easier to kill a page-one story when it is merely in the planning stages than when the blueprint is being approved.

It is also much cheaper.

ASSIGNING THE STORIES

Handing out assignments is usually done shortly after deadlines are set, although it can just as easily be accomplished prior to placing a schedule on paper.

In either event, it is a formidable task because, no matter what, the issue must be filled with some combination of text and artwork. Despite editors' wishes to the contrary, there are times when too few things are happening that are worth including in the house organs.

There are several things to do when story ideas are scarce. They include the following.

1. Look at past issues for the same month—There are numerous events at an organization that tend to take place the same time each year. Editors who are working on the September issue would be wise to review the previous three or four September publications. They might be reminded that these magazines all covered the annual blood and school registration drives. That adds up to two good story ideas.

2. Consult with the news bureau manager—News bureau managers should be good sources of ideas because they and their staffs have a rough idea of what press releases will be written over the next several weeks. Each release is a potential house-organ story.

3. Check the calendars of the senior officers—Names make news, and the senior officers are the biggest names in the organization. A perusal of their calendars could uncover important and/or interesting events.

4. Check the print and electronic media—Surely there are emerging issues in the automobile industry that are attracting press attention. These issues should be of interest to readers of the Jones Motor Company house-organ editor mentioned earlier because it is reasonable to assume that staff members will be asked about them. The editor should monitor the media—including the automobile trade press—and feel free to lift an idea or two.

5. Check other house organs—It is perfectly all right to entertain larcenous thoughts when reading other house organs. And it is easy to acquire the other house organs to look for interesting ideas. Simply write to the head of internal communication at concerns of your choice and ask to be placed on the mailing list for the employee publication.

I don't endorse a word-for-word pilfering of copy, but a study of what other editors are doing should trigger some layout, story, and feature ideas.

6. *Touch base with the personnel department*—This is where discussions about benefits, salaries, and related items originate. Editors normally hope that personnel operatives would be trained to notify internal communicators when changes in policy are made, but quite often the coordination gets lost between the cracks. The best protection against missing a major news story is to call the personnel department periodically to find out what is new.

7. *Keep a list of which departments are covered in each issue*—It is a good idea to have a chart with the names of each department listed vertically on the left-hand side and the names of each month across the top of the paper. Any time there is a story about a particular department, a check is placed in the appropriate box. An editor can look for large blocks of white space to determine which departments are overdue for some coverage. There may not be a lot of news on the surface at some of these units, but an hour of determined digging should uncover something worth writing about or photographing.

8. *Maintain contact with officers of the employee club*—This club is a source of information on athletic teams, parties, special trips, and discounts on a variety of purchases. Since these are topics of considerable interest to many employees, an editor should be able to tap this source for at least a story or two each issue.

9. *Encourage staff members to suggest stories*—A good way to do this is to give the "suggestor" a plug at the end of the article. Editors will use italic type at the bottom of the story to state, "This article was the result of a news tip by__."

Okay, the planning is behind us, stories have been assigned, and ample time remains before the crucial deadline days arrive. Let's look at the actual "action" steps in house-organ production.

WRITING

Gathering and writing news are probably the easiest tasks if the reporters are professionals. They know how to obtain data, evaluate it, and shape it into acceptable prose—and they should, if the schedule is organized well, have sufficient time to do all of the above properly.

They must, however, remember for whom they are working. They are not employees of a daily newspaper, investigative magazine, or any other outside publication. They work for a company house organ, so it is the company and not the general public that gets their loyalty. And it is the company that must be pleased. A picture of the chairman stepping out of a night club with an attractive starlet on his arm may make for entertaining journalism, but it doesn't belong in an internal publication. Nor does belligerent speculation on why earnings are down. House organ personnel must accept the fact that the only material that can be included in their publication is material management would want its employees to see. Everything else is verboten.

Since house organs are aimed at nonofficials more than at officers, editorial staffers must also approach each assignment from the viewpoint of the typical clerical employee. Two questions they should ask themselves in tackling subject matter are, What would the average staff member want to know about the topic? and What would management want them to know in order to become better informed and more productive?

EDITING

As stated earlier, the most intense editing should take place prior to sending copy to the printer. It costs nothing to make changes at this point—and the editor is seeing copy fresh, when it is generally easier to spot mistakes.

He or she should therefore review copy carefully to assure that it conforms to the publication's style, that it is correct, and that it is well written.

One way to protect against factual errors is to have the stories read by the people who supplied the information (and if any of them are not officers, get their department heads to look at the copy, too). The source and/or the department head should not read text in order to approve the way it is handled but, rather, to make sure there are no misrepresentation of facts.

GETTING PICTURES

House organ editors have two serious problems regarding photographs. First, they are too often given shots of three or four people seated around a table looking at some papers. Second, most of the individual shots they have of people are formal portraits taken from the same angle and showing the same amount of body (from the middle of the chest up).

How does one make these pictures interesting? The answer can be given in one word: variety.

Let's take the grouping of four people around a table. To repeat a comment made in chapter three, there is no need to have each of the quartet (or trio or quintet) shown full-face; profiles are refreshing changes. So have the photographer stand off to one side. Or let him or her stand on a chair and shoot down. Or kneel and shoot up. Or stand very close to the subjects—or far away.

As for the head shots, get rid of the formal portraits when possible. Photograph individuals talking on the phone, chatting with a colleague, reading a report, entering an office, typing, and so on. They don't spend their working days staring at a camera, so they shouldn't always appear that way in the company magazine.

If the subject works in another city and it's the formal portrait he or she sent you or nothing, rely on unusual cropping to draw attention to the shot. No laws will be broken if the top of his tie or her full head of wavy hair is not shown. Crop it close, from chin to hairline. Or narrow, from ear to ear. Or from afar so that we get a look at the person's waistline.

(There will, no doubt, be skeptics among the readership who will point out that the subject who has part of his chest, hair, or ears lopped off will object to the liberties taken with his $40 portrait. They are correct to an extent; not everyone will be annoyed, but some definitely take umbrage. My response to this is, What is worse; getting one person slightly disenchanted with the way his or her photo appears or boring thousands of readers with the same head shots issue after issue?)

DOING MAKEUP

After the galleys (long sheets of type) are edited, you are ready to do makeup. All you need are two clean sets of galleys, page blanks, the glossy photographs, time, imagination, and office supplies such as a ruler, grease pencil, scissors and rubber cement.

Two sets of galleys are needed because one is cut into separate stories and captions and the other is reserved for making changes for the printer.

Why glossy photographs instead of pictures that have already been sized and reproduced? Because we haven't sent them to the printer yet—and for a very good reason.

This is a critical point. Many editors forward their photographs to the printer as soon as they get them, but I think this is a mistake. Once the printer has them and engravings are made, the editor is stuck with a particular size unless he or she wants to go to the expense of having a new cut made.

I prefer to wait until I am doing makeup before I crop (determine the size of) the photos, because this gives me flexibility—which is the key to successful layout. If there isn't much copy on the page, I will crop the photos to appear long. If I have a lot of text, I will opt for horizontal shapes, which take less space.

Some people claim that this results in inferior photographs, but I disagree. Take a look at your local newspaper and pick any ten photos at random. Ask yourself if it would make a terrible difference in the effectiveness of each one if the pictures were lengthened or shortened by half an inch. Chances are it would make no difference at all.

But it could mean that copy doesn't have to be altered—at the company's expense—to make room for a picture that has already been sized. It is much better to play around with the measurements of a photograph—which doesn't cost you anything, since the "playing around" takes place in your office—until you find a layout that allows you to use the picture effectively and run the copy as is.

The first thing we do in laying out the magazine or newspaper is have the galleys cut up so that each story and caption is a separate item.

Second, we take the rough outline of the publication we adroitly prepared while we were getting copy ready for the printer. This is an outline all smart editors have—initially in their head and then on paper—which tells them which items are tentatively planned for which pages.

Third, we roll up our sleeves and actually do some layout work.

Let's begin with page 1 (or, in the case of a magazine, our first news page). We take the copy we identified as our lead items and start putting it on the blank page. First in one corner, then in another, and maybe then in the middle of the page. We keep moving the copy around until we are satisfied that we've hit upon a design we like. Then we add the other copy, leaving space for photos. (We originally had a rough idea in our head whether we wanted the pictures to be one-half, one-, two-, or three-columns wide, and we have left space accordingly.)

In the best of all possible worlds, each picture fits easily into the space that has been left for it, and no alterations need be made on the copy or layout. More often than not, that is exactly how it works out because most horizontals can fit into most horizontal openings—and ditto for vertical pictures and vertical holes.

In order to get a picture to fit exactly into the space that has been left for it, one uses a cropping wheel (see figure below).

A word about the cropping—or proportional-scale—wheel. This is a near-magical device that makes layout a tremendously enjoyable endeavor, not unlike playing with a puzzle. Basically, the wheel works on ratios, indicating, for example, that if a six-inch-wide photograph is to appear in a three-inch-wide hole, five inches of vertical space in the picture will occupy two and a half inches of space on the page.

Or let's pretend that we have left space for a two-column horizontal picture that will run 4 inches deep—and that two-column pictures are 4⅞ inches wide. We look at the picture, which measures 8 by 10 inches in its glossy form, and decide that we only need 7 inches of its width because the remaining 3 inches show unnecessary background. So we take the cropping wheel and put the 7″ line (A) from the inner circle (representing the 7 inches from the glossy) on the 4⅞″ line (B) on the outer wheel (representing the size we want the picture to be.) Then we look at the 4″ mark (C) on the outer circle (showing the size we want the picture to be) and see what the matching figure is on the inner circle. It is 5¾″ (D) which is the vertical space we'll include from the glossy.

In other words, we are saying that 7-inches

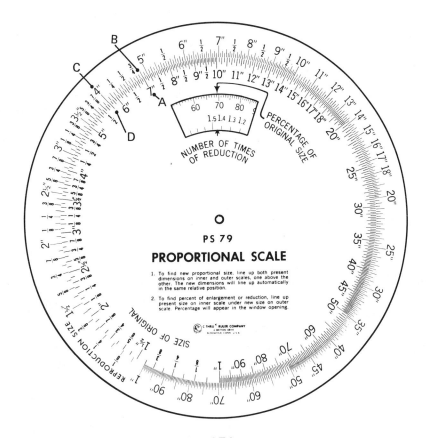

is to 4⅞ inches as 5¾ inches is to 4 inches.

We then look at the glossy to make sure that by using 5¾ inches we aren't cutting any important features out of the shot (such as someone's head). If everything that should be within the 5¾ inches is included, we are in good shape. If not, it's back to the drawing board. We would probably consider using 8 or 9 inches of the width so that the corresponding vertical figure would include more of the shot.

We can also remove some copy to let the picture be more vertical.

Or we can do another layout.

As editors become more experienced in doing makeup, they become better able to tell at a quick glance whether a picture will fit in a given layout or not. They may have to make some minor adjustments to get the picture cropped exactly as they want, but the overall task of getting a fit can be achieved.

In conclusion, each page is laid out in the same manner:

1. Place the copy down on the page.
2. Crop the photographs to fill the holes.
3. Make cropping or copy adjustments if necessary.

The critical thing to remember when doing layout is to give yourself as much flexibility as possible. There are three things on almost every page that can be either enlarged or condensed to give you makeup options:

• Copy

• Captions

• Photographs

As long as you are able to change the size of any or all of these elements, you can solve any makeup problem—and have fun doing it.

Another thing to remember is that you have options as to the number of columns to be used for a given piece of copy. Take a look at page 1 of *The New York Times*—or any other newspaper. Even though the copy is set one-column wide, some articles will appear under headlines that are two- or three-columns wide. This gives editors considerable flexibility in preventing each page from looking alike. The number of possible layouts is staggering.

It is because one is presented with so many choices that layout is considered an enjoyable activity by most internal communicators. They know that if their first idea doesn't work, there are countless other routes to aesthetic satisfaction.

Keeping one's options open is, therefore, the first goal of makeup. Other goals and rules that may also be of use to fledgling editors are the following.

1. Don't use too many typefaces—Being presented with a multitude of typefaces can make readers think they are looking at a jigsaw puzzle.

2. Don't change the look of the publication too often—Studies have shown that people feel more comfortable with the familiar than with the unfamiliar. Publications that are constantly changing their formats, typefaces, and makeup philosophies are constantly different to their audiences and unlikely to develop reader loyalty. People like it when they can recognize a publication without having to see its masthead.

If you are going to make a change—and there is nothing wrong with an alteration at one time or another—plan very carefully so that you will be well satisfied with the result, because the new look should be around long enough to become the old, familiar look.

3. Vary picture sizes—The only times you should have pictures of the same size are when you are cropping portraits for a yearbook or compiling a family photo album. Repetition in photo size in magazines or newspapers makes for an exceedingly dull appearance.

Pictures aren't alike in terms of visual appeal or importance; they don't have to be alike in size.

4. Put your most important copy or artwork in the upper outside corners—This isn't something that must be done on every page but people are in the habit of looking at the upper outside corner first, and editors must accept this fact.

5. Avoid bumping heads—This is sometimes hard to do at the top of a news page. Three ways to minimize the aesthetic damage when it is unavoidable to have bumping heads are to (a) use white space between columns—about two picas;

(b) use varying typefaces and sizes (italics, bold, condensed, and so on) within the same family of type; (c) put a box around one of the heads.

6. Don't be too gimmicky—The text and photographs are what readers should be concentrating on, not on an overly generous employment of cut-out designs, unusual typefaces, or photography tricks. Good layout should make the page or spread more attractive, but it should not play a starring role—only a supporting one.

Besides, the use of too many gimmicks isn't visually appealing. It's confusing.

7. Use subheads for long stories—Large chunks of copy not only look uninviting, they make for a waste of editors' time and efforts, because readers tend to focus on something else.

Generally speaking, an eighteen-paragraph story should have two subheads.

Don't however, put the subheads in the text before doing makeup, because you may end up with the subhead as the final line in one column or the top line in the next. That looks unprofessional. Wait until the copy has been laid out before deciding where breaks in the text would be most appropriate.

8. Don't lay out pages as separate items—With the exception of the first and the last, each page in a newspaper or magazine faces another. Make sure that you examine how they look together before sending them to the printer. Facing pages must be treated as one visual unit.

9. Don't be afraid of white space—Some editors feel white space is an admission of failure in terms of their ability to fill a publication. They are wrong. White space—especially in feature pages—is an aid and abetment to a visually attractive layout.

HEADLINES

A good headline induces people to look at a story; a bad one turns them off. There is room for humor, emotion, cleverness, and other gambits, but above all else, the head should tell readers what the story is about.

Editors should also try to have the headlines flush left and flush right in the space allotted to them. (*Flush left and flush right* means that the headline begins at the start of the left-hand column and concludes at the far right of the last column in which it appears.) It is not a must, but filling the space looks better than not filling the space. (If, however, you come up with a brilliant head, but it is not wide enough, you can either increase the type size or center the head.)

Humor is strongly recommended for feature-story heads, and anything that attracts attention without violating good taste is helpful for serious news stories, too. For example, take a look at this classic *New York Daily News* headline announcing the fifth marriage of the well-known, and short, Mickey Rooney:

Half-Pint Rooney
Takes a Fifth

In writing headlines, editors should know how many units are required to fill columns in each type size and what the counts are for each letter. There are some exceptions because of unusual typefaces, but, generally speaking, all lowercase letters count as one except for *m* and *w*, which count as one and a half, and *i, l, t, f, and j,* which count as one-half. All capital letters are one and a half, except *M* and *W*, which are two, and *I*, which is one. Some printers count punctuations and spaces between words as one, others as one-half.

A key aid in writing headlines to fit well is a thesaurus—or a fantastic vocabulary. If, as an example, "Johnson Appointed New Chairman" is too wide, try "Johnson Named New Chairman."

If

Six-Game Win Streak
Lifts Boosters to Second

is too narrow, try

Six-Game Victory Streak
Moves Soccer Team to Second

Some other suggestions about headlines are

• Use the present or future tense; avoid past-tense verbiage.

• Strive for active verbs.

- Don't break a line with a preposition.
- Use alliteration when possible.
- Use rhyming when possible.

Make sure, however, that the head relates to the heart of the story. There are headline writers who will focus on the last paragraph or two because they were the source of a clever idea, but a head zeroing in on a minor part of the story only confuses and annoys readers.

REVIEW

There are at least two times to review a house organ that has already been distributed to employees: immediately after delivery when the stories are fresh in the staff's minds and six months later, when you can give it a second look and benefit from hindsight.

The latter review can be a painful exercise because it often enables people to see things they missed in the heat of battle. Rueful "how could I have missed that" laments are a frequent by-product of such endeavors.

Regardless of the discomfort and frustration that accompany a review session, the critique is necessary if the editor wants better house organs in the future. Looking at a finished product and seeing how poor news judgment, amateurish makeup, less than Pulitzer Prize–winning writing, and boring photography impair the overall effect produces "I'll never do it again" vows, which make for improved publications in the future.

COMMON HOUSE-ORGAN PITFALLS

1. Too officer-oriented—Editors have to be reminded that even though officers generally have more interesting jobs than nonofficials—and are more likely to be engaged in newsworthy extracurricular activities—they are greatly outnumbered by the nonofficials. Too many stories about the officers will get a large number of the readers feeling that the publication isn't for them.

2. Too nonofficial oriented—This is what occasionally happens after editors or their bosses perceive a disenchantment with the abundance of officer coverage. Going too far to the other extreme can have the same kind of negative effect on reader interest. Even though there are more nonofficials than officials, employees in the former category aren't well known to a majority of the staff. A feature on the secretary in the purchasing department who works for the Red Cross on weekends could be of interest only to her close friends and some purchasing department personnel. Too many of these articles generate boredom.

3. Not enough information on negative issues—There are management teams who look upon the house organ as a morale builder. Developing team spirit and enthusiasm aren't bad goals to strive for, but they shouldn't be the sole *raison d'être* of a publication. If there is bad news about the organization or the field in which it operates, editors should tell it like it is. As we've discussed before, employees should be armed with the facts to defend the company position. More important, they should know all the important developments taking place around them, because this knowledge can make them better workers.

4. No attempt to show how departments interrelate—This is a serious no-no in large organizations, where many people know little about their employer save what goes on in their own department. They must be given the total picture so that they can develop a better understanding of their own role and shape realistic career plans.

5. Too inexpensive vis-à-vis other publications—It is very hard to convince employees that management cares about them when it spends small fortunes to communicate with shareholders, educators, government officials, and customers and next to nothing to communicate with the staff. Consistency is required. If an organization goes first-class on its annual report, the house organ should be given the same level of professionalism.

6. *Too head office oriented*—It is very easy to fall into the trap of heavily focusing on head office activities if that is where senior management and the internal communications staff are located. It takes a conscious effort to convince employees in the field that it is their publication too. All things being equal, the event away from headquarters has to be given occasional precedence over the happening at head office.

7. *Not much news*—This is what usually happens when house organs are understaffed or the editor is asked to take on too many additional responsibilities. Quality, of course, suffers, and one indication that the publication is going downhill is an overabundance of filler items. They're easy to spot. There are press releases from community organizations that are printed almost word for word. There are three pictures of an individual to embellish a profile that warrants only one. There is a shot or two of the president of the organization shaking the hand of one of the many important visitors he or she entertains. And too many stories occupy twice the space they deserve.

8. *Postage-stamp-size pictures*—I had a boss who would get on me every now and then when he felt I was cropping pictures too small. "You're running postage stamps," he would sneer, adding that bigger pictures always look better than smaller ones.

I remember a tongue-lashing I got from him when I ran a picture of a bank robber leaving a branch as a teller from behind the counter pointed at him and yelled; "Stop that man!" The teller's cry worked, because the robber was apprehended by the bank guard and a policeman half a block away.

In any event, I used the pictures across two of the five columns on page 1. This made my boss livid. "You have the best action shot in the history of the bank, and it's lost on the page. That picture should have run three, if not four columns. Don't you know that a large picture always looks more exciting than a small one?" he asked.

He was right. Four issues later, I had a picture of a construction worker standing on the forty-story-high beams of our new operations building. I ran it three columns wide and 5 inches deep on page 1 and got a lot of favorable oohs and ahhs.

In short, a good picture looks even better when it is large. Postage-stamp-size pictures look poor to mediocre because one can barely make out the faces, especially if they are group shots.

However . . .

There are exceptions to every rule, and it is, indeed, all right to run a lot of smaller pictures under certain circumstances. One of the best picture stories I ever produced, if I say so myself, was a cover and centerfold spread on a bank picnic I attended. There was a montage of seven pictures on the cover and fourteen in the spread, which, when you're talking about pages that measure only 8½ by 11 inches, makes for a lot of photographs in little space.

But it went over very well. One reason was that the pictures my photographer and I took were good action shots or clever candid portraits of cute children.

The second reason was at least as important. About six hundred people saw my photographer and me take some three-hundred pictures between us. They knew what we were snapping away for, so they immediately turned to the picnic-related pages when the magazine came out to see if they, a relative, or close friend were among those whose likenesses appeared. Had we run six large, attractive shots in the centerfold and two or three good ones on the cover—instead of the twenty-one we did use—it would have made for a lot of disappointed people.

On another occasion, I gave my photographer a break at a bank's annual cocktail party and proceeded to take about twenty or thirty pictures. One of the bank's messengers saw me and asked if I would photograph the group he happened to be eating with. I acquiesced and told the messenger and his cronies not to look at me, but rather to pretend I wasn't there and chat amiably. I then took six shots of the group, none of which was usable because at least half of the people were smiling into the camera on each picture.

The issue came out and got rave reviews because there were some innovative features in it, but the messenger was not among the publication's fans. He stopped me in the hallway a few days after the distribution date and said, "Gee, Mr. Cole, we were awfully disappointed that you didn't use the picture you took of my friends and me. One of the guys retired from the bank the following week, and it would have been nice to have the picture in the magazine."

I thought to myself that even though the issue was the best one we had produced up to that time, as far as the messenger and his three cronies were concerned, it was a failure. This is a good reason why it sometimes pays to squeeze a few more pictures into a spread—assuming they are good.

9. *Lack of originality in pictures*—One of my all-time-favorite examples of poor editing was a house organ from an organization that shall remain nameless, in which a two-page spread on an awards dinner appeared. The spread consisted of ten pictures, each one showing the president, second from the left, and three award winners smiling into the camera and shown from the waist up. The president had the same idiotic grin in each shot—which each looked identical anyway—and the whole spread was ridiculous.

10. *Overly obvious attempts at minority representation*—Some publications read as if the editor has decided that since 10 percent of the staff is over fifty-five, 20 percent is black, 55 percent is female, 5 percent is handicapped, and so on, the coverage of these groups in each issue should be proportional to their numbers. That's nonsense.

Editors *should* be aware of the minority representation at their organization and try to maintain some semblance of balance throughout the year. But they shouldn't try to touch all bases in every issue just for the sake of satisfying each group. Bending over backward to give different components of the staff coverage is obvious, it's insulting, and it prevents timely news stories from receiving the coverage they deserve.

If news developments are such that 90 percent of the space in one issue will go to whites, blacks, youths, the elderly, the handicapped, or whatever, so be it. Try harder to make up for the imbalance in the ensuing issues but don't suspend news judgment. The chances are the numbers will balance out by the end of the year.

11. *Too many cooks spoiling the broth*—Editors with too many people looking over their shoulders often find themselves making an indecent number of changes *after* copy is at the printer and pages are laid out. The result is unnecessary printing costs and lateness, thus pushing the subsequent issues off schedule. Worse, over-editing by too many superiors sometimes induces editors to suspend their editorial judgment by adopting an "I'll do anything you say in order to get your final okay" attitude.

FOR FURTHER EXPLORATION

1. Get five issues of your company's—or any company's—house organ. Critique them.

2. You are editor of a hospital house organ. Produce a list of ten feature-story ideas.

3. You are an editor sending a photographer on a picture-taking assignment. He's to get enough shots for a centerfold spread on the preparations for the annual meeting. What shots do you tell him to get?

4. You are the editor of an oil company's house organ. You have two assistants: an experienced veteran and a newcomer with no professional experience. What assignments would you initially give the new assistant?

5. Get a copy of a tabloid house organ. Pretend you are the editor and your boss told you to kill the lead article. Using copy from elsewhere in the paper—and bigger pictures—fix the first page.

15

SPEECH WRITING

THE speech-writing process—which includes finding appropriate platforms; gathering information; working with senior management; putting coherent, persuasive thoughts on paper; and coordinating follow-up promotional activities—is one of the most important public relations functions.

It's important for three reasons.

1. Speeches are almost always written for senior, as opposed to junior, executives. By definition, anything the PR department produces for senior management takes on added significance.

2. The speeches are given to important audiences; otherwise they would not be worth the senior executives' time.

3. There are really four audiences for every speech.

   a. The audience that hears it.

   b. Friends and business acquaintances of the above. It is safe to assume that if the members of the initial audience are influential men and women, they travel in circles abounding in other equally potent individuals. If the speech impresses audience number one, it is probable that the members of this group will share their reactions over luncheon dates, cocktail parties, and business meetings during the next several weeks and beyond.

   c. The audience PR people reach through the media. It is generally normal procedure for the news relations personnel to prepare a press release on the speech and send it to the media, along with a copy of the talk, for release after the speech is given.

   d. Any other constituencies the organization wants to reach. All it has to do is put the speech in pamphlet form—or on plain 8½-by-11-inch paper if the budget so dictates—and disseminate it. The reproduced version can go to shareholders, employees, government officials, customers, and so on, the sky or budgetary considerations being the limit.

BEFORE THE SPEECH

DECIDING WHAT WILL BE SAID

Most of the steps in speech production are fairly standard in that they follow the tried and true procedures of corporate- and nonprofit-sector wordsmiths of the past. Yes, there are variations in the skill one brings to the various chores, but the tactics followed in doing research, producing an outline, writing the speech, and then clearing it do not differ too drastically from organization to organization.

The same cannot be said for determining the basic thrust of the speech. This endeavor tends to be individualized, occasionally unscientific—or seat of the pants, if you will—and often influenced by factors over which the speaker and the writer have no control. For example, a political event can eliminate problems the speaker planned to solve orally, or it can create new difficulties that overshadow previous woes. Or worse, an officer of a rival concern gives a speech on the same topic two days earlier—and his or her speech has a better solution than yours.

There being no universally accepted methods of picking topics and deciding how they are to be handled, I can only offer suggestions that, hopefully, will make the task of writing easier.

First, it's important to know what kind of speech you would like to have presented to the audience in question. The talk's purpose could be

• To inform

• To entertain

• To inspire

• To convince or persuade

158

Second, it's wise to select a topic with which the speaker is familiar and comfortable. The danger of ignoring this rule is that no one will care what speakers have to say outside their area of expertise.

Picking timely subjects is part of the planning process, perhaps the easiest part. All it takes is an awareness of what is going on in the speaker's subject area and who is saying what.

A handful of questions can facilitate the thought-generation process.

• What are city, state, federal, or foreign governments doing to make our jobs easier or more difficult?

• What impact are technological developments having on our field?

• What impact will technological developments have on our field in the future?

• Are there any societal problems that our organization can alleviate—or is alleviating?

• What are our major external and business-related problems?

• What internal problems are we coping with that are shared by other concerns?

• What interesting trends are taking place—or will take place—in our field?

• Do we have any predictions for the future worth sharing with an audience?

• Are there any public misconceptions about us that need clearing up?

LEARNING ABOUT THE AUDIENCE

It is obvious that your company's president should not impart the same information—or employ the same approach—to an audience of stock analysts as he does to an assemblage of grade-school children. In order to avoid speaking over or under an audience's collective head, it is necessary to ask the following questions before—not after, but before—any thought is given to the message that is ultimately to be conveyed.

• How many people will be in the audience?

• Who will be in the audience?

• What do they know about the subject?

• What do they know about the speaker?

• Will it be a hostile, supportive, or neutral audience?

• Why is the audience there?

• How do they feel about the subject?

There are also some queries that should be raised about the event itself.

• What is the purpose of the event?

• Why did the organizers ask our (chief executive officer, executive vice-president, senior vice-president, or whoever) to speak?

• Where will the event be held and what will the physical arrangements be like?

• Will there be a question-and-answer period following the formal presentation?

• Who were the speakers at the event over the past five years?

• Will there be other speakers on the program?

• Who will introduce the speaker?

• Should we expect hecklers and, if so, inside the building or outside?

• Will the press be invited? If not, can we invite some journalists?

One question should be vibrating through each reader's mind at this point: Where does one go for the responses to the above queries? The answer is to the person handling the public relations for the event.

With the exception of the speaker, the speech writer, and possibly their spouses and immediate families, there are very few individuals more desirous of making the affair a resounding success than the person charged with handling the attendant public relations duties. He or she will therefore be eager to answer questions and happy to expend time in digging up additional data.

DOING PROPER RESEARCH

Research is the most important element in the speech-writing process. Facts must be marshalled to support contentions. The quality, quantity, and, above all, accuracy and timeliness of those facts—or the absence of data that should be included in any meaningful discussion of the subject at hand—are crucial make-or-break ingredients in the speech-preparation mix. Readers are advised to review the text on pages 10–12 and apply it to the preparatory work for speech writing.

One other caveat about research is don't—ever!—consider the fact-finding function completed when the information is at hand and an outline is starting to take shape. If the subject has any relevance—and it should—it is a fluid one that is constantly subject to change as new facts and figures emerge. Giving a speech on June 30 based on research that ended June 15 can be a source of embarrassment and possible humiliation to the person at the podium.

This thought applies to talks about historical subjects as well, because new information may have been found the day before the speech was to be delivered. Or some current event may prove useful in linking the topic to the present.

OUTLINING THE SPEECH

THE three main components of a speech are its introduction, the main body, and the conclusion. There are some who believe that the introduction should tell the audience what will be said, the body of the speech should say it, and the conclusion should tell the audience what was just said. This is an oversimplification, but it is not really too far off the mark.

THE INTRODUCTION

Of the three components, the introduction is the most versatile in terms of function. Its major purpose, of course, is to set the stage for the body of the speech, but there are a few preliminaries that must be taken care of before setting the stage for what is to follow.

First, is the acknowledgment of the host's introduction of the speaker. This may sound overly basic, but some speakers are so nervous, rehearsing up to the second they approach the microphone, that they pay no attention whatsoever to this personal introduction. This is a mistake. If the host's introduction is humorous, the speaker is given a good opportunity to build on the levity and have a pleased and attentive audience by the time he or she is warmed up.

It is also a good idea for speakers to learn about the individuals who will be presenting them to the audience. The biographical data could serve as ammunition for either a witty or a sincerely appreciative retort, whichever is required.

Equally obvious is the need for the speaker to recognize the individuals on the dais and/or the senior officers of the hosting organization.

No speech has ever been made either more or less memorable by the eloquence—or lack of eloquence—of the acknowledgments, but people expect them. To omit this detail would have the audience wondering why instead of concentrating on the ensuing oratory.

After responding to the introduction (if a response is necessary) and observing the formalities, the speaker should use the remaining portion of his or her introductory remarks to gain favorable attention, promote goodwill, win respect, and lead into the heart of the speech.

At this juncture some readers may well exclaim, "Gain favorable attention, promote goodwill, and win respect!!? That could take hours to accomplish. How does Cole figure to do it in three to five minutes?"

It's pretty easy. Don't forget, most of the audience knows in advance who the main speaker will be. It's not likely they would have shown up if they didn't have some interest in hearing what the man or woman had to say. And it is reasonable to assume that the individual making the personal introduction will sprinkle it with some words of praise.

Granted, these compliments may be exaggerations, marked by highly selective editing of the guest of honor's curriculum vitae, or reminiscent of great works of fiction. The point is that the speaker is presented in an extremely favorable light and it is a question of "he's impressive until he proves otherwise."

The speaker, therefore, doesn't have to try too hard to get favorable attention, promote goodwill, and win respect. He or she merely has to maintain the friendly and supportive mood that has already been created.

So how is it done?

Favorable attention and goodwill can be maintained by showing how the speaker is linked to the audience. Successfully tested methods include a discussion of past experiences in the host city or in the industry represented by most of the audience; a few sentences about how a current problem is putting everyone present in the same boat and a minute or two on how the speaker and audience share similar views.

Humor is another effective device—provided the speaker feels comfortable with it. Too many speakers feel it is obligatory to initiate an address with a joke or funny anecdote, only to lose their audience because their comic delivery and timing are poor.

If, however, the speaker is an adroit joke teller and the situation warrants it (that is, don't go for laughs at a funeral), by all means use humor.

It is not at all difficult—in fact it is quite simple—to take most jokes and apply them to the chosen topic. And there are scores of amusing stories directly related to the speech-giving process.

For example:

Before I begin, I have to tell you how I became the speaker this afternoon.

I was minding my own business in my office last month, when I received a phone call from (head of the hosting organization).

We exchanged pleasantries, and then he suddenly asked me how I felt about free speech.

"Why, I'm very much in favor of it," I responded.

"Great," he said, "you're giving one next month."*

Or:

This Roman gladiator was thrust into the arena to do battle with a particularly vi-

cious lion, one that had an impressive winning streak to its credit.

The gladiator leaped to the side of the beast, whispered in its ear, and watched smugly as the lion fled the arena in terror.

Asked the secret of his success, the gladiator replied; "I merely told him, 'After dinner you'll be required to say a few words.' "

An example of a joke that can be used in just about any situation to demonstrate enthusiasm and a willingness to stand up and be counted is the following:

Upon hearing that the star quarterback was killed in an automobile crash on the eve of an important football game, the second-string signal caller phoned his coach.

"Will I be able to take Tom's place tomorrow?" he asked.

"It's all right with me," the coach replied, "but you better check with the undertaker."

Keeping the respect given the speaker as a result of his or her title and the introduction is dependent in great part on how the speech is delivered and the choice of topic. If the orators speak well (and one would think that people likely to be asked to address major gatherings have received some tutelage early in their careers) and their topic is timely and interesting, it is decidedly difficult to lose any of the ground gained at the outset.

Having obtained attention, goodwill, and respect, the speaker is now ready to introduce the topic. There are no oratorical tricks required for this exercise; a simple "I'd like to talk to you today about . . ." or a reasonable facsimile thereof should more than adequately suffice.

But don't say, "I'd like to talk to you today about railroads" or "banking" or "intercollegiate sports," because that's not telling the audience much. Be more specific. Say, "I'd like to talk to you today about the need for less restrictive railroad legislation" or "the impact technology has had on contemporary banking" or "the abuses of recruiting in intercollegiate sports."

If the person for whom you are writing has other talks to give during the year to overlap-

---

*I used this a lot until a friend of mine who read the same book I got it from *(New Speakers Handbook* by S. H. Simmons) began embellishing speeches he was writing with it. We had to agree over lunch one day to put the story on the shelf for five years.

ping audiences, you might have to find a wide variation on the theme of "I'd like to talk to you about . . ." lest you be accused of repetition. One method is to go back to the introductory anecdote and explain how it relates to the theme of the talk. Another is to ask a rhetorical question. Still another is to come right out with a problem and then explore solutions.

THE MAIN BODY

The key to the main body of the speech is a central idea; what, in a sentence or two, is the speech all about.

In answering the question as the outline is being shaped, don't say that it is about railroads, but—rather—about the need for less restrictive railroad legislation. Put it down in a sentence. This identifies the heart of the speech and places limitations on it as well, so that the writer isn't trying to touch too many bases within the confines of a twenty- to twenty-five-minute time frame.

Now that the bare-bone central idea has been stated, it has to be surrounded by some muscle, tissue, and lesser bones. There are several ways to embellish the initial thought.

1. Use history—Why was there a need for regulation of the railroad industry? Who were the movers and shakers in putting new laws on the books? How did the current set of rules and regulations evolve?

2. Use examples—What are the rules and regulations? How do they stifle competition, impair the quality of service, or keep costs artificially high? What are the legislative and regulatory climates in other countries?

3. Use statistics—What is the cost of the rules and regulations to the railroads? To their customers? To the government? How many pages of legislative jargon are required to spell out the governmental fiats? How many people are required to enforce the rules and regulations and to monitor compliance?

4. Use authorities—Which respected individuals share the speaker's feelings on the proliferation of railroad legislation? What have they said on the subject?

5. Use anecdotes—Which stories can be used to show the harm caused by the overregulation? Any amusing tales about the inanity of the rules?

6. Use solutions—Which rules and regulations can be eliminated or watered down? How can it be done? Should the entire system be scrapped and rebuilt from scratch? What can the audience do to speed solutions?

Answering about half these questions should give the writer more than enough material for a speech. In gathering the responses, however, the author must constantly keep the audience in mind and produce the material that relates to their needs, strengths, desires, and problems. It is vitally important that the listeners be involved in the speech; that the writer constantly show how developments covered in the text impact on them—and how they, in turn, can impact on the developments.

THE CONCLUSION

First, it should be brief. Having said what should be said, there is no further need to hold the audience's attention. Wrap it all up in a few sentences, thank people for their attention, and sit down.

One of the more painful *bêtes noires* of a long-suffering listener is to hear the person at the microphone say, "In conclusion . . ." and then proceed to orate for another ten minutes.

A line I've used over and over in explaining the speaker's need to be brief is, "I realize I'm the only thing standing between you and a (whatever comes next)." Whether one likes this language or not, the philosophy is valid.

The people in the audience are busy individuals, and even though they're anxious to hear the speaker, they'd prefer to hear him or her quickly. Patience wears thinnest at the end of the talk, so that's another reason to keep the conclusion short.

There are several ways to bring one's remarks to a fast, but rousing finish.

1. Summary—Merely summarize the speech in two or three sentences.

2. Restatement—Take a pertinent sentence, one that contains the central idea and/or calls for some action on the part of the audience, and restate it.

3. Appeal—Specifically tell the audience what you want from them.

4. Anecdote—Close with a story that motivates, angers, amuses, or simply informs.

5. Rhetorical question—Ask one and hope the listeners respond the way you would like them to respond.

6. Personal reference—Close by stating what you hope the audience feels at the conclusion of the presentation.

7. Quotation—Use a statement from a Shakespearean play, the Bible, a political figure, a noted celebrity, and so forth that emphasizes your point.

WRITING THE SPEECH

ASSUMING the outline is a good one, converting it to text should not be a difficult operation. One way to enhance the outline's usefulness is to use full sentences rather than phrases or key words in itemizing different points. Writing the speech then becomes an exercise in filling in blanks rather than starting from scratch. Other suggestions are:

1. Get it down fast—Don't wrestle over every word in the first draft. Put your thoughts down quickly before you lose them, and worry about polishing the prose later on. You'll probably have to do one or two more drafts anyway, so the key objective of the first effort is to get something down for reshaping and remolding.

2. Make it conversational—Most neophyte speech writers are more experienced in composing for the eye than they are for the ear, which means that their initial drafts tend to read more like articles than speeches. So go over the initial version to make it conversational. Remember, a speech is transitory and requires a different kind of writing than an article, which can be read and reread. Repetition is not only helpful to a speech, it is necessary. And so is informality, because we all talk in a more relaxed fashion than we write.

3. Vary sentence length—A mixture of short, medium, and long sentences makes for easier listening than do sentences of the same length.

4. Adapt it to the style of the speaker—Most people have a distinctive manner of speaking. It's important for PR personnel to know how the senior officers in their organization think and talk so that the prose that is suggested for them matches their personal style. PR people should make it their business to study previous speeches of senior officers and to listen to them as often as possible in order to identify speech patterns and techniques of making a point. Speeches not only have to be well researched, well reasoned, and well planned, they have to use language and sentence structure with which the orator feels comfortable.

5. Clear it—The ultimate approval has to come from the person delivering the speech, but there are others who can provide helpful clues along the way. For example, in-house lawyers might be able to spot potential danger points if the speech touches on legal issues. Other in-house experts should look over that part of the text that touches on their areas of expertise to make sure there are no factual errors.

But be sure of the following points. First, that your "assistant editors" have enough time to read the drafts properly. Second, that they are told when they must get their comments to you.

And third, that you're seeking approval of facts, not writing or editorial assistance.

6. Maintain the proper introduction-body-conclusion ratio—There are no hard and fast rules on this, but a guide I favor is that 10 to 15 percent of the speech should be introduction. 5 percent should be conclusion, and the remainder should be the main body.

7. Pace yourself—Two weeks (or ten working days) is a reasonable time to block off for a major speech.

I would break this down to roughly three days each for:

• Research

• Writing and editing

• Clearing and rewriting

The remaining one day should be reserved for letting the speaker become familiar with (but not memorize) the text.

Again, I emphasize that while most of the research takes place in the early part of the two-week cycle, monitoring the subject must take place up to the time the speech is given. It is also worth emphasizing that good speeches have been produced in one day instead of two weeks because that was all the time the speech writer had. But it's nice to have breathing room.

FINDING APPROPRIATE SPEAKING ASSIGNMENTS

IT would seem silly, if not downright wasteful, if the thought, time, and mind-straining labor described in the previous pages resulted in talks to second- and third-rate audiences, when first-rate audiences remain unaddressed. But such occurrences are not rare.

Too often, speaking engagements are arranged solely because one organization asked another to provide a speaker for an upcoming event. The organization on the receiving end of the invitation is flattered and, after checking to see that there is no conflicting appointment for the designated spokesperson, acquiesces without further thought.

How much better it would be if the aforementioned concern *sought out* the speaking engagements that would give its management exposure to the largest and most influential audiences possible. Instead of speaking to the Podunk Chamber of Commerce on the fourth of April, for example, it could wangle an invitation to address the U.S. Chamber of Commerce on the same date.

It can be done, if not with the U.S. Chamber of Commerce, then with similarly prestigious bodies. The first step in the procedure is to identify the key publics an organization would most prefer to address in a given year. These constituencies may not necessarily be the most important publics in terms of sales or goodwill, but they are groups to whom certain messages must be communicated for one reason or another.

Having identified targets at which certain themes should be sounded, step number two is to find out where and when they congregate. Are there annual luncheons, dinners, or meetings that attract the opinion leaders in the targeted groups? Are there important organizations that have meetings that draw large numbers of press representatives?

Since the answers to these questions are affirmative much more often than not, it is up to the PR department to identify the best forums.

Here are some suggestions for doing just that.

• Ask senior management people which meetings impress them the most.

• Raise the same question with middle management.

• Read and watch the media to see which forums get the most attention.

• Ask journalists and community leaders for their opinions.

THE ROLE OF THE PR OFFICER AS A SPOKESPERSON

THERE was a time when some people believed the best PR practitioners were the ones who stayed farthest from the limelight; who produced outstanding speeches, publications, and press releases; and who cheered from the sidelines as others spoke for the organization. This is no longer so.

Reasons abound for thrusting PR practitioners into the limelight.

First and foremost, the PR officers often have no choice. As spokespeople for the organization, they may be expected to respond to charges at a public meeting, asked to chair gatherings, or serve as last-minute substitute speakers.

Why? Because PR people are—or should be—close to senior management. They should also be able communicators. It is therefore not unseemly for a representative of senior management who is looking for an emergency speaker within the organization to think of the PR department.

Second is the principle of leading by example. It is much easier to get reluctant executives in front of a microphone if the person voicing the request has performed the speech-making chore once or twice himself.

Third, experience as a speaker makes it easier to train and criticize others.

Fourth, appearances before diverse groups are excellent opportunities to gather information as well as dispense it.

In short, a mastery of speech writing should be matched by competence in speech giving. Happily, competence can be developed through practice; it is not a gift reserved for a select few. Neophyte PR practitioners would be well advised to seek speaking engagements (starting off with friendly audiences) and to take a public-speaking course or two.

I remember early in my tenure at one institution watching with dismay and embarrassment as the senior public relations officials made a mediocre presentation on what our department does. The appearances were part of a one-week program for future executives, and my colleagues were some of the many officials called upon to explain what they did for a living.

In an egregiously bold memo to the head of my department, I criticized the effort and pointed out that our presentation should have been vastly superior to those of other units because, unlike earlier speakers who were explaining their jobs, our people were up there doing them—that is, communicating. I lived to regret my audacity, for I was asked to be a panel member in subsequent sessions, but my contention remains valid. As professional communicators, PR people are expected to handle themselves better in front of an audience than other personnel. It is embarrassing and raises questions about their capabilities when they can't.

SPEAKERS BUREAUS

IT often falls to the PR department to manage the speakers bureau, which is designed to obtain goodwill for a concern by having its representatives share their expertise with important publics.

Here's how a speakers bureau works.

The PR person in charge of it writes a memo to all officers or department heads, asking them to identify the individuals in their units who (a) would be willing to speak to community organizations; and (b) have something worth saying. A list is prepared, naming the people who are available for speaking engagements, and it is cross-referenced by subject area.

The list is then put into booklet form and sent to community organizations. An accompanying letter would simply state that the individuals listed in the booklet are available to address local organizations and that interested parties should contact the PR department.

Communicators can further assist this goodwill effort by preparing canned speeches, and by coaching and critiquing the performances of company representatives. They can also send out press releases on the talks.

DO'S AND DON'TS OF WRITING AND GIVING SPEECHES

• **Don't** apologize for a lack of expertise or the fact that you are a last-minute replacement. This only makes people in the audience wonder why they are wasting their time listening to you.

• **Don't** lose your temper or get bellicose with hecklers. It lowers you to their level and minimizes any sympathy the audience had for you.

• **Do** rehearse if you're giving the talk—or urge the person for whom you have written the speech to practice. It isn't necessary that the text be memorized, but the speaker should be sufficiently familiar with the prose so that he or she can maintain eye contact with the audience without having any difficulty in finding the right place in the speech.

• **Do** have the speaker's text typed in large-sized letters. It is also a good idea to have the speaker's copy typed so that each sentence appears as a separate paragraph. This reduces the danger of losing one's place, too.

• **Don't** play with your pen, pull an ear lobe, or engage in other distracting mannerisms while speaking.

• **Don't** have too much research in the speech. It will sound like a term paper, not a talk.

• **Don't** have too many central ideas in the speech. If the audience can't summarize it in one sentence or two, they will have a rough time remembering the pertinent points.

• **Do** check the auditorium, dining room, and so on beforehand to make sure there is a microphone, podium, pitcher of water, and no glaring lights. Yes, that should be the hosting organization's responsibility, but you're the person who'll be standing in front of the audience with no place to put your speech. You owe it to yourself to worry about such things.

• **Do** feel free to embellish the talk with slides or film if the material and opportunities are present. But make sure you test the equipment before the speech—and that you have extra bulbs, wires, and other necessary spare parts.

• **Do** relax and be yourself—but not too much. You can't be too conversational because you're not engaging in conversation; you are talking, and two hundred people or thereabouts are listening. If you want to talk as if you're having a few beers with some friends, go out and have a few beers with some friends.

• **Do** insist that the person for whom you are writing the speech participate in the preparation of the text. There are executives who will ask for a speech, refuse to sit down with the speechwriter to express their views, and then complain that the resulting prose doesn't represent their thoughts. Such behavior wastes the executives' time as well as that of the speech writers.

• **Do** tape-record your planning sessions with the person who is to give the speech. You should still take notes, but the advantage of having the remarks on tape is that you capture the speaker's style and you may be able to lift a sentence or two verbatim for use in the final product.

• **Do** try for a provocative title. This can be helpful to the organizers of the event if they used a printed program and/or posters to try to attract a crowd.

• **Do** study audience reactions as the speech is being delivered. You may learn something for the next time you have to prepare remarks.

• **Don't** overexpose your senior officers. Five or six major addresses a year is quite sufficient. More than that could confuse audiences trying to recall what a particular speaker said several months ago. It could also tire your spokespeople and force them to spend too much time away from their desks.

• If there is going to be a question-and-answer period, **do** try to anticipate questions and suggest answers.

MUCH—but not all—of what has been said about speech writing applies to ghosting articles as well. Both endeavors consist of identifying something worth communicating, finding the appropriate vehicle through which the message is conveyed, and putting the message in marketable form. The difference lies in the form itself.

For example, speeches are written primarily for the ear; articles for the eye. As a result, the latter has more permanent form and requires less repetition. A sentence, once printed, is always available to the reader. There is also less need to get a person's personality into an article than into a speech. Readers aren't seeing authors produce the text, they are looking at inanimate type.

Speakers, on the other hand, not only have to impart meaningful information, they have to impart it in a lively manner. A beautifully written speech that is delivered in a dull monotone may not be as effective as a poor speech presented in animated and entertaining fashion.

Another advantage article writers have over speech writers is that they can use fancier prose. We all have more sophisticated reading and writing vocabularies than oral vocabularies, so readers aren't turned off by four-syllable words. Audiences might be.

Conversely, speakers have an advantage over authors in that their products are more timely. They can change their text up to a split second before each word is delivered. Authors may have a gap of a month or more between the time they bid their labors farewell and the moment readers see them.

Additionally, speakers hit two senses: the eye and the ear. Authors only have readers' eyes to work with.

Despite these differences, the similarities are greater in number and significance. In addition to the shared traits mentioned in the initial paragraph of this section, there are the availability of good vehicles and audiences—and the need for strong public relations assistance.

PR practitioners desirous of gaining the support of their organization's senior management often find that a good speech or article is the shortest route to respectability—and even acclaim—in executive corridors.

FOR FURTHER EXPLORATION

1. Take an article from a publication such as the Harvard Business Review, Harper's *or the* Atlantic Monthly. *Study the text carefully and determine what changes would have to be made if the author had to convert it into a speech.*

2. Your boss has been asked to give a speech on the importance of continuing one's education after getting a job. Prepare an outline for the talk.

3. Your boss is giving a talk at the employee club's annual Christmas party and has chosen to discuss the success of the company's athletic teams during the past year. He is a bit nervous and would like to use some humor in the introductory portion of the speech to break the ice. Come up with some ideas about sports and nervousness that you can work into the speech in a humorous vein. Put the ideas into speech form.

4. You are writing a speech about the dangers of overregulation of business by the federal government. Go to the library and dig up some quotes that will support your contention that the government should ease up.

5. Write a speech—you pick the topic.

16

ORGANIZING FOR PUBLIC RELATIONS

HOW should we organize for public relations?

Public relations beginners may daydream about being asked that question by a supervisor expectant of an insightful answer, but it is not likely that such a discussion will transpire early in their careers. They would be wiser to bet on the question being directed at a seasoned professional.

Nevertheless, all students of the subject should have an idea of how PR operations are organized so that they can have a better understanding of the practice. Additionally, an appreciation of why PR departments and agencies are set up in their current forms gives neophytes hints on the opportunities available to them and the steps they should take to realize them.

The beginners should also realize, however, that there are no universally accepted blueprints for public relations organization. Principles that apply to large corporations may have little bearing on the communications structure of a nonprofit neighborhood center.

Understanding and appreciation of certain guidelines are the recommended goals, therefore—not memorizing universal dictums.

AGENCIES VERSUS INTERNAL DEPARTMENTS

THE first question that comes up in discussing public relations organization is, Should we organize for public relations?

Why not, someone in the group may inquire, hire a public relations agency instead and refrain from using in-house personnel?

Why not, indeed!

There are numerous advantages to going the agency route, strong arguments for only using in-house operations, and no broadly accepted agreements on which contention carries the most weight.

Regardless of one's persuasion, however, students of PR should explore both sides.

THE CASE FOR AGENCIES

1. Independence—Outside counselors, while extremely desirous of establishing long-standing relationships with clients, do not live by one account alone. Unlike internal departments, which have a sole master, the agencies serve numerous clients at the same time.

This lack of total dependency on one entity tends to instill in them a certain amount of independence. And independent counselors are more likely than in-house operatives to deliver a statement to senior officials that is politely couched in terms along the lines of "your idea stinks."

This does not mean that internal departments are headed by sniveling cowards, but it does mean that agencies know they won't go out of business if they lose an account because they refused a request to do something unprofessional or unethical.

2. Broader press contacts—A public relations director for a hospital knows the medical and science editors at the daily media, and is familiar with magazines covering health. An automobile industry communicator knows automotive and transportation editors. Public relations agency officers, on the other hand, are likely to be well informed about a variety of industries and know journalists in every corner of a city room.

Being on a first-name basis with op-ed-page, sports, art, business, political, homemaker-page, travel, science, and other editors gives agencies a strong selling point. Any organization, no matter how confined its work, will want its PR operatives to work with a journalist covering another field occasionally.

For example, a college public relations officer may want to publicize a visit to a campus by some noted dancers. Or a communicator for a manufacturer of office machines may be asked to get coverage on the hiring of a famous athlete to head its fitness program for employees. Their tasks aren't insurmountable if they don't know anyone on the dance or sports beats, but they'll have an easier time of suggesting coverage if they can do so to a friend.

An agency with a client base crossing numerous geographic and industry lines won't encounter this kind of problem.

3. Broader experience—In addition to having a wider array of press contacts, agencies have lived through a more diverse set of PR experiences than departments covering only one industry. Regardless of the setting, a challenging PR assignment provides lessons applicable to all sectors. Generally speaking, then, practitioners covering a variety of clients will have had more experiences than those covering just one.

4. Greater economy—Organizations hiring an agency for a specific job pay for that work via fees and reimbursements for expenses. Using staff people for the same assignment requires expenditures on employee benefits, office space, equipment, and insurance. Assuming one doesn't find an agency that is guilty of establishing outrageous fees for its services, it is generally cheaper to use outside help than inside help for short-term jobs.

5. Wider geographic spread—Let us pretend we do public relations work for a New York–based paper company. Our chief executive officer is giving a major speech in Boston, and we want to get the press to cover the talk as well as conduct some interviews. We make some long-distance phone calls to alert the Boston media to the event, and then we fly up to the Massachusetts city to meet journalists and finalize arrangements for the interview. All in all, what with phone bills, airline tickets, a hotel room, and some meals, we're running up a pretty fancy tab.

If, however, we have an agency with a branch office in Boston, there would be no need for incurring such expenses. The Boston operative would handle all the arrangements locally and save the firm a lot of money and time.

Agencies with offices throughout the United States—and abroad—take great pains to point out the advantages of such networks. They make for a nice selling point.

6. Easy access to specialists—Agencies (especially the large ones) are able to have full-time specialists such as graphic designers, photographers, darkroom personnel, artists, editorial writers, and so on because the cost of their salaries is shared by many clients.

Companies with their own PR departments generally don't have all of these specialists available because they are not needed on a thirty-five-hours-per-week basis. This means they have to look on the outside and pay premium prices when such services are needed.

7. Cheaper in certain situations—What does a concern do if its headquarters office is in Ohio and it needs a public relations presence in New York, the media capital of the world—or it wants to place someone in London to handle the European press for its operations there?

Of the two alternatives—placing a full-time person in another city or using an agency—the latter is clearly the cheaper of the two. If the firm selects the agency route, there are no transfer expenses, no recruiting tabs if the firm decides to hire outside the organization, and no costs associated with finding, decorating, and paying for office space. Moreover, there may not be sufficient need for a five-day-per-week operation. An agency gives the firm the flexibility of paying for as much or as little public relations as it wants.

THE CASE FOR INTERNAL DEPARTMENTS

1. Greater knowledge of the concern—People who spend a minimum of thirty-five hours per week working for an organization should have a deeper understanding of its inner workings than those who aren't there thirty-five hours—and maybe not even seven hours—per week.

2. Greater availability—Company personnel are at their offices at 9 A.M., at 5 P.M., and most of the hours in between. If the president or chairman suddenly needs them, they're easily found and capable of extricating themselves from whatever was occupying their minds at the time of the summons. And they are rarely more than five minutes away from the senior officials' desks.

Agency operatives cannot offer anywhere near that kind of response.

3. *No conflicting demands*—In addition to the greater availability, in-house people have no conflicting professional demands on their time. If their boss says; "I want you to do nothing in the next ten days except work on the annual meeting speech," they can acquiesce quite easily.

What, however, can account executives do if they get the same kind of request from three different clients? They can, of course, farm out some of the work to subordinates, but that could result in a loss of quality.

4. *Greater ease in learning one industry as opposed to many*—People working for internal departments who would like to learn more about the industry they cover shouldn't have too much difficulty realizing their goal, because the reading of three or four books and a subscription to a publication covering the field should get the job done. There might even be time to take an evening course to expand their knowledge. If, however, they worked for an agency and handled accounts representing several different industries, their self-tutoring becomes much harder.

5. *Greater opportunities to talk with line and staff personnel*—Remember the point made in chapter five about chatting with people over a cup of coffee and what an advantage it gives to those charged with uncovering story ideas? The point was that one can't get by with merely asking key department heads if there is anything going on in their units worth publicizing. Key department heads aren't trained in news writing and, more often than not, they wouldn't recognize a story if they stumbled over it. If PR people are going to get ideas out of them, it is going to come from casual conversations in which the line people talk about their work and subordinates, and the communicators stop them when they recognize a potential feature or news article.

The law of averages dictates that the longer and more frequent the conversations, the greater the number of story ideas. And the laws of common sense tell us that those who spend at least thirty-five hours per week on company property will have more conversations with key personnel than those who are there less than ten hours per week.

PR practitioners *can't* rely on management

or non-PR personnel to suggest or initiate most of their assignments. If they do, they will find that their skills aren't put to much use and that some of the requests or suggestions that come their way should be ignored.

Generally speaking, the better public relations programs are the ones in which the communicators spot the needs for their services and initiate at least half of their own assignments. Internal department heads argue that they are in a much better position to do just that than outside counselors, whose infrequent discussions at the clients' offices are only with top management.

THE AUTHOR'S VERDICT

The most sensible conclusion is that both alternatives have strong arguments in their favor. There is no need, then, to treat the debate as an either-or proposition. Agencies and in-house departments can work very well together. In point of fact, they have.

The in-house people generally take care of the day-to-day duties, whereas agencies handle specific assignments. And frequent contact is maintained to allow for joint efforts on planning, goal formation, counseling, and evaluation.

My own feeling is that of the four alternatives—an internal department, an agency, both, or neither—both is best because it comes with all of the advantages cited on the preceding pages. Of course, it also comes with a heavy price tag, so this alternative should not be used by all kinds of concerns and in all kinds of public relations climates.

If forced to choose between the first two alternatives, I am obliged to admit that my more than fifteen years of experience as a member of internal departments renders me somewhat biased toward having one's PR personnel on hand thirty-five hours per week.

I base this opinion on the feeling that the arguments in favor of in-house practitioners—especially the fifth—carry more weight than do those in favor of outside counselors.

But, again, I emphasize that the issue need not be an either-or one.

ONE of the problems with generalizing about internal departments is the confusion over names. One concern's "public relations" may be another's "public affairs." Still others may refer to the unit dealing with external publics as "external affairs," "external relations," "corporate communications," "communications" or "public information."

According to *O'Dwyer's 1979 Directory of Corporate Communications*, 30 percent of the 2,375 companies sampled used the title "public relations," 20 percent used "communications," 8 percent used "public affairs," and 8 percent used "advertising/public relations."[1]

Rather than spend too much time on semantics, beginners must learn to accept the fact that confusion is likely to reign throughout the century and that they should focus instead on a study of the functions. The principal functions at most (public relations) departments are

- Press relations
- Speech and article writing
- Internal communications
- Government relations
- Community relations
- Consumer relations
- Philanthropy
- International public relations

Those departments in the private sector will also have an investor relations unit (with responsibilities for shareholder publications), while the corresponding unit at non-profit organizations will likely deal with special publics such as alumni (for colleges and universities), the medical profession (for hospitals), and the handicapped (for organizations working for physically or economically disadvantaged individuals).

Were I to organize a public relations department for a corporation, I would divide it into four units. One would be responsible for press relations and internal communications. Another would cover speech and article writing and investor relations. A third, entitled public

affairs, would cover government relations, community relations, consumer relations, and philanthropy. And the fourth unit would be responsible for the organization's advertising activities.

In addition, a mini-unit reporting directly to the department head would handle the administrative duties; that is, budgeting, payrolls, reports to senior management, employee benefits' paperwork, memberships, and so on.

On paper, the department's organizational structure would look something like the figure on the following page.

I'd lump press relations and internal communications together because many of the stories being worked on for external media are likely to be of interest to internal audiences. It is possible that much duplication of effort can be avoided by having one person write two versions of the same article.

It makes sense to keep the speech writers and annual report people together, since their functions require outstanding writing skills matched by a detailed understanding of the organization's operations and external environment.

The public affairs unit should house the people working on government, consumer and community relations, and philanthropy because all interface with external publics.

And, as stated in chapter three, advertising should be included in the overall group—which I'd call corporate communications—because advertising and public relations work best when their efforts are coordinated.

So much for pipe dreams. Let's see how it's done in the real world at four large corporations, which shall be nameless at the request of their spokespeople.

At One Bank—One multinational bank has three units that report to the director of corporate communications, plus a person responsible for administrative matters.

The first unit, called public relations, covers press relations, international public relations, speech writing, and investor relations.

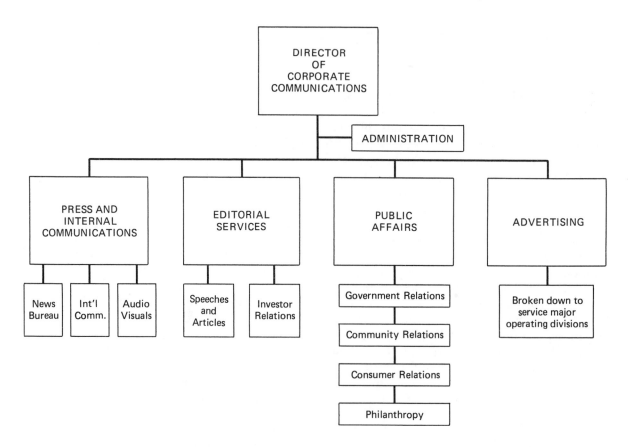

The second covers internal communications. In addition to producing house organs for various departments in the bank, internal-communications staffers also prepare management and marketing newsletters and assist junior-level officers in writing speeches. (The public relations unit only authors speeches for members of senior management.)

The third unit, corporate responsibility, covers urban affairs, philanthropy, consumer affairs, and government relations.

At Another Bank—A second multinational bank has three departments that handle parts of the public relations function. The larger of the three is called corporate communications and has three sub-units, plus a person responsible for administration.

The first subunit is press relations. The second is called field services and provides public relations assistance to bank offices operating outside the headquarters city. And the third covers speech and article writing, investor relations, and internal communications.

The legal department, which is separate from corporate communications, oversees gov-

ernment relations activities and personnel operating as lobbyists in the state capital and Washington.

The third umbrella department is called social policy. In addition to helping to shape bank policy on external issues, this department also oversees the institution's urban affairs activities.

Neither bank includes advertising with public relations, although one once did and the other is contemplating such a move. Both have approximately one hundred people in corporate communications. In the first institution, the department head reports directly to the president and chairman; in the second, he reports to a vice chairman.

At An Insurance Company—Moving away from the banking world, a large New York City-based insurance company has a public affairs department that is designed to "develop and direct programs in the areas of advertising, communications, and corporate responsibility to create and maintain a favorable reputation among (name of company) policyholders, employees, tenants, the media, academic and community leaders and groups, and the general public." It employs ninety-five people.

Reporting directly to the vice-president in charge are four units: advertising, corporate communications, corporate social responsibility, and consumer affairs, as well as a seven-person administrative services section.

Corporate communications, in turn, is further divided into four subsections. They are communications consulting services, corporate audiovisual media services, editorial services (including internal communications and press relations), and external communications.

In the Energy Field—One major firm has a public affairs department with three major components: government relations, investor relations and information coordination, and public relations.

Rather than have government relations activities provide assistance to the company on an across-the-board basis, the public affairs department doles out assignments to separate subunits, which work directly with major divisions of the company. For example, one government relations unit operates only on behalf of the international division, two others cover domestic operating divisions, and a fourth works with the chemicals and special projects divisions.

In addition, government relations has a support group that shapes programs to back the company's positions on legislative and regulatory issues—and an administrative and coordination section. This latter operation prepares reports on developments in Washington and coordinates internal meetings on key issues.

The investor relations arm prepares financial communications, interfaces with investor publics, monitors news about energy from all over the world, and coordinates the dissemination of public information. In assessing global news, the company spends approximately $500,000 annually on an elaborate news-monitoring and information retrieval operation. Not only are the major wire service dispatches read carefully, but more than eight hours of television news is recorded on cassettes each day.

The third major component, public relations, is similar to government relations in that it adheres to the "client" approach of organization. There are six subunits providing a full range of public relations services to six major

line units of the company. In addition, there is one section coordinating media relations, another for internal communications, and one responsible for cultural programs and promotion.

THE NONPROFIT SIDE

In order to explore the nonprofit side of the coin, let's take a brief look at college and hospital public relations.

College units are headed by an individual generally named vice-president and director of university relations, external affairs, or public relations. Or he or she may be named assistant to the president. Other titles that have been given college departments include community relations, college relations, and college affairs.

There are six key functions of a college PR operation. Depending on the size of the school, each one may be headed by an experienced officer—or one person may be responsible for two or three of the activities.

First on the list is development (fund raising). In some schools this is set apart from public relations; in most others it is part of the overall PR function.

Next (and from here on the order is of no importance) is press relations. This can be subdivided into sports information, student information, and academic affairs.

Third is publications, the branch of the department that produces the college's brochures, faculty newsletters, annual report, and so on. This unit should also involve itself in the planning, editing, and production of *all* literature produced by the school—because, theoretically, the best editors on campus work in the publications section.

Fourth is the alumni affairs office. Some schools place this unit with development personnel, since many donors are former students. Others, however, feel that graduates represent a small portion of potential supporters and that alumni relations should therefore be a separate function.

Next is special events. Graduation ceremonies, inaugurations of new presidents, community relations, visits to the school by dignitaries, and a speakers bureau are some of the things special events people deal with.

And sixth, assuming the college is sufficiently endowed, is audio-visual services. Many colleges and universities recognize that films and videotape are key media for campus publics. They've reacted to this development by establishing in-house production facilities similar to those in the corporate sector.

Hospitals tend to place the highest priority on press relations, community relations, internal communications, and development/trustee relations.

Those that are teaching hospitals will also have someone handle alumni relations in addition to one of the foregoing functions.

Whereas PR staffs at some of the country's major colleges and universities can contain as many as fifty people, it is rare that the PR unit at a hospital will have more than six or seven professionals.

AGENCY ORGANIZATION

PUBLIC relations agencies range in size from one- or two-people operations to mammoth entities staffed by hundreds of people around the globe. Some specialize in certain industries; others are active in all sectors. And some, in recognition of the fact that many outsiders view public relations and advertising as allied functions, are the PR wings of advertising agencies formed solely because some clients expect help on press releases, speeches, and so on, in addition to the preparation and placement of advertisements. Conversely, there are some PR agencies that also provide advertising assistance to their customers.

Despite the variety of size, specialization, and geographic scope, agencies do not differ too much in the way they are organized. These operations are generally headed by a chairman and/or president, with an executive vice-president directly underneath to supervise the day-to-day operations. If the firm is very small, these officers will also serve as the account representatives, handling all the public relations functions from the writing of a short press release to the plotting of major campaigns.

If the firm is medium-sized or large, there will be two or more account groups, placed together according to industry or geography and headed by an account group manager. Each account group, in turn, will have account executives who oversee the client relationships. Reporting to these executives are account supervisors and account personnel.

As one moves to the larger public relations agencies (the Hill and Knowltons, Burson-Marstellers, and Carl Byoirs of the world), one generally finds specialized departments such as the following in addition to the account groups:

- Production (handling releases and mailings)
- Creative (art, graphics, audio-visuals)
- Research (library, polling)
- Major media contact (for print and electronic media)
- Financial (preparation of annual reports, 10-K forms, proxy statements, and so on)
- International (for clients with overseas operations—as well as to oversee subsidiary operations abroad)

Options are also open to agencies on the manner in which they bill clients. The first choice is the imposition of a fee or retainer as the sole source of funds. Ranging in size from four to seven figures per year, the charge is looked upon as money paid for availability. On top of this, PR counselors can charge for the cost of the staff used on a project, executive time and supervision, overhead costs, out-of-pocket costs, and even profit.

Given these options, there are no standard billing practices among agencies. Some include one or two of the foregoing items in their bills; others include more.

There is no special reason why there should be universally accepted billing patterns, because fairness standards are honored if for no other reason than that competitive pressures and codes of ethics from organizations such as the Public Relations Society of America dictate that they be honored. Besides, clients are in the driver's seat by the simple process of examining the monthly charges and supporting documentation. They can ask hard questions and, if they don't like the answers, they can switch accounts.

What is standard are detailed discussions between agencies and prospective clients so that arrangements are clearly understood by both parties before a relationship is started. For example, some firms may opt for the flat-fee route so that they know what they can bill the client each month, whereas others prefer flexibility out of fear the client may say, "Oh, by the way, we're opening a new office in Buenos Aires and will need one of your people there for two months."

According to a study report by the Counselors Section of the Public Relations Society of America, many firms prefer to say something like this in the early discussions: "Our fee for seeing that the work gets done is x dollars a year. We will of course bill you without commission for any out-of-pocket costs or expenses. The work actually performed by the staff will be billed at the rate paid to the employee, plus the normal overhead factor. From what you have told me, the job ought to be in the area of y dollars a year total, but that's subject to variations depending on what we run into. On the basis of experience, I would guess that variation would not be more than 10 percent."[2]

Regardless of the wording, all billing arrangements are made clear in advance; including details such as how the bills are to be presented, what documentation is needed, and whether clients are to be billed when agency operatives wine and dine journalists who are of importance on a number of accounts. (Many firms only bill the client directly if the purpose of a lunch or dinner is to sell a journalist on a particular story about the client. If the get-together is merely to establish or maintain a relationship, the client is not billed.)

It is vital that no questions be left unanswered, because no one wants to see good—and productive—working relationships turn sour over something as trivial as a long-distance phone call.

FOR FURTHER EXPLORATION

1. Give three examples of when an agency and an in-house department would—and should—work well together.

2. How would you organize a twenty-person (ten professionals) PR department for a nonprofit cultural center?

3. How would you do the same for a nation-wide retailing firm?

4. What arguments could you cite for placing the audio-visual unit with press relations personnel? With internal communications personnel? How could you justify creating a separate department for this function?

5. Given your estimate of societal changes in the eighties and nineties, what changes do you envision for the future in terms of public relations department organization?

17

WHAT MANAGEMENT LOOKS FOR IN PR PEOPLE—AND VICE VERSA

SINCE this book is aimed at beginners in public relations, this chapter will zero in on what managements want from neophytes. Those who have worked in the field for several years may benefit from the other chapters dealing with specific functions, but they don't need a primer on management's wants and needs. The chances are they've been through the interview mill once or twice and learned some useful things along the way.

Let me state at the outset that I plan to take myself off the hook by pointing out that not all managers are alike when assessing candidates. So even though some of the points in the ensuing text strike readers and the author as being Solomon-like in their wisdom, there may very well be interviewers who wouldn't hire people following my advice, even if they offered to work for the minimum wage.

WHAT MANAGERS LOOK FOR

LET'S start off with a few basic assumptions before getting very selective.

1. Bright people with a good education—There are so many disciplines with which a PR practitioner will become involved, that a well-rounded education is very important, the more well-rounded the better.

Think about all the topics discussed up to now. Working with them requires exposure to economics, history, literature, political science, sociology, science, and the arts. If there's some home economics, physical education, typing, and shorthand thrown in, that wouldn't hurt either.

Those who had to go to work immediately after high school—or were unable to attend college for some other reason—may well wonder if the absence of a degree permanently bars them from a career in public relations. The answer is no, though they will probably have to settle for a lower-entry-level position than applicants with identical work experience but a college degree as well.

There are numerous instances of PR officers who began their careers as secretaries, messengers, or file clerks. If people in those positions are bright and ambitious, carefully observe the performance of professionals, do a lot of outside reading, and maybe even take an evening course or two, they can make up for their lack of formal schooling. As a matter of fact, there are those who feel the education one gets watching professionals in action, doing selective reading, and taking on additional work assignments is much better than the education students get in a classroom.

In a novel entitled *Winners and Losers* by Martin Quigley, there is a wonderful character named Sam Dellafield who heads a growing construction company. Asked by a bright, but not formally educated, young officer on the rise about the value of college, he replied,

> Not having a college education—of course, that's a handicap. It's a gap in your background you'll have to fill in the hard way as you go along. What I used to do, out on a job in some wilderness, was get the Sunday New York Times and read everything in it—foreign news, national news, politics, the business pages, theater news, the book reviews. Hell, I even used to read some of the books. You do that, and you can make small talk at any cocktail party, which seems to be the principal accomplishment of most of these educated monkeys that I hire.[1]

There is something to his answer, though a college education has an edge over *The New York Times* in the woods. A lack of a degree *can* be overcome by an understanding of what's going on in the world and an awareness of what led up to these developments.

2. Bright people with a good education and a degree in public relations, communications, or journalism—It is not a must, because there is much to be said for the wonders of on-the-job training, but formal tutoring in a PR discipline is a definite asset. It means an applicant won't have to be schooled in basics and that he or she has most likely learned to employ the tools of the trade. All other things being equal, a PR degree has to give a job candidate an edge over a competitor without one.

This doesn't mean potential communications executives should pore through college catalogues to determine where the best PR or PR-related programs are offered. It's possible that while some people are obtaining an advanced degree in the field, others who will compete with them for jobs in the future are gaining professional experience that could be more useful in the marketplace.

My advice to young people choosing between a good PR job offer and a graduate program in the field is to take the job and figure out a way to embellish it with outside study.

If, however, you are faced with a good graduate program and a mediocre job that will not polish your skills, I think the academic route has the stronger appeal, provided full-time matriculation is economically feasible.

And just as people who opted for a good job in the first example could take a course or two on the side, participants in graduate programs should look for part-time employment in the field or gain practical experience by volunteering for work in the school's PR office or on the student newspaper.

3. People with good experience—There is no surefire advice on how to get good experience, so a pair of suggestions will have to suffice.

a. *Lower your demands*—Competition for entry-level positions is decidedly intense, and good jobs often go to the lowest bidder. Those who are turned off by the prospect of a year of peanut butter sandwiches for dinner could miss out on a reasonable diet of steak later on if they hold out for a high starting salary.

b. *If you can't sell your skills to an organization, give them away free*—Beginners desperately need experience so that they have something to talk about or show when looking for a good job. Those lacking in professional experience to refer to would be well advised to volunteer for editorial or PR work in order to develop skills and produce tangible materials to display to recruiters.

For example, if your neighborhood civic group has a newsletter for its members, volunteer to be the editor. If your local Little League, church, or theater group wants its activities publicized, take a step forward and announce that you'll do the press releases.

This boldness not only enables you to polish and refine skills while waiting for the big break, it provides you with clippings for a scrapbook and shows that you can perform basic PR chores.

(By the way, if you're going to put the press releases you write into a scrapbook, make sure you follow these up with the articles that appear as a result of the release. This demonstrates that whatever writing ability you have can translate into the all-important knack of being able to place news.)

There are many men and women happily ensconced in good beginners' jobs who owe their positions to a portfolio filled with parent association newsletters, neighborhood organization press releases, and the like. While their volunteer status labeled them zero-dollars-per-year people as they awaited their first job offer, their scrapbooks showed that they could meet deadlines, write readable copy, and/or obtain media coverage. These are skills that command money in the marketplace.

4. Flexibility—PR people deal with many publics and many tools. To belabor a point made earlier in the text, any public and any number of PR tools can stand head and shoulders above the rest in any given crisis. Individuals flexible enough to deal with different publics and to trot out a variety of tools when substitute solutions are required have reasonable expectations for a long career in PR. Those who believe that each problem has only one solution are not long for the field.

The importance of flexibility can be demonstrated by the voicing of but a pair of questions:

a. What do you do if a large, page-one story in your house organ is killed just as you are about to give final approval to the printer—and the publication must be distributed by the end of the week?

b. What do you do if your boss wants you to spread information on a new product and none of the brilliant press releases you sent out has been picked up by the media?

Feeling sorry for yourself will not bring you any closer to an acceptable solution. New approaches are needed and they are needed fast. Flexibility is the ticket to coming up with novel answers. And so is the next ingredient desired by recruiters.

5. Creativity—Flexible people are capable of bringing additional techniques to a problem-solving exercise; those who are flexible *and* creative can bring in techniques that haven't been used before.

Equally important, we often need something different if for no other reason than to be different. With the exception of government-approved monopolies, there are few private- and public-sector operations that have an entire field to themselves. Any idea that will single out an organization in a positive manner is an idea that will be well received by one's bosses.

It is worth repeating the statement made in chapter five that creativity can be developed. Books on the subject (see Bibliography) can be valuable primers in helping people learn how to generate ideas.

6. Writing ability—As was noted in chapter five, public relations practitioners will, sooner or later—and probably sooner rather than later—have to put words on paper. Those who feel uncomfortable arranging words into readable sentences will have to overcome their unease. Studying good writing, taking a course or two, practicing, and practicing some more, are the necessary steps to glibness and comfort in front of a typewriter.

7. Pleasant personality—In order to disseminate information, PR operatives must first gather it. Some of the data are available to them on a silver platter courtesy of the media, pollsters, trade associations, government agencies, schools, and other sources. Gathering facts and figures from these assorted wellsprings is called secondary research. Some also label it "pretty easy."

They do not, however, apply this tag to primary research. This form of information gathering, which requires researchers to go out and obtain data from original sources, is difficult, time-consuming, expensive, and absolutely necessary.

But how many people are willingly going to answer questions voiced by a person they actively dislike? Not many. And, more important, how many will call a PR person they abhor and dispense information without being asked for it? Far less.

A pleasant personality is a must if people want opportunities for casual chats that can lead to the birth of a significant story.

8. Inquisitiveness and news sense—Having colleagues acquiesce to requests for lunch, coffee, or an after-hours cocktail is a key first step in getting the news one needs to function properly as a PR representative.

Asking the right questions and recognizing news when it presents itself is an equally valuable second step.

Both elements of this pivotal component of the news-gathering process require advance work. In shaping questions, PR people must identify all the things they would want to know about a topic before they can properly evaluate its news value. Sitting down beforehand and forcing oneself to produce a minimum number of questions—say ten or fifteen—is one way to get the productive juices flowing. Another is to think of different publics and try to guess what they would want to know about the topic.

Identifying news when it is discussed by another person comes from (a) studying the media and knowing what interests them; and (b) recognizing the unusual.

(It is important, by the way, to compile a list of questions before going on a job interview. There are numerous recruiters and PR directors who focus as much attention on each job seeker's questions as on their answers. The feeling is that those lacking in inquisitiveness or aggressiveness to ask intelligent questions will probably fail to exercise these traits on the job.)

9. Salesmanship—How can applicants sell the organization they hope to represent if they can't sell themselves? My personal feeling on the subject is this: Regardless of how impressive one's résumé is, if the applicant doesn't give me an additional reason during our talk to want to make a job offer, I rapidly lose interest.

Aggressiveness and confidence are key ingredients here; so are planning and organization. Candidates should have a good idea—

hopefully before the interview and definitely during it—of the characteristics needed to perform the job well. Assuming they possess these characteristics, they should make it their business to move the conversation to a path that will allow them to make this fact known.

10. Knowledge of—or interest in—the field in which the firm operates—Regardless of the field in which PR neophytes acquire a full-time job, it is the field in which they will spend a minimum of thirty-five waking hours per week. If several of these hours have to be devoted to learning about the field, a newcomer's productivity is decreased, and he or she has a higher-per-productive-hour starting salary than an informed person.

This is not, however, a barrier to gainful employment. Intelligence, a good personality, and some of the selling points cited on the preceding pages can overcome a lack of experience in the field. But the knowledge gap must eventually be narrowed, so a lack of interest on top of a lack of familiarity is justifiable reason for rejecting a candidate.

An addendum to these ten points is the following checklist of twenty-six skills and qualities employers are looking for in entry-level people, according to a special report in *Public Relations Journal.*

1. Writing proficiency
2. Organization
3. Ability to speak and communicate well
4. Ability to channel energies and work hard
5. Good attitude
6. Pragmatism
7. Flexibility
8. Understanding of general business practices
9. Good personality
10. Practical experience in related field
11. Variety of personal interests
12. Knowledge of current events
13. Awareness of societal trends
14. Good educational credentials
15. Broad range of academic disciplines
16. Self-reliance
17. Knowledge of how to think
18. Avid reader of books, newspapers, magazines, etc.
19. Basic knowledge of all media
20. Background in social sciences and liberal arts
21. Intelligence
22. Curiosity
23. Imagination
24. Initiative
25. Accumulation of high-quality writing samples
26. Presentable[2]

The report also said;

Give yourself 75 points if you checked number 1. Writing is the single most important skill in public relations, employers say. It is involved in every public relations function and every prospective employer looks for it first. Score one point each for numbers 2 through 26. Some of these are intangible qualities, but all are important to prospective employers. A score of 100 indicates you are an ideal public relations job candidate. Less than 100 indicates need for improvement. Less than 75 indicates you had better consider another occupation.[3]

WHAT TO LOOK FOR FROM MANAGEMENT —BESIDES A JOB OFFER

THE old adage "Beggars can't be choosers" comes to mind here. The sad fact is that the public relations field, glamorized in films and novels—and cursed by a spillover from would-be investigative reporters who left college bent on uncovering another Watergate and found they couldn't even uncover a job opening—has more candidates per opportunity than the candidates would like.

But we're all dreamers, and the day may soon come when more than just a select and overly talented few will be able to sift through job offers. That's when candidates can start acting sassy and ask, "Do you meet my standards?"

Even if that day doesn't arrive for a while, it is beneficial for job holders and seekers to think about the behavioral traits they'd like to see in management anyway—and not only for the bursts of pleasure that accompany such daydreams. The real purpose of this fantasizing is that having identified the desired characteristics, PR personnel could try to turn their wishes into reality via a little tutoring of senior executives.

Here are the things PR practitioners should expect from management.

1. A philosophy and performance record worth talking about—As we discussed in chapter one, public relations can't lead an organization, it can only reflect its policies and performance. Beginners ready to launch lengthy careers in the field should determine the qualities they would like to see in their employers and then see how perceived performance and philosophies measure up to their goals.

Remember, if a concern is courting you, you are in the driver's seat. You can request the same volume of information interviewers seek from you and you can postpone decisions until your questions are answered to your satisfaction. Where an organization has been, how it got there, why, what are its prospects for the future, what is its role in the communities in which it operates, and how it regards the field of public relations are legitimate concerns of sought-after individuals. Getting complete answers will shed considerable light on the kind of communications program that will spring forth from the firm's headquarters site and the ease or difficulties PR people will encounter in meeting their goals.

2. A willingness to include PR executives in management committee meetings—Public relations is a management function. The sooner senior executives accept this the better they and public relations officials will work together.

This doesn't mean that communications specialists should exercise veto power over decisions affecting different publics, nor does it mean that they should play leading roles in shaping decisions on products, services, plant relocations, prices, and so on. But they should be able to offer opinions on public responses to alternative plans and they should sit in on planning sessions from the outset so that they can formulate strategies to make management's actions known.

There are also some side benefits to having PR personnel sit in on management committee deliberations.

First, their presence at the upper councils' brainstorming sessions will allow the communicators to learn who are the real powers in the executive corridors. It's possible that the individuals with the fanciest titles are not the ones with the greatest influence over group decision making. And knowing who the opinion leaders are can be very helpful when new public relations programs are being finalized and recruiting allies is the order of the day.

Second, participation in management meetings bestows upon the PR practitioners an importance in the eyes of others. After all, how can some executives treat the department with disdain and/or arrogance if the president and chairman look to its head for guidance on a variety of issues?

Third, it allows PR people to spot early danger signals and put out minor brush fires before they become blazing infernos. One of the more frequently sounded laments by communications executives is that they are only called in when the fire is out of control. The initiative is clearly taken away from them in such situations, and their only options revolve around how they can react to the moves of others.

If, however, the PR department is involved in a program from its conceptual stages, it could anticipate moves of others and counter them before they are launched.

Two reasons often cited by managers for barring senior PR officers from high-level discussions are:

a. Public relations is not a management function. We can tell the department what to do when it's time to call on it for assistance.

b. Public relations practitioners are too close to

the press. If we let them sit in on our deliberations, what we say will be in tomorrow morning's newspapers.

I say bah! humbug! to both these assertions. First of all, anyone who believes that the act of preparing and sending information to and from key publics isn't a management function doesn't place too high a priority on satisfying major constituencies.

As for the fear that PR people will blab behind-closed-doors secrets to the media, I say proponents of such thoughts must have very low opinions of the senior officers who hired the top communicators.

I recall listening in disbelief once as an executive assured me that although he had the highest respect for my discretion, he didn't want me or any other PR types sitting in on management committee meetings because there could be leaks to the press.

"Arnold (not his real name), the reason you would be angry if any of the deliberations appeared in print is because you don't want our competitors to know what we're doing," I retorted. "Right?"

"Right."

"Yet every person on the management committee has friends at competitor firms whom they've known at least as long and as well as I know certain journalists. They don't need a middleman; they can take the information directly to a rival. Why aren't you concerned about them inadvertently or deliberately revealing privileged information?" I asked.

He didn't have an answer to my questions, but I'm still not sure I shook him from his deep-seated distrust of PR people.

Fortunately, he is only one of a very small handful of businesspeople who feel that PR counselors are not to be trusted. Most realize that communicators who deal without a full deck of facts are at a severe disadvantage in trying to represent an organization effectively.

3. A willingness to participate in the planning and implementation of PR programs—Management can't adopt a hands-off policy, because without its blessing, PR campaigns lack clout, direction, leadership, and necessary information. Equally important, if management doesn't help pinpoint goals and help shape strategies, they may be less inclined to perform their required roles as spokespeople because they don't agree with the programs established by the PR department.

PR departments need more than management's stamp of approval, they need its commitment and involvement so that others in the organization will also participate.

Still another advantage of top management's active involvement is the positive effect it has on the many people at whom an activity is directed. Psychologist A. H. Maslow, in his theory of motivation, defines five classes of needs; they are, in order of importance according to Maslow, physiological, security, belongingness, esteem, and self-actualization.[4]

There is nothing like a personal call from or friendly conversation with the chairman or president of an organization to satisfy an individual's need for security, belongingness, esteem, and self-actualization.

Some final words on the importance of management enmeshment in external relations. It should include not only participation but monitoring as well. Senior executives can't wait until the conclusion of a PR campaign to evaluate performance and results, because minor irritations could sprout into full-scale disasters without careful reviews at key checkpoints. Disasters, in turn, incur the wrath of the officials, which could then lead to reprimands and less than Olympian annual salary reviews.

But much worse than that, a wrathful management could make middle- and lower-level officers excessively gun-shy about participating in future campaigns—or sticking their necks out if they are somehow forced to be part of a communications effort.

I know of one major corporation that had a body of senior officers who pointedly—and successfully—avoided press interviews out of fear that their comments could antagonize their bosses. The motivating rationale—until it was finally shaken by senior management—was that a good interview is ignored by one's superiors, whereas a bad one (or bad sentence in an otherwise favorable interview) attracts censures. With more downside risk than opportunities for gain, discretion was considered the better part of valor.

This leads to the next point.

4. An understanding that not all public relations activities will be 100-percent successful—There is a tendency at some organizations in the private and public sectors to become more disturbed over a negative result than delighted by a beneficial development.

Managements must learn to temper their preoccupation with setbacks, especially if they occur in a program that is an overall success. If not, they will generate a "why bother?" attitude on the part of subordinates, who may come to feel that involvement in external affairs is a "no-win" errand.

This doesn't mean that management should settle for a 75-percent growth rate when a better performance is attainable, but it does mean that negative results should be treated in the proper context.

Public relations officers who want personnel below the CEO to continue taking part in the programs they create must advise their chairman and president to opt for an approach along the lines of "Those results were good, and I'm grateful for your contributions. And if we had done this and this instead of that and that, we could have been even more successful."

5. A willingness to provide guidance and leadership but leave the nuts and bolts decisions about public relations to the professionals—Senior executives who spend their time moving commas around and suggesting photo angles to photographers are, in effect, cheating their shareholders, customers, and employees. Observers would justifiably expect their valuable and costly time in the office to be devoted to loftier pursuits, while leaving the basic PR endeavors to editors, photographers, and other communications personnel. At the risk of offending certain senior executives, their intrusion in editing, picture-taking, and writing functions can often result in poor copy and artwork.

I was involved in an incident some years ago that demonstrates, I believe, the senselessness of non-PR types making communications decisions. The incident was prompted by my being struck with the thought that year-end earning releases, which are laboriously produced by lawyers, accountants, and news relations specialists for financial analysts and financial editors, should not be given a headline and reproduced in house organs for employees. The

level of understanding among the latter group simply doesn't match that of the former.

"Why not," I suggested to my boss, "rewrite the earnings release in laymen's terms so that staff members can understand it?"

My boss was skeptical because it was a rash departure from standard practice, but he said I could do it if the accountants and lawyers approved the rewrite. I then prepared a new version, the opening sentence of which read something like the following:

> The year 1969 was a good one for (name of institution) and its employees alike, as earnings topped the $100-million mark for the first time and expenditures for salaries crashed through the $75-million barrier.

The remainder of the story explained, in very simple terms, how and why these developments occurred.

Surprisingly, the legal department approved the story without delay. Then I got a call from a senior accounting officer.

"Bob, you'll have to kill the story. My boss [the head of the department] doesn't like it," he said.

"Why?" I asked. "Were the numbers wrong?"

"No, the numbers were fine."

"Were the facts wrong?"

"No, no problems there," replied the accounting executive.

"Then why do I have to kill the story?"

"It's your lead, Bob. You're talking about salaries and earnings in the same sentence."

"Why shouldn't I, they're the two most important features in our performance."

"Yes, but they're on different sides of a profit-and-loss statement. You can't put them in the same sentence."

"Why not?" I retorted. "I can put America and Australia in the same sentence, and they're in different parts of the world."

"It just can't be done."

"Will you or I or anyone else go to jail if the story appears?"

"No, but my boss doesn't like it. He says you're talking about apples and oranges and he can't approve it."

Seeing that I was getting nowhere fast and knowing that my caller and his boss both seriously outranked me, I decided to curtail the conversation and seek my own boss's counsel.

But he, anticipating many battles with the accounting department over the upcoming annual report and not wishing to waste any victories on the house organ, suggested that I give in or find a way to convince the accounting department head on my own.

I figured an end run might work, so I called a junior personnel officer, who served as an advisor to the employee newspaper, and asked if he had any suggestions.

"Let me get back to you in a few minutes," he said.

Whereupon he called the head of the accounting department. "Were the facts in Cole's story correct?" he asked.

"Yes."

"Fine, that's all we want to know from you. Thanks for your help."

And the story ran the way it should have run.

6. An awareness that public relations can't always have a positive or direct effect on earnings—The PR department does not generate income for an organization, nor do its actions directly result in loss of earnings. It may help to maximize gains and minimize losses, but it is exceedingly difficult to measure the impact of PR efforts accurately.

Given the lack of monetary measurements of its work, PR departments can be in serious trouble at budget-planning or salary review time—unless its organization's management realizes that more than numbers are needed to evaluate its performance.

Fortunately, most senior executives do realize this and are able to plan budgets based on need and reward employees based on ability and performance.

The management teams that tend to rely on bottom-line contributions alone will have well-paid line departments (assuming earnings are up) and underpaid staff personnel. After a few years of this, it will have underqualified staff personnel as well, because the talented people will find better-paying jobs elsewhere.

A related managerial error is to tie departmental budgets and salary increases solely to an ability to meet certain goals during the course of one year. Unless these goals can be

established with an eye toward the long-term, departments will concentrate only on the short-term and leave the distant future to the distant future. Sometimes you have to take a backward step to achieve a significant victory down the road, but with a management that only looks at performances with a "what have you done for me lately?" attitude, those important strategic steps won't be taken.

7. A recognition that social performance of employees should be part of the annual review process—One of the best ways for managements to encourage staff members to participate in external affairs and thus ensure that organization performance matches its rhetoric is to ask the question, "What have you done to improve our image in the community during the past year?"

Admittedly this can't be done with all employees, because many are not in positions to make meaningful contributions during working hours, but it could demonstrate that the concern's guiding forces consider image building a vital prerequisite to the realization of other goals.

Another question that might be asked on an employee's review is, "What have you done to improve the organization's image or prospects for greater success beyond this year?"

8. An acceptance of the fact that PR can't perform miracles—A company with the best public relations performance in the world can nevertheless have poor press and a bad image for a very simple reason: Its products or performance leave a lot to be desired.

Unfortunately it's a lot easier to rant and rave over imagined inadequacies of communicators than to reshape philosophies and redesign goods and services. As a result, there are some managers who will react to a bad image by firing or reorganizing PR departments—not unlike professional football team owners, who fire the coach after a losing season.

Management must realize that PR reflects performance; it doesn't direct it. Communicators can't control external events such as wars, recessions, floods, and famines; they can't convince customers that poor-tasting tomato juice is delicious, and they can't get the media to look the other way when earnings decline 94 percent. They can't even guarantee a lot of press attention when plans for a new and major expansion are announced, because the release may go out the same day a foreign government is overthrown or a major earthquake occurs.

Public relations practitioners are not magicians. Managements that hold realistic expectations for their communications staffs and recognize the role unforeseen events can play tend to get better mileage out of the units that serve as their eyes, ears, and mouth.

FOR FURTHER EXPLORATION

1. You belong to a neighborhood theater group that does not have a publicity chairperson. You would like to serve in that capacity because you figure it will look good on your résumé and will be good practical experience. The head of the group isn't sure a publicity chairperson is needed. He asks you why you think the organization needs one and what would be the goals of such a publicist. What is your answer?

2. You are being interviewed for a job as assistant editor on the house organ of a giant retailing firm. Compose a list of ten questions you will ask the interviewer. (While the questions should be designed to obtain information, their main purpose is to show you off.)

3. Your local newspaper decided it would like to do a feature on a head of a purchasing department of a major corporation. Through luck and timing, you arrange to have your firm's purchasing director be the one who is interviewed. You

think the resulting article is favorable, but the purchasing executive's boss is upset about one quote. Taken slightly out of context, it implied that the purchasing department is smaller than it actually is. She complains that the interview shouldn't have been held and she's not sure it is a good idea to cooperate with the press in the future if the article in her hand is indicative of the quality of news writing today. What do you tell her?

4. Prepare an action plan for a clerk in the PR department of a major breakfast food company. He does not have a college degree but he would like to compensate for it by making himself appear to be more valuable in the eyes of his supervisors.

5. A prospective employer asks you how you would go about helping his firm acquire a good reputation as a corporate citizen. How would you respond?

18

HOW TO BREAK INTO PUBLIC RELATIONS

THE job-hunting process involves producing a résumé, sharpening skills while awaiting an offer, taking advantage of opportunities to improve techniques at current places of employment (if there are any current places of employment), identifying targets, and actually pounding the pavement in search of new or better employment.

THE RÉSUMÉ

ONE is always hesitant about offering advice on résumés because there are few generally accepted rules and a large number of opinions on their proper preparation. The fear of having someone follow one's suggestions, send the résumé out in response to a job ad for which he or she is ideally suited, and then have the résumé end in the wastepaper basket because the recruiter totally disagrees with the suggestions weighs heavily on the minds of those tempted to share their opinions on the subject.

Nevertheless, the responsibility to discuss job hunting—and because of that, résumés—in a book aimed at newcomers to the field tilts the scale slightly in favor of my sounding off.

The following are Cole's rules on résumés, based on hearsay, comments from recruiters, recollections of books I've read, and personal opinion.

1. Strive for scannability—Chances are reasonably certain that most of the job ads answered by beginners or those in the field for less than five years will attract upward of fifty résumés. Some may pull in as many as two or three hundred if they sound especially attractive.

There is no way in the world that the person doing the screening is going to read every word in every résumé, even if he or she established that as a goal at the outset of the hunt. Instead, the screener will briefly scan the résumés, looking for reasons to put them in either the "let's take a second look later" pile or the "reject" pile.

The author of each résumé should try to help the reader by employing good organizational skills. Capitals, items in the margin, underlining, divisions, and subdivisions are all valid devices for aiding the reader to "know" the person behind the text after a brief glance.

As an example of how to make a résumé become more scannable, take the subject of working dates. I prefer that they be out in the margin so that a reader can know in two or three seconds how long the person has worked and how much time was spent at each job.

A respected executive recruiter, however, once scoffed at my résumé and told me to put the dates under the names of the firms that had employed me. "Who you worked for is much more important than for how long," he said.

He's right that employers are more important, but I think I'm right in putting dates in the margins—and capitalizing the name of the employer and underlining the job title. This gives scanners three items to see quickly.

Look at the beginnings of the résumés on the next two pages.

I like the second résumé better because it allows people to quickly see who John Doe has worked for, how long he spent on each job, and what his titles were. If the initial readers are impressed by these facts, they will look at the rest of the text with more than a passing interest. If, however, the readers can't find out in a first or second glance who a person has worked for, for how long, and the job titles—and if there is a pile of one hundred résumés still to be read—there's a strong possibility they won't waste time searching for the desired information; they're going to place the résumé in the "reject" pile or, failing that, to a pile to be looked at later on *only* if a sufficient number of likely candidates hasn't emerged from the first go-around.

2. Place your work experience before your college experience—You are not applying for admission to school; you're trying to get a job. What you have done is therefore of greater importance than what you have learned, regardless of your alma mater's status.

190

JOHN DOE
44 Elm Street
Dobbs Ferry, N.Y. 10845
(914) 749-1522

Background
& Objective:
Experience includes work as journalist and public relations officer. Seeking executive position managing public relations/communications for progressive organization.

EMPLOYMENT RECORD

REPORTER DISPATCH
One Gannett Drive   White Plains, N.Y. 10801
From...June 1977 to present
Title...Reporter
Duties...Cover manufacturing industries in Westchester; do features on business people; serve as assistant Sunday business section editor.

MOBIL OIL CORPORATION
150 East 42nd Street   New York, N.Y. 10017
From...Dec. 1974 to June 1977
Title...Assistant Editor, Mobil Oil News
Duties...Assist in production of monthly newspaper for Mobil Oil employees. Do news and feature article writing, photography, proofreading, and layout.

IONA COLLEGE
North Avenue   New Rochelle, N.Y. 10804
From...June 1972 to Dec. 1974
Title...Public Relations Officer
Duties...Assist in preparation of monthly faculty newsletter; write press releases on athletic teams and students; handle publicity during Iona College's participation in 1974 N.I.T. Tournament; supervise staff photographer.

JOHN DOE
44 Elm Street
Dobbs Ferry, N.Y. 10845
(914) 749-1522

Background & Objective:	Experience includes work as journalist and public relations officer. Seeking executive position managing public relations/communications for progressive organization.

Employment
Record

June 1977
to present

REPORTER DISPATCH
One Gannett Drive   White Plains, N.Y. 10801

Reporter
Cover manufacturing industries in Westchester; do
features on business people; serve as assistant
Sunday business section editor.

Dec. 1974
to June 1977

MOBIL OIL CORPORATION
150 East 42nd Street   New York, N.Y. 10017

Assistant Editor, Mobil Oil News
Assist in production of monthly newspaper for Mobil
Oil employees. Do news and feature article writing,
photography, proofreading, and layout.

June 1972
to Dec. 1974

IONA COLLEGE
North Avenue   New Rochelle, N.Y. 10804

Public Relations Officer
Assist in preparation of monthly faculty newsletter;
write press releases on athletic teams and students;
handle publicity during Iona College's participation
in 1974 N.I.T. Tournament; supervise staff
photographer.

3. Don't feel you have to list items such as age and marital status—It is not mandatory that these personal items be included in a résumé, so don't put them down if you think the data will reduce your chances of getting a job.

For example, you might think the fact that you're the mother of a preschool-age child will hinder your chances of obtaining a full-time job. More likely than not the fact that you're a member of the working mother lodge will surface during a first, second, or third interview. But by that time, the people you've been talking with, who may have been biased against working mothers, may like you too much to let it make a difference.

4. Be brief but don't leave the pertinent facts out—Always strive for brevity but don't forget that the major purpose of the résumé is to sell its author. In describing duties performed in the employment record category, there are certain things worthy of inclusion, even if they come at the expense of conciseness. They are

• Number of people supervised
• Suggestions made or activities introduced to successfully reduce costs
• Special assignments handled above and beyond the call of duty

5. Don't be too fancy—Some people use colored stock, an ink other than black, or engraved type to embellish a résumé; others pointedly eschew the practice. A little spiffing up of the product is a good idea when you have had an impressive ten years experience under your belt, but it is not necessary at the beginner's level. For one thing, there isn't much text to get excited about, and for another, recruiters think it is presumptuous of neophytes to have a more expensive-looking résumé than they have. Making the résumé look neat and scannable is sufficient challenge for beginners.

6. Newcomers don't need an opening statement on background and objectives—The function of the opening statement is to tell prospective employers quickly what kind of experience the applicants have had and where they want it to take

them. It is a helpful technique and should be employed by people who have been in the field at least five or ten years.

There are two reasons why experienced people should employ a statement at the beginning.

First, no matter how scannable the résumé is, a statement at the outset is the best way to summarize to the reader just what the author is all about. This is especially so when the person behind the résumé has had diversified experiences.

Second, people with five or ten years in the field should have a good idea as to how their career goals shape up. If they don't, one may logically assume they haven't been paying attention during their working hours.

Neither of these arguments apply to beginners, however. Additionally, beginners should not let themselves be confined by career goals. For example, if a public relations school graduate states on his résumé that he is looking for a job as a writer in a news bureau, he might feel awkward answering ads in quest of a community relations associate or assistant editor on a house organ—even though both of these positions would be good for him.

The gentleman in question can, of course, say he is looking for a beginner's job in public relations, but the statement is so obvious that it raises the question as to whether it needs to be stated.

7. Do list extracurricular school activities, especially if they are related to the field you are trying to enter—Work on a college newspaper or as the public relations representative for a student organization is definitely worth mentioning. Granted there is no remuneration associated with such activities, and the monetary value placed on your work by others remains zero, but the involvement shows that the applicant has clearly dealt with some of the challenges faced by professionals in the performance of their daily chores.

8. Don't be afraid to list hobbies—I often wondered why certain "experts" suggest listing hobbies on a résumé, because I always felt that what a prospective employee does on his or her own time is

193

none of my business. Indeed, I rarely, if ever, paid attention to applicants' hobbies, though I suppose if someone listed "sado-masochism," it would have given me pause. Then one day a student of mine made an interesting observation on the importance of listing special interests, and succeeded in converting me. She pointed out that while urban-area organizations are generally more than willing to leave employees to their own devices after working hours, those situated in small towns may want to know what potential staff members' interests are for the simple reason that many social functions in town are company sponsored. She was right.

SHARPENING SKILLS

THERE are three basic skills that neophytes can and should work on at home while waiting for—and even after—that first big break.

They are:

• Writing
• Photography
• Editing

WRITING

1. Clip newspaper articles and rewrite them.

2. Clip feature articles and rewrite the leads. Go back to the list of leads in chapter five and use each one for each of the stories selected.

3. Go to a library or bookstore and get a book of news-writing exercises. Do them.

4. Go to an event and "cover it" by writing a news or feature story. If you have no opportunities to be where the action is, watch the evening news on television and write news stories based on what you have seen and heard. Then compare your prose to that of the next day's newspapers.

5. Read and study the media. Pick the best writers and study their style.

PHOTOGRAPHY

1. Take pictures—both indoors and outdoors.

2. Take the same pictures from six or seven different angles and distances. Pick the best ones and determine why you think they are best.

3. Look at pictures in the newspapers and think of how you could have taken a better shot had you been given the photo assignment.

It is possible that readers may ask themselves at this point why it is necessary for beginners to know photography when they are planning to earn a living with a typewriter, not a camera. One very obvious reason is that all public relations officers will occasionally have to select photographs for a publication or to accompany a press release. Knowing what makes good and bad pictures will help them in the selection process.

Another reason is budgetary. It is decidedly cheaper to send one person to gather news and take pictures on a story assignment than to send two. Public relations directors who are cognizant of this fact believe that young practitioners with writing *and* picture-taking skills are more valuable than those who can only write.

EDITING

1. Take a batch of newspaper articles and reduce each by five lines without losing any factual content. Just remove excess verbiage. Then take another pile of stories and add five lines to each. (Sometimes editors have holes to fill and no time to gather additional facts. They fill the holes by adding some words to the end of one line and other words to other lines.)

2. Get some photographs that can be cropped as either horizontal or vertical shots. Crop them to fill holes 4½ by 3 inches, 4½ by 4 inches, 4½ by 5 inches, 4½ by 6 inches.

3. Take some random newspaper articles and photographs and lay them out so that they fill a new page.

4. Take seven photographs and design a two-page picture spread with them.

In addition to doing all of the foregoing at home, would-be PR officers should volunteer to serve as newsletter editors or publicity chairpersons for local nonprofit organizations. As stated in the previous chapter, job seekers need tangible evidence of their skills to show potential employers. If you can't build up a scrapbook from your work as a professional, do so as a volunteer.

IMPROVING OPPORTUNITIES FOR ADVANCEMENT AT WORK

IN addition to doing self-improvement exercises at home, budding PR giants fortunate enough to acquire starting jobs in the field should make it clear to their bosses that they want bigger and better things. Don't be obnoxious about it, because a certain amount of time is required to learn your job and the organization—and your boss may have had to put his or her time in the trenches and thus feels that others should do the same. But expressions of ambition are a good idea.

Don't be afraid to:

• Ask questions about other people's jobs. In addition to demonstrating an interest in the organization, such curiosity will help you learn more about the organization and enable you to shape realistic goals about your next job or two.

• Volunteer for additional work. There is considerably less pressure on you when you're doing something not in your job description. You won't get fired if you err in the endeavor, so the risk is minimal. And if you do it well, you have shown your boss that you're ready for more challenging assignments.

• Suggest additional things for you to do. This not only shows aggressiveness and ambition, it demonstrates that you are capable of recognizing opportunities to be of service. As we discussed in chapter sixteen, most managers are incapable of spotting needs for PR assistance. Showing that you can identify such needs has to make you more valuable in the eyes of your boss.

IDENTIFYING TARGETS

MOST PR beginners aren't terribly selective as to which industry or nonprofit-sector area they aim their job-hunting efforts at. Nor should they be. It is rare that a person's first employer is a person's only employer nowadays, so most people look on initial jobs primarily as a source of necessary experience.

If the first job is where a beginner stays for life, fine. But the important thing is to get some experience so that decisions about where to go next can be based on a decent amount of firsthand observation.

Then, after having a job or two under one's belt, rational thought can be directed toward which field would be the most preferable. Key ingredients in the decision-making process are interests, geographic preferences, and opportunities.

It makes sense that people do better when they work in fields that interest them as opposed to areas that bore or confuse them. Outside reading, academic courses, and participation in societies or associations allied to the line of business come a lot easier if the subject matter is of interest.

Job hunters should take geographic factors into consideration if there are parts of the country or world that are especially desirable or undesirable. For example, individuals not interested in living in the southwestern United States should avoid energy public relations, because many firms in the field are either based in or have offices in Texas. Those who prefer rural or suburban environments might opt for hospital or college PR, since so many schools and medical institutions are located outside urban areas.

(Speaking of geography, people anxious to get a newspaper job prior to breaking into public relations might consider temporarily leaving major media centers such as New York, Los Angeles, Chicago, and Washington and looking at opportunities elsewhere in the country. While it is true that most newspaper jobs are in the larger cities, the ratio of applicants to openings is much lower in rural America. A perusal of the classified advertising section of *Editor & Publisher,* a weekly magazine that covers journalism, generally reveals several job openings in smaller cities and towns. Those willing to give up theater, French restaurants, and a variety of museums for a year or two—as well as endure salaries below media center standards—might be able to pick up good working experience which they can leverage into better jobs in urban areas.)

Once a field or two are identified, newcomers should read the key trade journals, get data from trade associations, and pore over annual reports. It shouldn't be too difficult to discover who are the industry sector leaders and which organizations are in greatest need of public relations assistance.

LOOKING FOR A JOB

THERE are six basic ways to look for a job, and PR professionals will, during the course of their careers, hear numerous arguments explaining why one method is better than all of the others combined.

While I have strong opinions on the relative merits of each one, I firmly believe that all should be used by beginners.

Why? Because all have worked at one time or another for people in the field. To shun one technique despite its alleged inferiority to others, at a time when competition is very keen, doesn't make sense.

The job-hunting methods are the following.

1. Spreading the word among contacts or friends— There are several advantages to telling people you know in the field that you are in the job market.

• It doesn't cost anything. If you are competing for a job with people who have been referred by an agency or executive recruiter—and your means of entry, on the other hand, has been a personal contact—your competition is at least 10 percent more expensive than you because they come with fees. All other things being equal, the job is yours.

• Your contacts probably know the people attempting to fill jobs in their organizations better than you do. If your contacts tell a recruiter nice things about you, their comments will carry much more weight than any similar statements you might make.

• Contacts are likely to hear about job openings before they are advertised and/or given to a personnel agency. If you can get an interview in the early stages and you do a very good job of selling yourself, it is possible that the interviewer may decide to halt further screenings and make you an offer on the spot.

2. Going to personnel agencies and executive recruiters— Employment agencies and executive recruiters are organized to help people find good jobs. They charge fees for placing indi-

196

viduals (usually, but not always, picked up by the concern doing the hiring), so being employed by this method generally makes you more costly than if you came in via a contact.

But the agencies and executive recruiters have several important selling points.

• They save companies time and effort in screening candidates. As an employer, I know that if I run an ad and/or ask my friends to supply names, I'll have to pore through many résumés before selecting those deserving of further investigation. Some of the applicants with impressive résumés may, however, have the personality of a wet towel. An alert agency would spot this personality blemish and spare me the aggravation of a wasted interview. And it will carefully screen for other faults, because its professional reputation is on the line every time it submits a candidate's name. If an agency recommends a couple of loony-toon characters, it knows that recruiters will call another agency the next time an opening presents itself.

• Because agencies spend portions of their day calling organizations in a given geographic area to ascertain employment needs, it stands to reason they will know about more job openings than the average individual.

• Many PR practitioners who are doing the searching for a new person in the department got their jobs through an agency. Their inclination, therefore, is to go to that agency when there is a job to be filled.

Yes, agencies often require applicants to spend time in crowded waiting rooms. And they almost always ask people to fill out forms seeking information clearly covered in the résumé.

But they have successful track records in placing people. Otherwise they would be out of business, because they need a minimum number of placements each year to pay the rent, salaries, and other overhead items. If they have succeeded with others, it's possible they can succeed with you.

3. Letter writing—Those who use this approach identify the organizations for whom they would like to work, then write to their presidents, public relations directors or personnel directors. These letters can ask for an interview or simply voice the request that the enclosed résumé be kept on file and referred to when an opening arises in the future.

This method doesn't have a high rate of reward because, obviously, many of the recipients don't have any positions to fill.

It can, however, be effective when the reader is impressed with the writer's ambition, or the timing is right and a vacancy exists, or the résumé is actually filed for future referral.

The advantages are that there are no agency fees involved and the letter generally holds the attention of the targeted reader for at least two or three seconds. Sometimes much longer.

Thousands of people have obtained interviews via the letter route,* and a good percentage of these people have taken advantage of the door-opening technique to get jobs. Letters work.

4. Visiting personnel offices—This is not unlike the letter-writing approach in that one never knows if an opening exists, and the success average is therefore low. It is also time-consuming, since it often involves lengthy periods of boredom in waiting rooms.

The advantages, in addition to the absence of an agency fee, are that résumés are kept on file and you get a look at the organization in action.

When PR directors in quest of a new body in the office have exhausted their contacts and examined the résumés in their own files, they usually call personnel departments for help and eventual permission to go the advertising or agency routes. Given budgetary pressures, the personnel department very likely will respond thusly: "Don't place an advertisement or call an agency yet; let us see what we have in our files first."

Since opening a drawer and surveying its contents is faster and cheaper than placing an ad or paying an agency's fee, the PR director will have no objection to the personnel department's response.

---

*Having an interview for an interview's sake isn't a bad thing to do, even if no job exists. Interviewees get experience in selling themselves, learn from their mistakes if they say something foolish, and get a feel for the types of questions asked.

5. *Visiting college placement offices and those of professional societies*—Most colleges have placement offices designed to facilitate their graduating seniors' entries into the working world. A good percentage of them can also be used by alumni who have been coping with the job market for several years and still need assistance in getting placed.

These offices should be used, with the understanding, however, that most, if not all, of their referrals will be for entry-level jobs.

The placement arms of professional societies and associations list jobs at all levels, and they should also be consulted. Many people pay stiff annual dues to belong to an organization solely in order to receive job-listing bulletins.

6. *Answering advertisements*—The nice thing about this activity is that in most cases there is an actual job opening waiting to be filled. Candidates should read their local newspapers and, regardless of where they live, the Sunday *New York Times,* Section 9 (classified ads). If they have acquired some experience along the way, they should also look through the Sunday *New York*

Times, Section 3 (business section) and the Tuesday and Wednesday editions of the *Wall Street Journal.* Other job listings worth looking at are in the Sunday *New York Times,* Section 4 (for hospital, college, and library PR jobs), *Public Relations Journal, Editor & Publisher,* and college placement offices.

Applicants should be aware, however, that some ads aren't real; they are prepared by personnel agencies and executive recruiters looking for potential clients and/or private- and public-sector organizations curious to see what the job-hunting market has to offer.

Don't be discouraged if you answer several ads each week and receive no responses. Most ads are legitimate, and it is only a matter of time before return letters start arriving.

My own opinion is that using contacts is the best of the six methods. But it can't be emphasized enough that job hunting should *never* be an either-or endeavor. All methods have worked for others, and all can work for you. Time permitting, the ideal job-hunting approach is the one that uses every available option.

FOR FURTHER EXPLORATION

---

1. If you are looking for your first job, find it.

2. If you are looking for a better job, find one. Good luck.

NOTES

Chapter One
[1] Rex F. Harlow and Marvin M. Black, *Practical Public Relations* (New York: Harper & Row, Publishers, Inc., 1947), p. 10.

[2] Summary of lectures and discussions in the "Short Course in Public Relations," conducted by the American Council on Public Relations, Harvard Club, New York City, 1942.

[3] Benjamin Fine, *Educational Publicity* (New York: Harper & Row, Publishers, Inc., 1943), pp. 255.

[4] Anonymous journalist.

[5] Verne E. Burnett, *You and Your Public* (New York: Harper & Row, Publishers, Inc., 1943), p. 1.

[6] Scott M. Cutlip and Allen H. Center, *Effective Public Relations* (Englewood Cliffs, N.J.: Prentice-Hall, Inc., 1971), p. 18.

[7] Interview with David Finn, February 1980.

[8] Joseph T. Nolan, "Protect Your Public Image with Performance," *Harvard Business Review,* March–April 1975, pp. 135–142.

[9] Thomas W. Thompson, "Managing Communications through Planning," special report in *United States Banker.*

Chapter Six
[1] "What Motion Picture Theatres Want from Sponsored Films," Modern Talking Picture Services, Rickefeller Plaza, New York, N.Y. 1977.

[2] Ibid.

[3] Judith M. and Douglas P. Brush, *Corporate Video: Burgeoning Role for PR* (New Providence, N.J.: International Television Association, 1977), p. 15.

[4] Ibid.

Chapter Seven
[1] Raymond Van Houtte, *Responsibilities of Bank Directors* (Saint Louis: Director Publications, Inc., 1974), p. 45.

Chapter Eight
[1] *The American College Dictionary* (New York: Random House, Inc., 1970), p. 715.

Chapter Nine
[1] Ralph Nader, *Unsafe at Any Speed* (New York: The Viking Press, 1965), preface.

[2] The Conference Board, *The Consumer Affairs Department: Organization and Functions* (New York, 1973), p. 12.

[3] Ibid., p. 13.

[4] "Consumer Affairs Climbs the Corporate Ladder," *Industry Week,* July 10, 1978, pp. 55–56.

Chapter Ten
[1] *Giving USA: AAFRC 1979 Annual Report* (New York: American Association of Fund-Raising Counsel, 1979), p. 6.

[2] "How to Target Your Charitable Giving," *Business Week,* February 4, 1980, pp. 118–120.

[3] *Giving USA: AAFRC 1979 Annual Report,* (New York: American Association of Fund-Raising Counsel, 1979), p. 41.

Chapter Twelve
[1] Oscar Beveridge, *Financial Public Relations* (New York: McGraw-Hill Book Company, 1963), p. 142.

[2] Ibid., p. 152.

Chapter Thirteen
[1] Lee L. Morgan, "Letters," *Dun's Review,* January 1979, p. 27.

Chapter Sixteen
[1] Jack O'Dwyer, *O'Dwyer's Directory of Corporate Communications* (New York: J. R. O'Dwyer Co., Inc., 1979), preface.

[2] Counselors Section, *Fees, Charges and Overhead in the Practice of Public Relations* (New York: Public Relations Society of America, 1972), p. 12.

Chapter Seventeen
[1] Martin Quigley, *Winners and Losers* (Fhiladelphia: J.B. Lippincott Company, 1961), pp. 158–59. Used by permission of Harper & Row, Publishers, Inc.

[2] "The Employers: What Do They Really Want?" *Public Relations Journal,* July 1978, pp. 11–14.

[3] Ibid., p. 13.

[4] Leonard L. Berry and James H. Donnelly, Jr., *"Marketing for Bankers* (American Institute of Bankers, American Bankers Association, 1975), p. 71.

BIBLIOGRAPHY

PUBLIC RELATIONS—GENERAL

BERNAYS, EDWARD L. *Biography of an Idea.* New York: Simon & Schuster, Inc., 1965.

BUDD, JOHN F., JR. *An Executive's Primer on Public Relations.* Radnor, Pa.; Chilton Book Co., 1969.

CENTER, ALLEN. *Public Relations Practices: Case Studies.* Englewood Cliffs, N.J.: Prentice-Hall, Inc., 1975.

CUTLIP, SCOTT M., and ALLEN CENTER. *Effective Public Relations.* 5th ed. Englewood Cliffs, N.J.: Prentice-Hall, Inc., 1978.

HARLOW, REX F., and MARVIN M. BLACK. *Practical Public Relations.* New York: Harper & Row, Publishers, Inc., 1947.

HARVARD BUSINESS REVIEW. *Public Relations.* A *Harvard Business Review* Reprint Series. Cambridge, Mass.: Harvard College, 1975.

HILL AND KNOWLTON EXECUTIVES. *Critical Issues in Public Relations.* Englewood Cliffs, N.J.: Prentice-Hall, Inc., 1975.

LERBINGER, OTTO, and ALBERT J. SULLIVAN. *Information, Influence & Communication.* New York: Basic Books, Inc., Publishers, 1965.

LESLY, PHILIP. *Lesly's Public Relations Handbook.* 2d ed. Englewood Cliffs, N.J.: Prentice-Hall, Inc., 1978.

MARSTON, JOHN. *Modern Public Relations.* New York: McGraw-Hill Book Company, 1979.

STEINBERG, CHARLES S. *The Creation of Consent: Public Relations in Practice,* New York: Hastings House, 1975.

STEPHENSEN, HOWARD. *Handbook of Public Relations.* New York: McGraw-Hill Book Company, 1971.

PRESS RELATIONS AND NEWS WRITING

ALSOP, JOSEPH and STEWART. *The Reporters' Trade.* New York: Reynal & Co., 1958.

BERNSTEIN, T. M. *The Careful Writer.* New York: Atheneum Publishers, 1975.

DAUBERT, H. *Industrial Publicity.* New York: John Wiley & Sons, Inc., 1974.

GOMPERTZ, ROLF. *Promotion and Publicity Handbook for Broadcasters.* Blue Ridge Summit, Pa.: Tab Books, 1977.

JACOBS, H. *Practical Publicity.* New York: McGraw-Hill Book Company, 1964.

KLEIN, TED, and FRED DANZIG. *How to Be Heard: Making the Media Work for You.* New York: Macmillan, Inc., 1974.

MARTIN, DICK. *Executive's Guide to Handling a Press Interview.* New York: Pilot Books, 1977.

WEINER, R. *Professional's Guide to Publicity.* New York: R. Weiner, Inc., 1978.

GOVERNMENT AND COMMUNITY RELATIONS

ESTES, RALPH. *Corporate Social Accounting.* New York: John Wiley & Sons, Inc., 1976.

GOULDEN, HAL. *How to Plan/Produce/Publicize Special Events.* Dobbs Ferry, N.Y.: Oceana, 1960.

HIEBERT, RAY. *Political Image Merchants.* Washington, D.C.: Acropolis, 1971.

HUMAN RESOURCES NETWORK. *The Handbook of Corporate Social Responsibility.* Radnor, Pa.: Chilton Book Co., 1975.

LEIBERT, EDWIN R., and BERNICE SHELDON. *Handbook of Special Events for Non-Profit Organizations.* New York: Association Press, 1972.

LUTHANS, FRED, and RICHARD M. HODGETS. *Social Issues in Business.* New York: Macmillan, Inc., 1976.

McGRATH, PHYLLIS S. *Redefining Corporate-Federal Relations.* New York: The Conference Board, 1979.

SCHRIFTGIESSER, KARL. *The Lobbyists: The Art and Business of Influencing Lawmakers.* Boston: Little, Brown & Company, 1951.

VAN HOUTTE, RAYMOND. *Responsibilities of Bank Directors.* Saint Louis: Director Publications, 1974.

CONSUMER RELATIONS

AAKER, DAVID A., and GEORGE S. DAY. *Consumerism: Search for the Consumer Interest.* New York: New York Free Press, 1978.

GAEDKE, RALPH, and WARREN ETCHESON. *Consumerism: Viewpoints from Business, Government and the Public Interest.* San Francisco: Canfield Press, 1972.

GARDINER, JONES, and MARY and DAVID GARDNER. *Consumerism: A New Force in Society.* Lexington, Mass.: Lexington Books, 1976.

JOHNSON, HELEN D. *The Consumer Help Manual: A Reference Book for Consumer Complaint Centers.* New York: New York State Consumer Protection Board, 1976.

MURRAY, BARBARA B. *Consumerism: The Eternal Triangle; Business, Government and Consumers.* Pacific Palisades, Calif.: Goodyear Publishing Company, 1973.

NADER, RALPH. *Unsafe at Any Speed.* New York: The Viking Press, 1965.

PHILANTHROPY

AMERICAN ASSOCIATION OF FUND-RAISING COUNSEL. *Giving USA: AAFRC 1979 Annual Report.* New York, 1979.

CONRAD, DAVID LYN. *Techniques of Fund-Raising.* Secaucus, N.J.: Lyle Stuart, 1974.

GOULDIN, JOSEPH C. *The Money Givers.* New York: Random House, Inc., 1971.

HARRIS, JAMES J., and ANNE KLEPPER. *Corporate Philanthropic Public Service Activities.* New York: The Conference Board, 1976.

LISTON, ROBERT A. *The Charity Racket.* Nashville, Tenn.: Thomas Nelson, Inc., 1977.

MIRKIN, HOWARD. *The Complete Fund Raising Guide.* New York: Public Service Materials Center, 1972.

NIELSON, WALDEMAR A. *The Big Foundations.* New York: Columbia University Press, 1972.

SCHNEIDER, PAUL H. *The Art of Asking.* New York: Walker & Co., 1978.

ZURCHER, ARNOLD. *Management of American Foundations.* New York: New York University Press, 1972.

FINANCIAL PUBLIC RELATIONS

BEVERIDGE, OSCAR. *Financial Public Relations.* New York: McGraw-Hill Book Company, 1963.

CATES, D. *Bank Investor Relations.* Chicago: Bank Marketing Association, 1975.

HERRICK, TRACY. *Bank Analysts Handbook.* New York: John Wiley & Sons, Inc., 1978.

KIRSCH, DONALD. *Financial and Economic Journalism.* New York: New York University Press, 1978.

MARCUS, B. *Competing for Capital.* New York: John Wiley & Sons, Inc., 1975.

ROALMAN, A. R. *Investor Relations Handbook.* New York: AMACON, 1974.

INTERNAL COMMUNICATIONS

D'APRIX, ROGER. *The Believable Corporation.* New York: American Management Association, 1977.

DARROW, R. *House Journal Editing.* Danville, Ill.: Interstate Printers, 1975.

DEMARE, G. *Communicating at the Top.* New York: John Wiley & Sons, Inc., 1979.

DEUTSCH, A. *Human Resources Revolution.* New York: McGraw-Hill Book Company, 1979.

GOLDHABER, G. *Organizational Communication.* Dubuque, Iowa: W. C. Brown Co., 1974.

INDUSTRIAL COMMUNICATIONS COUNCIL and TOWERS, PERRIN, FORSTER & CROSBY. *Case Studies in Organizational Communication.* New York: Industrial Communications Council, 1975.

ROSENBLATT, S. BERNARD; T. RICHARD CHEATHAM; and JAMES T. WATT. *Communications in Business.* Englewood Cliffs, N.J.: Prentice-Hall, Inc., 1977.

SPEECH WRITING

CROCKER, LIONEL. *Effective Speaking.* New York: American Institute of Banking, 1958.

LARSON, ORVIN. *When It's Your Turn to Speak.* New York: Harper & Row, Publishers, Inc., 1962.

REID, L. *Speaking Well.* New York: McGraw-Hill Book Company, 1977.

SIMMONS, S. H. *New Speakers Handbook.* New York: The Dial Press, 1972.

ORGANIZING FOR PUBLIC RELATIONS

BURGER, CHESTER. *The Chief Executive: Realities of Corporate Leadership.* Boston: CBI Publishing Co., 1978.

THE CONFERENCE BOARD. *Managing Corporate External Relations: Changing Perspectives and Responses.* New York, 1976.

CONNORS, TRACY. *Nonprofit Organization Handbook.* New York: McGraw-Hill Book Company, 1979.

DRUCKER, PETER. *Management: Tasks, Responsibilities, Practices.* New York: Harper & Row, Publishers, Inc., 1974.

MAYER, FRANK. *Public Relations for School Personnel.* Midland, Mich.: Pendell Publishing Co., 1974.

PUBLIC RELATIONS SOCIETY OF AMERICA. *Careers in Public Relations.* New York, 1979.

ROSS, ROBERT D. *The Management of Public Relations: Analysis & Planning Public Relations.* New York: John Wiley & Sons, Inc., 1977.

WHAT MANAGEMENT LOOKS FOR IN PR PEOPLE—AND VICE VERSA

OSBORN, ALEX F. *Applied Imagination.* New York: Charles Scribner's Sons, 1953.

INDEX

H

I

J

K

L